DEEP SEA SAILING

H.R.H. the Duke of Edinburgh with the author aboard *Samuel Pepys* in London River

Erroll Bruce

DEEP SEA SAILING

STANLEY PAUL
London

STANLEY PAUL & CO LTD
3 Fitzroy Square, London W1

AN IMPRINT OF THE HUTCHINSON GROUP

London Melbourne Sydney Auckland
Wellington Johannesburg Cape Town
and agencies throughout the world

First published November 1953
Second impression 1959
Third impression 1961
Fourth impression 1967
(Revised edition)
Fifth impression 1971

Printed in Great Britain by litho on antique wove paper
by Anchor Press, and bound by Wm. Brendon,
both of Tiptree, Essex
ISBN 0 09 053471 9

CONTENTS

	Prefaces	9
	Foreword by Robert Somerset, D.S.O.	13
I	Planning a Cruise	15
II	The Craft	24
III	Fittings and Equipment	34
IV	Maintenance	49
V	Emergency Repairs	56
VI	The Crew	71
VII	Preparing the Crew for Sea	81
VIII	Watchkeeping and Routine	93
IX	Food and Water	104
X	Safety at Sea	120
XI	Navigation	132
XII	Cruise Strategy, Weather and Currents	148
XIII	Wind and Sea	169
XIV	Bad Weather	182
XV	Comfort and Health	195
XVI	Meeting Other Ships	206
XVII	Yacht Business	219
XVIII	Storm at Sea	226
	Index	241

20 tables, 28 diagrams, and 8 maps, in text

ILLUSTRATIONS

H.R.H. the Duke of Edinburgh with the author
aboard *Samuel Pepys* in London River   *frontispiece*

facing page

1   *Dayspring*, a converted Ramsgate trawler   32

2   *Cohoe II* at the start of a Fastnet race   32

3   A lifebuoy that a fully clothed man can get into in a
rough sea   33

4   *Fabius* sets out past Anglesey in the Irish Sea race   33

5   Jury mast   48

6   Jury spreader   48

7   Light, airy and dry conditions for repair work below
in *Aloha of Hamble*   49

8   A steep little sea that brought down the mast of an
ocean racer before she reached the open sea   49

9   *Ilala*, rigged as a Chinese schooner, with Hasler self-
steering gear   96

10   Racing speeds up the tempo and demands more of the
crew, as shown in *Griffin II*   96

11   Coming up to the Fastnet rock in *Belmore II*   97

12   Three thousand miles of ocean ahead for *Samuel Pepys*   112

13   Setting storm canvas on board *Wyvern* during a gale off Start Point   113

14   *Lisoletta V* racing to windward in the Skagerrak   160

15   Racing at sea before the wind   161

16   Always ready for emergencies   161

17   A big wave breaking in the open sea   176

18   A dangerous harbour entrance in an onshore gale   176

19   *Rapparee* dips her main boom   177

20   Building a jury spar in mid-Atlantic   177

21   Dry decks in *Bolero* running before a gale   224

22   A mid-Atlantic roller   224

23   Concentration in the darkness on board *Belmore I*   225

PREFACE

In 1950 I enjoyed an exciting sailing race across the North Atlantic and was soon afterwards sent for by Lord Fraser of North Cape, then First Sea Lord at the Admiralty. He asked many questions about the handling of the yacht, and finished by saying, 'What you have learnt of the sea in small craft is not your private property, so I trust you will hand it on to others.'

Such a wish by one of the most distinguished seamen of our times demanded compliance. Yet it seemed to me then that I needed far more experience both of the sea and of expressing ideas on paper before achieving a book of any value. I began to collect notes and practise the craft of writing with that eventual aim.

During the next year or so I lived aboard a yacht with my family when not at sea in the course of my profession, and besides sailing spent much of the time sifting and analysing my experiences of small boat sailing. I am still not certain whether this was not rather a one-sided foundation for family life, considering the austerity aboard, the protracted hours of my night study and typing, and my long absences when racing; but whatever she felt, I could not have done the work without the help of my wife, and the environment maintained incentive. I was able to develop ideas not only from frequent sailing, and from reading and re-reading numerous books on sailing, but also enjoy discussions in person or by letter with many contemporary sailing men of vast experience, in particular K. Adlard Coles, J. H. Illingworth, R. Somerset, H. Barton and R. Stephens, besides experts in subjects that affect the yachtsman at sea, such as the provocative medical research opinions of Dr. J. Harper, the dietary views of E. Warner and the discussions on sea clothing with M. C. Compson, and many others. To all of these I am grateful.

The more I searched for knowledge and confirmation, the greater seemed my ignorance, and the less true seemed any dogma about what is right or wrong at sea in small craft.

In 1952 the Royal Naval Sailing Association again invited me to take charge of their yacht *Samuel Pepys* with the clear objective of winning the Bermuda and Trans-Atlantic races. This task needed some definite doctrines in each aspect of seamanship involved, so in the cruise that prepared for and included these races the tentative theories that I had developed could be used, not as dogma but as a basis on which to plan and act. That cruise was the most enjoyable and successful I have ever known, and if any particular confirmation shone out most vividly it was the truth of the age-old doctrine that the success of a cruise depends much more upon the feelings of individuals on board than any other factor. Ian Quarrie, David Coaker and Lance Wise were superb shipmates, and formed a competition crew that could feel proud of itself against any opposition.

After that cruise, and having celebrated twenty years since commanding my first sailing craft out of sight of land, it seemed that perhaps there might be something worth handing on to others; yet I still doubted my ability to express these experiences with sufficient clarity and vividness. Then I came within the influence of a yachtsman and publisher, W. H. Johnson, who first flattered my writings inordinately until I believed that readers would understand what I had to say, and then patiently suggested modifications in spelling words, arranging sentences and describing ideas, so that they really might understand.

Orkney, 1953   E.B.

PREFACE TO NEW EDITION

In 13 years since completing the first edition of this book it has been my good fortune to enjoy a couple more stirring races across the Atlantic Ocean, besides a great deal more sailing on many seas and oceans. It has also been my privilege to meet many more sailing people of great experience. Basically the doctrines I set down then as a guide to deep sea sailing have stood up to these further tests, but equipment and techniques have progressed greatly.

When the book was first published, many experienced yachtsmen who had sailed offshore successfully without lifelines, safety harness, liferafts and so forth, criticised what they considered was my obsession with safety equipment. Today such a view would be rare, and ocean racing authorities, for instance, normally demand attention to safety at least up to the standards I had suggested. Therefore, part of the original purpose of the book no longer exists, so in this modified edition I have cut out many pleas for what is now common doctrine among deep sea yachtsmen of all countries, and brought in more about developments of yacht seamanship in recent years. I have also been able to bring in photographs of several more fine craft in which I have enjoyed deep sea sailing.

One man who encouraged me to stress proper seamanlike precautions for safety was Robert Somerset, who wrote the foreword of this book. Surely the dangers of the sea were cruelly emphasised when he, one of the greatest deep sea yachtsmen of his era, was drowned at the time his yacht was lost at sea in a gale.

Lymington, 1966   E.B.

A FOREWORD BY ROBERT SOMERSET, D.S.O.

There must inevitably be very wide gaps in most yachtsmen's experience, however extensively they have cruised or however many races they have sailed. For instance, it would be perfectly possible to sail twice round the world without being unlucky enough to encounter a gale of more than Force 8, as real storms are fortunately rare except in high latitudes, winter months and in the hurricane seasons.

Furthermore, there are few men who can claim great experience both in first-class racing and in voyaging off-shore, though since the development of ocean racing to its present high pitch this is less so than formerly.

But the most serious gap in the knowledge of most of us is that there is hardly anyone who can compare from first-hand observation the behaviour of more than a few different types and sizes of yachts under the full range of conditions that they have to meet at sea. In forming our ideas of what is best we therefore have to depend much on the reports of others, and consequently there will always be a large demand for books on sailing that are written by those who really know.

Certainly no one is better qualified to produce such a book than Erroll Bruce. A submariner for many years, like so many who have gained for the Royal Naval Sailing Association the unsurpassed reputation as yacht sailors it holds today, he is used to seeing the sea much closer than is possible in a big ship. He has also cruised and raced in all sorts of boats in many parts of the world.

For most people, though, his name will chiefly be connected with *Samuel Pepys*, for in his charge she has proved herself one of the most formidable craft in her class in the world today. In a passage from Bermuda to New York in 1950 *Samuel Pepys* came unscathed through a really severe gale, such as can seldom have been weathered by so small a boat without damage. In two hard-sailed races across the North Atlantic, not to mention many other off-shore races, there can be little that Erroll Bruce has not learnt about getting the very utmost from both vessel and crew.

Ocean racing is merely cruising raised to an intenser pitch in which all thought of comfort is sacrificed to efficiency and speed. All the same principles apply and I feel sure that Erroll Bruce's ideas are likely to be equally valuable to all who go to sea in small yachts, whether they are interested mainly in racing or in the equally fine sport of cruising off-shore.

I

Planning a Cruise

F EW things in this world can give more lasting satisfaction than the achievement of a cruise in a small yacht. The more ambitious the cruise, the greater is the satisfaction. A man must have some object that impels him to set out. This is obvious. Yet it must be clear in his mind just what his object is; otherwise his ship may be prepared for one thing, his crew expecting another, and all the time he is hankering after something quite different.

The object.

There is a wide range of objects that have sent men sailing across the oceans in small craft. Slocum resolved to sail around the world in 37-foot long *Spray*, just to show himself that he could do it, as he felt that he had not cunning enough properly to bait a fish hook. Graham crossed the Atlantic alone in 30-foot long *Emanuel*, after over-strain from his work at home, so that he could cruise in new waters far from the telegraph office. Robinson set out in 32-foot long *Svaap* so that he could wander around the world in search of strange islands and interesting people. The Fisks, man and wife, sailed their *Debonair* to New Zealand in 1950, so that their young children, who were aboard, could start their life in a vigorous new country. Voss admits that he set out to sail round the world in a 38-foot long canoe *Tilikum* to achieve this feat in something smaller than Slocum's *Spray*. Robert Somerset has crossed the Atlantic many times in *Jolie Brise* and *Iolaire* largely because he likes the life at sea. In recent years more pleasure craft have set out to race each other across the oceans than have cruised for any other reason; a very high proportion of these ocean racers have achieved the object of their cruise, largely because it is in the nature of a race to know precisely where the destination lies.

As man is a land animal, any ocean voyage is a difficult matter for him. Before starting his preparations, he will do well to decide precisely what he wants to do and where he will go. That is unless he has such wealth that he can afford to prepare for anything, and act according to the whim of the moment.

Cruising.

Cruising really means voyaging upon the seas, so that strictly a race across the seas is a cruise, while an expedition which consists largely of visiting harbours, creeks and bays is a marine excursion. However it has been recent practice to call any peregrination afloat a cruise, even if the greater time is spent not cruising but at anchor. This is distinguished from the occasions when yachts are competing against each other in cruising from one place to another, by so-called 'ocean racing'; this is in spite of the fact that some of these races do not lead across oceans but have their courses in the English Channel, North Sea or Bay of Biscay.

Perhaps the greatest joy of a cruise, in the modern accepted sense, comes from the sense of independence, in an age when ashore man has built up such a complex system of life that few people are ever dependent upon themselves. When cruising one can move, not just when the hands of the clock point to the figures printed in a time-table, but when conditions and feelings make it right to move. At sea one's actions are controlled not by convention or the needs of a soulless mass, but by the needs of the ship and the individuals aboard her.

The pleasures of a cruise, whether it is a way of life upon the seas or is a convenient way of visiting interesting places, can be almost unlimited; yet equally the discomforts can be well-nigh interminable. The difference between these two extremes depends upon seamanship; that is seamanship in the widest sense, meaning the art of living upon the sea. Perfection in the art depends not only upon what is done when afloat, but to an equal extent upon the thought and preparation beforehand. It is folly to ignore the experience of others in the past; part of the pleasure of any cruise comes from reading and listening to what others have encountered, followed by the delights of anticipation in planning a cruise for oneself.

There are very few places in the world that have not been visited by yachtsmen; yet it is surprising that some still set out for a cruise, when the experience of their predecessors could have told them that the season made it nearly impossible, that the course selected was dangerous or that other factors would ruin the pleasure of the cruise. Before deciding on any cruise it would be well to read all that can be found about the seasons, winds, ocean currents and local information of the places to be visited. Much can be found from the different volumes of the *Admiralty Sailing Directions*, which are packed with factual information, although the opinions are always assiduous in stressing the dangers, so that a reader depending on these alone might be left with the impression that going afloat anywhere was a grave hazard. There are numerous books with excellent accounts of cruises by yachtsmen, some of which go to the opposite extreme and almost suggest that no difficulties need ever be encountered; the more of these several accounts that are read, the greater will be the joy of one's own cruise.

Ocean Racing.

It is in many ways simpler to enter an ocean race than to plan an independent cruise to the same place, as so much of the planning will have been done by the body organising the race. The organisers will have seen to it that the course is practicable; they will decide a suitable date for the start; they will arrange for the reception of vessels at their destination, and sometimes even lay down a standard of craft and equipment required for the race. The value of these services is so great that vastly more people have gained pleasure from sailing to far places than would have been the case if the sport of ocean racing had not developed. Man is gregarious by nature, and if some like periods of solitude or isolation at sea, they seem equally to enjoy discussing their experiences with others of a like mind.

Racing puts the knowledge of the most experienced competitors at the disposal of all entering, who can watch their methods, often follow their tracks, and afterwards discuss the reasons for various actions. The planning of a cruise may be simplified by entering a race, yet successful competition requires a far higher standard of seamanship than does cruising, when speed is immaterial. That most experienced seaman E. G. Martin wrote, 'Ocean racing is magnificent. It seems to me to confront a skipper with the most difficult problems with which a man can be faced at sea.'

Yet ocean racing does more than to confront skippers with difficult

B

decisions, and their crews with hard work and wet shirts. Racing a yacht hard as part of a good crew is an experience that once felt some will hanker after for ever. Perhaps these feelings are reserved for those that truly love the sea with its ever-changing moods and constant surprises. Racing at sea can bring out the best qualities in people; it gives scope for adventure such as is hard to come by in any other sport. Each haul on the halyard or sheet, every cold douche of discomfort, each long night hour at the tiller, is for the good of the ship. She returns the offering ten-fold with the lasting joy of satisfaction that each individual gains from being part of a team that works together whole-heartedly.

On the map an ocean looks one vast expanse, perhaps coloured in one unchanging shade of blue. A race over such a distance, probably sighting nothing but sea the whole way, might seem sheer drudgery. Yet there is nothing monotonous in a long race; no two patches of sea feel quite the same; no sequence of weather is ever the same; and the unremitting effort to keep the yacht sailing at her best provides endless variety in employment.

Preparations.

The success of a cruise will depend inevitably on the care and imagination with which every detail of preparation has been carried out. Once a ship is in deep waters far from land her very survival, and that of her crew, may depend on these preparations. This could scarcely be shown more powerfully than in W. E. Sinclair's intriguing book *Cruises of Joan*. An experienced seaman, who had sailed his small yacht to Madeira and the Baltic, he describes how he planned to cross the North Atlantic *via* Iceland. After three whole months preparing his craft he records the decision as the season grew late, that unless he started not fully prepared, he might never start at all. Starting partly unprepared is a common habit, he rightly explains, and perhaps it is good enough in summer for coastal waters with shelter fifty miles away. But an ocean passage is different. In the final chapter Sinclair describes how he was forced to abandon and lose his ship in mid-Atlantic. It is an invaluable warning of what such a cruise entails.

An ocean passage is still far from dull for those who have successfully prepared and rehearsed every event that they encounter on the voyage.

Seasons.

The seasons are far less simple than just summer and winter in each hemisphere, with their corresponding good and bad weather. Parts of the North Atlantic, even no further north than the coast of Spain, are infested with icebergs and fog in June. All tropical oceans, except the South Atlantic, experience fierce storms during part of their summer season.

A careful study of the weather during the various seasons must therefore be made as one of the first stages in the preparation of a voyage. It seems elementary not to set out against the direction of an ocean monsoon, or close to the time when the monsoon may change, yet that has been done, while others have blundered into the area of hurricanes and typhoons. No seaman who has ever experienced the devastating violence of a tropical revolving storm would any more consider risking his ship and crew within their known areas and seasons, than he would sail his vessel into an atomic minefield. The United States Atomic Energy Commission in their report at the end of 1952 stated that a moderate hurricane has the kinetic energy of 1,000 atom bombs of the type dropped on Japan.

Costs.

Very few yachtsmen have unlimited supplies of money, so financial necessity alone entails detailed planning, without which costs cannot be guessed. Many cruises have come to grief when money ran out unexpectedly and prematurely; the grief must have been heavy indeed if, as so often happened, the cruise was abandoned at the stage where costs were heaviest, yet the value of the vessel was least.

Costs depend very much on forethought, thus an essential replacement of equipment might be bought for very little at home, yet mean six weeks' delay, or the cost of cables and air freight, in the Azores. Many set against their costs the hope of a large return from writing a book of their experiences; unless the writer is already experienced as an author, or has something really new to tell, this result is most unlikely. It must be remembered that quite excellent accounts of yacht voyages to almost anywhere are already numerous; the standard is high, and it is likely that the effort put into writing a book after the voyage would have been more profitably employed in really careful preparation beforehand.

It is a safe guess that the more fortuitous the preparations for a cruise, the greater will be the cost above what the owner was expecting to spend, and the more will be the extravagance in unnecessary expenditure.

Bases.

For any extensive cruise a vessel will need bases away from her home port, where she can find stores, refit her gear, and perhaps be hauled out of the water. The cost of goods and labour varies enormously in different places, so that information about the possibilities of any place saves much money. One of the most valuable things in any possible base is the presence of a friend or agent who can give accurate information in advance; wandering quietly into a place in the hope that it can provide the needs of the ship is an exorbitantly expensive means of cruising. Thus recently various English yachts cruising and racing in American waters achieved great economy by basing their cruises on Bermuda, which is in the sterling area, and to which stores could be sent from England without import restrictions. Others bound for American waters, refitted at Antigua after crossing the Atlantic, as the weather was suitable and the cost a small fraction of what would have been spent in America.

Stores.

There was a time when the stores of a whole fleet, other than the needs of ordnance, comprised no more than hemp, canvas, simple bosun's ironmongery, rum, biscuit and salted meat. Since then we have developed a more complex way of life, and our needs are much greater, even if it is uncertain whether the happiness of man has increased correspondingly. The problem of the stores to be carried by a vessel, and replenishments needed during her cruise, requires detailed study. Happy indeed is the seaman who is never short of any essential, yet carries nothing on board that is never needed. To achieve this happiness, he must first know the purpose, destination and general requirements of the cruise. It is commonplace for a vessel to be delayed longer from her purpose by the lack of some small but essential item of stores than by many head winds or calms. The more complicated the gear and equipment, the greater is the stores problem; it has been suggested for instance that for every hour saved by motoring during a calm, four hours are wasted finding spare parts to make the engine work.

Freight and Road Transport

It often happens that a cruise or race can only be achieved, due to shortage of time, by sending the yacht part of the way, carried in a ship or towed on land in a trailer. No good seaman likes these methods very much as it exposes his vessel to more risks than when she is well handled afloat, and it is risk largely beyond the control of the owner. A yacht is designed to float, and encounters quite different strains and stresses when lifted out of the water. The best that can be done by the owner is to ensure that she travels in a cradle that distributes the strains fairly, and he must protect all the equipment and gear carefully. After a short journey on a road trailer on one occasion, all the standing rigging of a yacht's mast which rested on her deck had been stranded due to insufficient packing to cope with the jolting. Another yacht, supported in a metal cradle when travelling in a fast liner, suffered considerable damage to hull and fittings from vibration.

Programme.

There are so many factors to be worked out in achieving a satisfactory and enjoyable cruise that some sort of programme is necessary at an early stage of the preparations, unless it be a single-handed cruise when time is unlimited, or the owner is wealthy enough to buy the entire services of all those on whom his cruise depends. This programme should first be sketched out broadly, becoming filled in with more and more detail as the planning progresses. Some claim that they hate being tied to any pre-arranged programme, yet curiously enough it always proves easier to alter a carefully considered plan than to do what one wants when no clear plan exists; often enough the cruise without a real plan or object develops into a continuous struggle to catch up with circumstances that are beyond the control of the yacht's crew.

Even for a simple cruise of short duration there is much to be arranged, so a straightforward statement allows the crew the best chance of making useful preparations. A sample programme for a very simple cruise in countries and ports unknown to the crew is shown in Table I*a*.

Dar-es-Salaam,
East Africa,
6th September, 1946

INDIAN OCEAN CRUISE

September 10th (After dark)	Sail from Dar-es-Salaam. Provisions for one week.
11th	Arrive Bagamoyo. Crew will stay ashore due to malarial mosquitoes.
13th (After dark)	Sail from Bagamyo.
14th	Arrive Zanzibar Island Complete with one week's provisions.
14th (After dark)	Sail from Zanzibar.
16th	Arrive Pemba Island. Crew will stay ashore.
18th (After dark)	Sail from Pemba Island.
20th	Arrive Mombasa (Kenya).

Table I*a*. Simple Cruise Programme for a small boat.

Another programme is shown in Table I*b* for an ambitious cruise that entailed sailing long distances and visiting many places within a short period of time. This was the final programme produced before starting the cruise; it included all the essential dates and places on which detailed planning could be based, yet still left periods for cruising when the destinations could be arranged locally without affecting any arrangements for stores, correspondence or detailed planning.

	ATLANTIC CRUISE, 1952		Plymouth, 17th March, 1952
Date		*Programme*	*Address*
Monday	7th April	Lower yacht into water Ship mast Fit out	
Saturday	12th ,,	Sail from Plymouth for trial cruise Visit South coast ports as convenient	
Sunday	20th ,,	Arrive The Nore Crew to refit yacht at Sheerness or Chatham	H.M.S. *Abercrombie*, Chatham
Monday	28th ,,	Sail up River Thames	Tower Pier,
Wednesday	30th ,,	Arrive Pool of London	London
Thursday	1st May	Enter London docks for shipment in M.V. *Brittany* (Ship may be 4 or 5 days late embarking cargo)	M.V. *Brittany*, Royal Mail House, Leadenhall Street, London, E.C.3
Saturday	3rd ,,	*Brittany* sails (May be 4 or 5 days late)	
Thursday	15th ,,	Due Bermuda Disembark and cruise in Bermudian waters Embark provisions for 6 weeks	Royal Bermuda Yacht Club, Hamilton, Ber- muda
Friday	23rd ,,	Sail from Bermuda Exercise in Gulf Stream	
Thursday	29th ,,	Arrive America. Clear customs and immigration at New London, sail at once	
Friday	30th ,,	(Storm Trisail race, if in time)	
Monday	2nd June	Arrive New York Measure for handicap and slip at City Island or New London	Messrs Ratsey and Lapthorne, City Island 64, New York
Thursday	5th ,,	Sail for cruise in Long Island Sound	
Friday	6th ,,	Montauk race (Off Soundings Club)	
Saturday	7th ,,	Shelter Island race (off Soundings Club) Cruise in Long Island Sound	
Friday	13th ,,	Oyster Bay to Newport race	
Wednesday	18th ,,	Arrive Newport, R.I.	Ida Lewis Yacht Club Newport, R.I., U.S.A.
Thursday	19th ,,	Inspection by Cruising Club of America at Brenton Cove	
Saturday	21st ,,	Bermuda race	
Thursday	26th ,,	Due Bermuda Complete with provisions for 5 weeks	Royal Bermuda Yacht Club, Hamilton, Ber- muda
Tuesday	1st July	Start of TRANS-ATLANTIC race (May be delayed one day)	
Sunday	27th ,,	Due Plymouth	Queen's Harbour- master, Plymouth
Wednesday	30th ,,	Yacht to be handed over ready for next race	
Thursday	31st ,,	Special crew 'pay off'	

Table I*b*. Sample Programme for an elaborate cruise.

II

The Craft

IDEALLY one should build a vessel fit to carry out the voyage con-
templated. Some have the good fortune to do this. Often it comes the
other way round, and a man already owning a vessel plans a cruise
that he feels within her power. Thus Conor O'Brien was invited to join
a mountaineering party in New Zealand, and having recently designed
and build himself *Saoirse* for the waters off the Western Irish coast,
decided to test her further with the long voyage round Africa and then
run down the Easting to New Zealand. G. H. P. Muhlhauser, having
resolved to push out and have a look round the world, selected
Amaryllis as suiting his purpose best. Most fortunate of all have been
those who like John Guzzwell have been able to build with their own
hands a dream ship, such as his *Treasure*, and set out with her for an
extended voyage across oceans. Robin Kilroy spent twenty years and
more considering his perfect off-shore sailing cruiser before he designed,
built and sailed across three oceans, his unusual *Boleh*, with the bows
of an Arab dhow and the body of a Chinese junk.

Requirements.

The requirements of any yacht sailing in deep waters, whatever the
purpose of her cruise, can be reduced to three essential factors:
- (*a*) Safety.
  > So that she may remain afloat and intact whatever weather
  > she meets.
- (*b*) Control.
  > So that she may reach her destination.
- (*c*) Space.
  > So that she may carry her crew with sufficient stores and
  > comfort to maintain them and the ship.

Size.

It is clear from actual results that safety in the open sea does not depend on the size of the craft. Under certain conditions the reverse is the case, and a larger vessel becomes more difficult to handle. Discounting freak cases, such as the open rowing boat in which Captain Ridgway and Sergeant Blyth crossed the North Atlantic in 1966, many ocean crossings have been made safely in really small craft, that were fit for sea. The 20-foot *Nova Espero* was scarcely suited to an ocean voyage when the Smith brothers sailed from Nova Scotia to England in 1949, as her cabin top was no more than a dinghy lashed into position; yet by building a water-tight cabin she was made quite seaworthy for her return across the Atlantic a year later. An even smaller vessel, *Little Western*, also made the double Atlantic crossing safely. This was through the same difficult waters in which the 47-foot ketch *Shanghai* was lost after successfully cruising 16,000 miles from China to Copenhagen; here too the 42-foot yawl *Lief Ericsson* disappeared. Going even further up the scale in size, the *Kobenhaven*, nearly 4,000 tons, and one of the largest sailing vessels ever built, was lost with all hands in the Southern Ocean during the 1920s.

However, if size is not essential for safety, it does determine the amount of space available for living, stores and equipment. *Sopronino*, under 20 feet long, crossed an ocean safely in 1952, providing some comfort for her crew with one man on watch at sea; yet she would not offer much of a home for two men during the days in harbour. There are many craft of some 30 feet overall length in which two or three people have enjoyed protracted cruises, such as Dr. and Mrs. Pye's voyage to the West Indies in *Moonraker*, 29 feet overall length. To find a vessel whose ocean voyage failed through inability to carry sufficient stores, one must go right down the scale to a 13-foot boat in which William Andrews was forced to abandon an Atlantic crossing. He was picked up by a passing steamer, and his evidence is all the more valuable as he tried again in a similar sized boat called *Phantom Ship*, which also failed to complete the voyage from lack of stores; however he did succeed in crossing from New England to Lisbon in a 14-foot boat, besides another Atlantic crossing from Beverly Harbour to the Channel in a dory. In recent years two men have found their different methods of squeezing themselves and their stores onboard even smaller boats. The American Robert Manry, in the summer of 1965, sailed from America to England direct in his 13 ft. 6 in. boat *Tinkerbelle*, arriving in a wave of publicity. The day before this the Englishman John Riding arrived in Bermuda after a very lengthy crossing from England *via* Spain, the Azores and the trade wind route in his *Sjo Ag* of only 12 ft. 6 in., which is certainly the smallest boat to cross the Atlantic Ocean. There have been yachts far bigger than this whose ocean voyages have come close to failure from shortage of water or food, but these examples show incomplete planning, and not lack of space.

Type.

The expression 'a fine ocean-going type' is used frequently by yachtsmen; yet often it refers to vessels so clumsy that their ocean-going ability would be limited. A search through the plans of sailing yachts that have made successful ocean passages shows truly amazing variety of types, ranging from Voss's dug-out canoe *Tilikum*, six times as long as her beam, to Slocum's *Spray*, probably first built as an oysterman, with massive timbers and a beam nearly half her length. They range from Adlard Coles's very light displacement Tumlare type *Cohoe*, which raced across a stormy North Atlantic in twenty-one days, to the very heavy displacement ex-Havre pilot vessel *Jolie Brise*, which made this passage four times, first under E. G. Martin and then R. Somerset. It is much more likely that there is an 'ocean-going type' of man, who will make a successful voyage in any sound vessel, than that any special type of vessel is alone suited to the deep sea.

The best type of vessel for deep sea sailing depends on the object and purpose of the voyage. Many yachts intended for the open sea developed from the lines of the fishing trawler. Yet the sailing trawler's purpose was to act as a vast fly-wheel and drag her nets at a steady speed through water; she needed space to stow dead fish, and provide the very barest existence for the large crew which was normally busy working the nets, an operation assisted by a low freeboard amidships. Few yachtsmen want to carry around all the bulk of a fly-wheel, which means big sails and heavy gear to move her; nor do they share the accommodation needs of dead fish, or enjoy such a low freeboard that the decks are needlessly awash. An age-old description of the Beaufort wind scale records Force 8 as the condition when smacks take shelter, yet in deep water cruising a moderate gale must be encountered quite often.

For ocean going, a craft must be fit to suffer strong gales, and even storms, with their 6o-knot wind speeds and exceptionally high waves. This needs strength, but the stresses increase vastly with the size of a craft, besides increasing at a lesser rate with its weight. In this respect the dug-out canoe, after a cork, would be the most seaworthy. A compact, strongly built, yet light hull will be safe as it rises and falls with the waves; however, this readiness to follow the capriciousness of the waves will be uncomfortable in rough weather. Aboard a larger, heavier craft the motion will be less violent, but the stresses greater; also the mitigating comfort of less motion is lost if the craft's steadiness means that the waves wash over her.

The type of fast cruiser that has developed on each side of the Atlantic through the incentive of off-shore racing is a thoroughly sound seaboat. She is far more easy to manage, and more fun to sail, than the yachts that developed from work boats.

Freeboard.

Many of the work boats had low freeboards due to their function. Some of the racing type of yacht of fifty years ago make excellent seaboats with the one exception that they lack freeboard. A seaman, at all costs, must keep the sea from the inside of his craft, and prefers to keep it off his decks. The higher the freeboard of his yacht, particularly in the important midships section, the easier it is to achieve this object. It is good freeboard, perhaps more than any other feature, that makes a yacht comfortable and safe in the open sea.

Stems.

Much has been written about the advantages, or even essential need, of a straight stem and long run of keel for a sea-going yacht. This probably dates from the period when this type of yacht was the only reasonable alternative; the racing yacht with cut-away fore-foot, long over-hangs, low freeboard, short keel and vast spread of scarcely manageable canvas, was certainly not suitable as an open sea cruising yacht. She could not even heave to, but this was due more to her sail plan than to her profile.

It is a mistake to assume that all the features of the racing yacht of that time were unfit for the open sea, while all those of the work boats are deep sea features; a long bowsprit is just as bad as an exaggerated

over-hang; forecastle galleys are as bad as over-lean bows. Going into
a sea the long lean bows of a racer slam into the waves, but the ponderous weight of a trawler's massive stem wallows like a bulldozer as its
perpendicular line gives no warning to the bow of a coming wave.

A well-designed bow with a moderate over-hang, smooth curves
leading to some power in the shoulder, and free of bulky weight, will
go to windward far more comfortably than either. So long as her hull
and sail plan are balanced, she will heave to readily. Many straight
stemmed, long keeled vessels steer abominably, while a yacht with a
short deep fin keel in the right place is often exceptionally steady on the
tiller.

Sterns.

Losses among working craft at sea show that the danger of pooping
is a very real one, which may be fatal to the vessel and her crew. All
those who have experienced a severe pooping realise this to the full, and
often hold that some particular type of stern is responsible, or that some
other type is immune. Yet facts do not support this as vessels with
counter, transom or canoe stern have all experienced pooping in
rough following seas.

The dangerous pooping waves are those which rear up astern and
break right over the boat, perhaps even causing her to broach-to. One
thing that may make a wave rear up and break in this way is the wake
of a fast moving craft. So speed affects the chance of being pooped,
but the wake varies with the lines of the whole ship, and not just the
stern alone; thus a yacht with clean lines can go faster before she is
liable to be pooped than can one that stirs up a tumult astern. However,
if her stern is heavy, or lacks the buoyancy to rise quickly to a steep
following wave, her chances of pooping are increased.

Cockpits.

The cockpit is a recess in the deck that provides extra security
to the helmsman and hands required on deck. Robinson, having sailed
half way across the Pacific, tore out the cockpit of his 32-foot *Svaap*,
designed by John Alden; he preferred to board it over and have extra
space below decks. Few would agree with such a drastic step. The logbook of the great schooner *Fleetwing*, in the first yacht race across the
North Atlantic, records how she shipped a sea which washed from the

cockpit six men, the entire watch, who were never seen again. Her cockpit was shallow, but a flush deck provides even less security.

If rough weather is to be expected, and no deep sea voyage can be expected to miss this altogether, there should be a cockpit that really does give a good chance for the men on deck, perhaps sleepy and exhausted, to remain inboard. This means a cockpit of ample depth to keep a man's centre of gravity below the top of the cockpit. Seas will inevitably come inboard, so the cockpit must be water-tight to prevent water running through into the bilges. Graham's struggle with a great storm 500 miles off the New England coast of America nearly led to the loss of *Emanuel*; he admits that had he been on deck when a British cruiser closed his yacht, he would probably have abandoned her. *Emanuel*'s unseaworthiness was due to her open cockpit.

For safety in open waters, the cockpit should be only as large as is necessary to shelter the watch on deck. A bigger cockpit provides less security, and leaves a larger hole for the sea to fill. If the cockpit really is small, even when full of sea water it will not endanger the stability of a small sailing vessel with deep ballasted keel. However, except in the warmest of weather, it is uncomfortable to steer for long sitting in the water, so a self-draining cockpit is a great advantage. In a boat with a low freeboard it may be necessary to choose between a deep cockpit and self-draining; then safety should come before convenience, and a good bailer provided.

Rig.

Robinson, having sailed round the world in the ketch *Svaap*, wrote that the ketch was the finest rig for a small ocean-going boat. O'Brien also sailed round the world in a ketch, and considered it a poor rig, except that the position of the masts helped the accommodation plan. O'Brien, too, made his rig complicated, so as to give his crew of paid hands something to do on long passages. Every rig has had its successes, or perhaps it is that in spite of certain rigs, someone has succeeded with them.

Purely from the sailing point of view, the sloop is the most efficient and simple rig for the general variety of sailing conditions. If the vessel is so small that with sloop rig both sails are still easily handled, there seems little advantage in splitting up the rig into smaller sails. The need for ease in handling will depend on the size of crew to be carried, so the sloop which suits a strong racing crew might be better rigged as a cutter or ketch if the same vessel is normally to be sailed single-handed. Accident has always to be considered, such as the loss of a mast, so it might be held best for an ocean cruiser to be rigged with more than one mast. However when the ketch *Joan* lost her mainmast in the Atlantic, the undamaged mizzen did not stop her being abandoned. The very simplicity of a single mast may mean that its rigging can be better watched.

As few yachts will have a crew of paid hands which, like O'Brien's, need occupying, the most important factor for the safe and speedy handling of a sailing craft is the reliability and simplicity of its rig. If the skipper knows that he ought to lower the mainsail, but is reluctant to give the order as he doubts the ability of his crew to tame the unwieldy lurches of the gaff on a dark, wild night, then the rig is not safe.

An important consideration on a long passage is chafe. After sailing across the Atlantic and back in his gaff-rigged cutter *Karin III*, G. C. L. Payne wrote about his gaff flogging against the cross-trees, knocking off the port spreader on one occasion, and causing much seam-sewing. Having myself sailed 10,000 miles in the 30-foot length Bermudian sloop *Samuel Pepys*, which included two Atlantic crossings, and experienced no chafe at all except to the spinnakers, I know that this rig has powerful advantages. There was a time when the slides of the mainsail with a tall Bermuda rig were prone to jam, making it impossible to lower the sail in an emergency without sending a man aloft; equally there was a time when the steam engine was so uncertain that no seaman would venture to sea without sails in addition to his engine. Both these are passed.

Accommodation.

Just as the hull form and rig of many cruising yachts in the past were based on work craft, developed for quite different purposes, the accommodation plan seems often to have been based on houses, in which quite a different way of life is practised. A vessel must be very large before her living space approaches the capacity of a house, yet far smaller ones were often divided up, like a house, into compartments with doors; but each so small that the result was as dark and confined as a rabbit warren.

The accommodation must be planned to suit the purpose of the vessel. If she is often to be at sea for long passages, the space below decks will seem quite small after only a day or so. The feeling of restriction is best mitigated by making what space there is seem as roomy as possible, avoiding extra bulkheads and sub-divisions. Light and air are still welcome below, however much there may be to spare on deck.

A place must be found for each function, and every item of equipment. In practice the living space within a ship depends less on its cubic capacity than on the habits of the crew.

The most important functions of the accommodation are:

(*a*) Preparation of food for the crew.

(*b*) Rest for the crew.

(*c*) Navigation of the yacht.

Each of these has equal importance in the cruise of the ship, but there is no doubt that the first is the hardest. Cooking, and the preparation of food, therefore deserves the position below where the motion is least, and the supply of air and light is best. The cook needs the use of both hands and somewhere to use a large number of tools and apparatus. It is also important that the members of the crew eating their meals can sit comfortably within easy reach of the cook's position. So in a craft designed for comfort at sea, the accommodation plan should be built up round the galley, which needs to be in the best position of all.

Bunks are vital, and although they are in use for more time than the galley, very little skill is required in their use. The nearer they are to amidships the less will be the motion in a sea-way, and the easier sleep will become; in any small yacht, bunks are likely to be untenable at sea before the mast, although this position may necessarily be used in harbour when all the crew need to sleep at the same time, with no one on watch.

Bunks must have ample length to be comfortable, at least 6 inches longer than a fully stretched man; but in a sea-way they are most comfortable when a modest width allows the body to be wedged in firmly between the sides. With lee-boards of ample height, such as 10 inches above the mattress top, the best width is no more than 20 inches and they may become narrower at the foot without loss of comfort. A highly sprung mattress can be most uncomfortable at sea, and with such a fitting I once had to sleep on the cabin deck as the springs seemed to exaggerate the motion. A hard mattress is not uncomfortable with some practice, but projections into the bunk at body level, such as are frequently found, will produce chronic outcrops of bruises in any bad weather.

Navigation is considered in detail in a later chapter, but its accommodation requirements for cruising are comparatively modest, as far less jugglery is needed for the under-cover mechanics of navigation than is required for cooking. The art of navigation will be carried out in every part of the ship, but the mere calculations and plotting do not take very long, so a position of far greater motion can be tolerated for this than for cooking. Most of this work is of a simple routine type requiring a few books and some easily operated tools, of which the pencil is the most important.

The navigator needs a weather-proof position where he can be wedged in a sitting position with the use of both hands. In front of this there must be a fixed or portable shelf 22 inches by 28 inches for his plotting.

Most of the real problems of navigation are likely to have been solved before the voyage even starts, and new ones that arise will be solved just as much by a good meal and comfortable bunk, as by manipulations at the chart table.

However, for serious ocean racing the standard is so high that winning will usually require elaborate equipment and ample space to make full use of it.

Survey

Successful cruises across oceans have been undertaken by small sailing vessels of almost every size, shape and type from 12 feet length upwards; some were better for their purpose than others. It may sound all too easy, and sometimes it is easy, if everything has been considered beforehand. But on a long voyage any weakness will show up; the ocean is merciless. *Marabu*, setting out for a 10,000 miles cruise in 1952, ran into a gale right at the start, in which a man was washed overboard but fortunately recovered twenty minutes later; *Vertue XXXV*, only 25 feet overall length, had covered over 3,000 miles of an Atlantic voyage before she met her worst gale, described so vividly by Humphrey Barton. *Temptress*, 34 feet length overall, was near the Azores, where the ocean chart records, 'Storms almost unknown', before Edward Allcard met his worst gale after sailing her single-handed twice across

Plate 1. *Dayspring*, a converted Ramsgate trawler of 56 ft., here shown in fine weather, later demonstrated the need for the Beaufort scale maxim that in force 8 smacks take shelter

Plate 2. *Cohoe II*, a yacht of 35 ft., seen here in the foreground in fine weather at the start of a Fastnet race, was quite at home in force 8

Plate 3. A lifebuoy that a fully clothed man can get into in a rough sea. The man is about to be hoisted by the line seen attached to his safety-belt lifting strop

Plate 4. *Fabius* of 34 ft. overall sets out past Anglesey in the Irish Sea race. Those in the cockpit are well protected

the Atlantic. No one can foretell when these trials will come, so right from the start the skipper must be able to rely implicitly on the condition of hull, spars and standing rigging.

Before a man sets out for a long cruise he must know a good deal about a great many subjects. He will probably be an expert in some, while in others he will have only a working knowledge. Some, for instance, have set out without the knowledge of sextant navigation, confident of learning it before reaching the first landfall 3,000 miles away. This might be a reasonable risk, but there is no room for any risk at all over the ship's condition. Unless the owner is himself sufficiently experienced in yacht construction, the fee for a professional survey will be well worth paying. It will be an infernal nuisance to the owner to have someone prodding and boring holes all over his ship, and is best done well before fitting-out commences. Numerous voyages have come to grief, perhaps with loss of life, certainly with great cost in money, which could have been saved by the employment of a first-class yacht surveyor, many of whom advertise their names in the yachting papers.

III

Fittings and Equipment

AN elaborately fitted yacht is not necessarily the best equipped for deep water sailing. It may even be an advantage, on preparing for a long cruise, to simplify the ship by reducing fittings of which the advantage is doubtful or the reliability uncertain. A labour saving convenience that fails in bad weather may cause more work to regain control of the vessel than was ever saved by its use; fitting a safety device may lure an owner into a false sense of security till the gadget fails in an emergency. There is little advantage in apparatus which saves time in doing its function, yet requires twice that amount of time in maintenance.

Purpose.

It is so easy to be attracted by some ingenious gadget that does a job cleverly, or even by some contrivance that shows fine workmanship or a polished finish. Yet a yacht bound on a long cruise has no room for anything that does not assist the purpose of the cruise, whether that purpose requires maximum comfort for the crew, maximum speed for the craft, or perhaps the ability to navigate under some special circumstances. The criterion for any equipment carried is whether it is an effective contribution towards the purpose of the voyage. For almost any ambitious cruise, when there will be no yacht chandlers, mechanics or fitters just around the corner, the first essential for any equipment is that it can stand up to its job without failure.

Weight and space.

In a small yacht space and weight will limit the amount of equipment that can be carried. This amount may be far less than it would be convenient to have on board, so some degree of priority must be given to equipment, depending on the purpose of the voyage. In assessing this order of priority all the equipment required for life on board must be considered, and perhaps even the size of each of the crew with the bulk of food, water and clothes needed to support him. However, this chapter deals only with the ship's mobility, the equipment needed for the safety of the crew, navigation and signalling is considered elsewhere.

Sails and rigging.

In a yacht that cruises with sails as her main motive power, obviously these, and the rigging that enables them to be spread, have the first priority. A sailing yacht bound for an ocean cruise may have automatic steering, a refrigerator and echo-sounding, but she is poorly equipped if her rigging is not absolutely sound, and her outfit does not include some sails in first-rate condition.

The life of a sail depends largely on its treatment. The after part carries the heaviest strains and stresses, so should be guarded most carefully; any small hole or failure of the stitching will increase these strains and may well lead to a blown-out sail that with care could have lasted many thousand more miles. When full of wind and properly set, the strain is evenly distributed over the sail, but during any evolution such as reefing, lowering or tacking, far greater strains may come on to sections of the sail and damage it. The sails can be nursed by careful treatment, such as never allowing them to flog. A crew that frequently gets the yachts in irons when tacking, that fumbles the sheets, and takes an unnecessary time over hoisting and lowering, will prove expensive in canvas.

Yachts have successfully cruised far with almost every type of rig, but the amount of work involved and even the overall speed of the ship depend largely on the amount of chafe the gear suffers. Fore and aft rig is designed primarily for reaching and beating into the wind, when its efficiency is high; a deep sea cruise is likely to include long distances running before the wind, when the fore and aft rig is far less efficient as sails and moving spars almost inevitably come up against the shrouds of the mast which supports them, causing chafe however much the rigging is draped with baggy-wrinkle.

Down-Wind Rig.

When running before the wind the sails and their moving spars would be best placed on the lee side of the mast that supports them;

this not only makes it easier to avoid chafe, but keeps them in a state
of stable equilibrium, so that a slight change of course or shift of wind
will not bring the whole apparatus crashing over to the other tack.
The square sail achieved this well in larger vessels, but attempts to
adapt the fore and aft rig in a small vessel to carrying a square sail have
not been satisfactory; both the large sail and the heavy spar aloft are
unwieldy, while chafe between the spar and the mast remains a major
problem. Nor is this extra apparatus really necessary, as many yachts
have made long down-wind passages satisfactorily without any extra
equipment, using a pair of headsails boomed out forward of the mast.
Each of these sails can be of a size readily handled by the crew, yet
their combined area will be ample to drive the ship; both can be jibs
or genoas of the ship's normal complement of sails, so the only extra
equipment needed is a second light spinnaker pole.

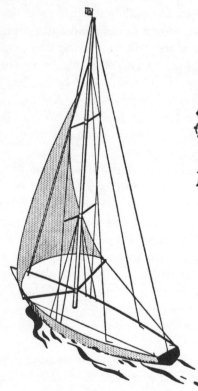

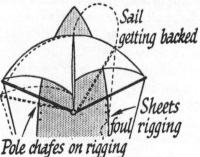

Fig. III, 1. Twin foresails
boomed to the mast make a
good deep sea running rig,
except that the tolerance of
wind direction is limited

Fig. III, 1, shows how twin foresails can be set with their poles secured to the mast, as is required by ocean racing rules. The limitation of this arrangement is that it will tolerate only a small variation of wind from right astern, before the lee pole comes against the rigging and the weather sail loses its driving area or falls in. A far more seamanlike rig, when not handicapped by racing rules, is shown in Fig. III, 2, where both spinnaker poles are pivoted at a point nearer to the tack of the

Fig. III, 2. Twin foresails boomed before the mast allow a wide variety of wind direction and keep spars and sheets clear of the rigging

Full spread of sail presented to wind

Spars always clear rigging

Sheets always clear of rigging

sails; this position keeps the spars well clear of the rigging, and the weather sail spread fully, through a wide variation of wind direction. Chafe is reduced to a minimum, self-steering is easily rigged, and in the event of a man falling overboard this is the very simplest running rig for turning the ship under control. Yet no code of racing rules at present allows this rig, and even that shown in Fig. III, 1, is only allowed by the Royal Ocean Racing Club when the total sail is not greater than the rated sail area of the vessel; however, a far larger area of sail is permitted with mainsail and spinnaker set.

The racing spinnaker spreads a fine area of sail to drive the ship but that same area may be heavy work for a cruising crew to handle on a dark night. Worse than that, the intense concentration needed to

prevent the balloon spinnaker from falling in makes it a poor sail
when cruising in anything but very settled conditions. Even with a full
racing crew this rig is not really satisfactory, as the many chafe spots
shown in Fig. III, 3, make it expensive on sails. The greatest danger

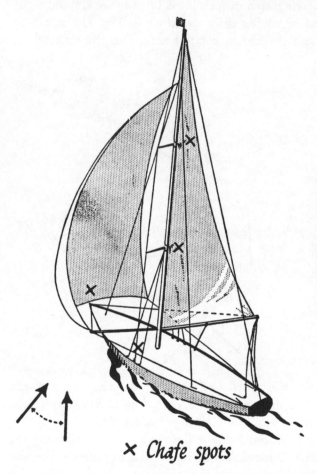

Fig. III, 3. Mainsail
and spinnaker is a poor
down-wind rig as chafe
is widespread and only
a small change in wind
direction can be toler-
ated. With the boom,
guys, snarl net and
numerous scotsmen are
needed for this rig in
the open sea, rounding
up in an emergency
takes a long time

× Chafe spots

when running in a sea-way is that the main boom will gybe accidentally,
so it is necessary to rig a fore guy to bouse the boom forward against
the motion of the ship and a kicking strap to prevent its vertical swing;
even then an accidental gybe in a heavy following sea may occur
with the finest helmsman. This happened to *Gulvain* when running
before a gale in the Transatlantic race of 1950, damaging her upper

spreaders and so putting her into a dangerous condition which was only overcome by exceptional seamanship.

Apart from the risk of an involuntary gybe, should a man go overboard the ship is rather like a bicycle going down hill with both of the rider's arms in slings. During the 1951 Pacific race to Honolulu, a man went overboard from *L'Apache* when running in a Force 5 wind; the main boom was guyed forward, and with the complications of a racing spinnaker besides all the little local attachments to prevent chafe with this unseamanlike rig (forced on the crew by the rules), the man was a long distance astern before the ship could be got on to the wind under full control.

Storm sails.

Effective storm sails are an essential part of the equipment of a yacht cruising off-shore. They need to be of a size and cut to enable the vessel to sail on all points in strong winds; it is particularly important that the design is such that they can be readily set in bad weather, as otherwise they become almost useless. Storm sails are often made with such heavy material and clumsy fittings that the very act of hoisting the sails is too hazardous and strenuous to be worth while. Sound sails can take a powerful force of wind when filled, yet may blow to pieces in a few seconds as they start to flap when being handled, so good design is more important than ponderous weight.

Rigging.

A well-fitted yacht of good design should need no extra size in the standing rigging for a long off-shore passage. Even when yachts have been driven hard during bad weather when ocean racing, a sport which has fostered tall Bermuda masts and tolerated no extra windage from outsize rigging, the loss of a mast has infrequently occurred, and even then was more often due to the failure of a fitting than the rigging wires.

The life of a halyard depends partly upon the number of times its sail is hoisted so in fickle weather conditions an occasional failure is always a possibility. With the violent motion of a small yacht, perhaps carrying no sail due to such a failure, it requires superb courage and seamanship for a man to go aloft to reeve a new halyard, but it is far better seamanship to have rigged spare halyards before the vessel left harbour should the length of her voyage be such that this accident may happen.

Sail material.

The material from which sails are made should be strong for its weight, withstand all climates and abrasion, resist stretching and be proof against rot when stowed away wet. All this means that synthetic cloth has a big advantage over natural material, and improvements are steadily being made in its qualities.

Ropes and cordage.

A sailing yacht owner has been known to invest in a new engine when his yacht's rigging was far beyond the equivalent stage of needing a re-bore. This is bad seamanship if the ship is ever intended to carry sail, as should the mast come down the torn rigging tangled round the screw will make the new engine little help to the yacht's safety. To keep the rigging in first-rate condition over a long period of time it will probably prove an economy to fit stainless steel wire rope.

On a long ocean cruise, sheets and guys get more wear than in many a season of week-end yachting, so wear will be heavy. Yet it is expensive in sails and crew effort to use them until they part, as the gust which blows out the sheet will damage the seams and fibres of the sail left slatting, so that an emergency call may be necessary to the hands resting below. If space for spare cordage is restricted then it is important to fit the longest wearing sheets and guys, and synthetic materials, such as Terylene, have proved able to do the job best; they are certainly economical in crew effort compared with any natural fibres, and may even prove economical in cost.

Shock cord.

Shock cord is a tough elastic rope, with a core of many parts of rubber. It is made in many different sizes and strengths. This is most valuable material for reducing wear and chafe, and seems to have taken the place of baggy-wrinkle as the main equipment for the reduction of wear and tear from long sea passages.

Pumps.

An important part of the sea-going equipment of a yacht is her bilge pumps. The yacht's hull and cockpit should be water-tight so that very little water ought to get into her bilges; but 'ought' is not a very authoritative word for a small craft in a rough sea. Sooner or later there will be leaks from hull fittings, such as engine cooling water inlets, sanitary outlets and shaft bearings; or seams may open up or heavy water come aboard and force its way below. The struggle recorded by Humphrey Barton in the book *Vertue XXXV* to keep afloat his storm damaged and partly flooded ship gives a vivid impression of the essential need for a good pump. For such a vital piece of equipment, one is not enough and a second pump should always be fitted. It may be possible to use a lavatory outlet pump or fresh water pump to get water out of the ship, but they are not designed or fitted as bilge pumps, so would normally not be very effective. Not only must good pumps be fitted, but they must remain effective when the need is greatest; this situation often coincides with violent motion which will have stirred up any loose rubbish in the bilge, dislodged any clothing or books incompletely secured, and done its best to choke the pump suctions, which must be sited where they can easily be cleared, remembering that when the time comes they will be deep under water. If a man can strip and clear a choked bilge pump suction with his head half under a swirling emulsion of dirty water, oil, sodden pulp and wool, he is a very fine seaman; if he ensures that this situation does not arise, he is a much better one. One way to help this is to fit a pump of the type that can take a good deal of flotsam without choking.

Engines.

The question of whether an auxiliary engine is important in a sailing yacht when deep sea cruising is purely a matter of personal feelings. Many people have managed all they wanted to do perfectly well without one, and feel that the smell of petrol or diesel oil is an abomination; others feel that it can act as an extra hand or more in helping with their task.

Unless the vessel be built with power as a considerable part of her design, an engine is unlikely to save much time on a long cruise, except perhaps for crossing the Doldrums; but it can allow entry to many harbours which could not be visited without auxiliary power; especially this applies to coral islands with a continuous current flowing out through the narrow channel into the reef.

Yachts designed to motor as well as sail can carry enough diesel fuel to give quite an effective ocean cruising range, as was demonstrated by Ann Davison when crossing the Atlantic alone in *Felicity Ann*, for which she was awarded a Seamanship Medal of the Royal Cruising Club. But a diesel engine takes up a great deal of space which some would prefer to use for other purposes, especially when speed is not important. For some it is infuriating and thwarting to lie restless in an ocean swell with the yacht's rolling unchecked by the slightest whisper of a breeze, and they would want to be able to avoid this by motoring off to ease the motion. Yet for others, one of the greatest joys on an ocean passage is that moment of sheer delight when the first caress of a breeze fondles the hot cheeks after a tiresome calm.

If an engine is fitted mainly as an insurance against difficulties, it is important to ensure that it is always kept fit for this task. For instance, the skipper whose man overboard methods depend upon the use of his engine will be giving himself a dangerous sense of false security if his engine does not start at the critical time.

Engines in boats have lost lives as well as saving others. The greatest danger comes from carelessness with petrol, although wood carelessly impregnated with diesel oil has its dangers too. When the yacht *Halcon Negro* was bound for Rio de Janeiro in 1949, she found herself becalmed and set down towards a rocky island. To avoid this danger, an attempt was made to start the engine, but instead the petrol ignited, causing the loss of the ship and death of her owner. Perhaps, in this case, the simple use of an anchor might have proved the greatest security.

For those who feel happier, or more secure, with an engine and its fuel onboard, both should be cared for thoroughly and competently. Others will take delight in achieving their object without an engine. Either may show equally good seamanship.

Electric light.

All that has been written about the disadvantages of an engine must apply to electric lighting if it has to be generated on board. Yet if an engine is fitted for propulsion, then the addition of another as a generator is purely a matter of the space available. So long as electric fittings and wiring are water-tight, the advantages of electricity, both for navigational and domestic lighting, is overpowering. When *Tai-mo-shan* sailed from Hong Kong to England she was fitted with a small engine to generate electric power, but no mechanical means of propulsion.

Even if there is no space for any engine, or its fuel cannot be accepted on board, secondary batteries carefully used can have sufficient capacity to keep electric lights going for a good time between charging the batteries in harbour. The lead-acid type of battery is heavy for its capacity, but light-weight alkaline accumulators, such as those made by Venner, will carry a large capacity in a small space with little weight. They also seem able to stand up well to rough treatment, salt-spray, and can be fully discharged without damage. Simplest of all in principle is the power cell, in which some fuel such as hydrogen is supplied to one electrode, and oxygen to the other. They are vastly expensive, but perhaps one day so many will be made for space craft that they come within the reach of ocean cruisers; then we will be able to have brilliant navigation lights, read books all through the hours of darkness, and perhaps cook by electricity as well. Meantime craft without means of generating power have to use their batteries very carefully.

It might well be possible to generate electric power to charge the batteries with a windmill, such as is commonly used in windy parts of the country ashore; a small rate of charge can be obtained by a hand operated generator, which is a nuisance to work, but still less trouble than the frequent refilling and cleaning of paraffin lamps.

Ground tackle.

In a small vessel where weight is important Danforth or C.Q.R. anchors are normally used, as they have the holding power of other types of anchor of far greater weight. On a long ocean voyage the anchor should be stowed below as in bad weather a partly loose anchor can do serious damage moving around on deck. But the shape of the C.Q.R. becomes awkward to stow and it takes much more space than a stripped Danforth type.

The advantage of chain cable in giving additional holding power to the anchor is such that it is almost universally used in British waters. In American waters a nylon warp is frequently used with the anchor in yachts up to 60 feet long; experience has found it to be quite satisfactory when combined with a short length of cable attached to the ring of the anchor to take chafe. It will be necessary to veer more nylon to get the same fair pull on the anchor as would be achieved with chain cable, yet anyone would prefer to heave in 30 fathoms of 3-inch nylon to half that amount of $\frac{1}{2}$-inch chain with a 40 pound anchor on the end of it. The spring of the nylon prevents snubbing, and it has been found that the rope stands up to chafe remarkably well; a scotsman—such as an old piece of canvas—should be used where the warp passes through the deck fairlead.

A great advantage in carrying a nylon anchor warp in a small sea-going yacht is that the same rope can be used as a storm warp (see Chapter XV on Bad Weather).

Harbour Dinghy.

The purpose of a dinghy for a cruising yacht is to give dry-shod and safe access to the shore when anchored in sheltered waters. It should not be considered part of the off-shore life saving equipment of the yacht, unless it is a really substantial lifeboat and is secured in davits from which it can be readily lowered; this limits it to really large yachts. The small yacht dinghy is utterly unsuited to saving life at sea; if the yacht should sink in bad weather, the conditions will not be fit for a dinghy; if the yacht catches fire or explodes, it is most unlikely that the rigid-type dinghy can be got into the water in sufficient time; if a man goes over the side at sea, an attempt to save him with the dinghy will probably cause the loss of the dinghy's crew as well as the man.

The 54-foot overall length ketch *Hamrah* met tragedy in this way during 1935. Her owner went overboard in bad weather 600 miles east of Cape Race, and as the yacht turned his eldest son jumped into the sea and swam to support his father weighed down with sea boots and oilskins. The ship came up within 15 yards of them, and although a lifebuoy was thrown across, the crew were just unable to reach the men in the water as she drifted astern. Again the ship gybed, her main boom breaking as it swung over. While the rest of the crew were hoisting the mizzen, in desperation the owner's younger son launched the dinghy into the sea, where it soon swamped. With half the crew over the side, the rest could not get the partly disabled ship under control before father and both sons were lost.

The small yacht's dinghy therefore is needed purely for harbour work, and at sea is safest stowed inboard even for the shortest passage. It is important that it should be as light as possible, so that it can be readily hoisted aboard. To achieve its purpose of taking men and stores ashore it should be stable and have a good reserve of buoyancy, besides remaining afloat when swamped. This suggests a broad, flat-bottomed boat with built-in buoyancy, and this shape is likely to have the advantage that when stowed bottom up on deck it makes a safe working platform. An alternative is an inflatable rubber dinghy, quite separate from the liferaft, as these are particularly safe, even if it is very hard to get ashore entirely dry in one's best clothes. Most things in small craft must be something of a compromise, but there should be no compromise with safety, and events have proved that the cruising yachtsman is more likely to drown from his dinghy in harbour than from his yacht in the open sea; this is especially so when returning to the yacht late at night with the dinghy overcrowded and the occupants too full of a good dinner to be at their best for swimming in cold water, while their life-jackets are likely to be in the yacht.

However, one should perhaps treat statistics with care, as figures also show that more people in Britain drown from accidents to cars and bicycles than due to sailing boats; while perhaps an even greater need for wearing lifejackets is in one's bath ashore, as even more people drown in their bath tubs; I fear that the records even show drowning fatalities in washing machines, where lifejackets would be little help.

Protection from the weather on deck.

Very few sailing yachts are constructed to give much protection to the helmsman or crew in the cockpit. Usually any permanent structure would interfere with the helmsman's view or the handling of the ship, also the designer and owner must reduce any superstructure whose wind resistance would make the vessel sluggish getting to windward. A canvas screen or dodger round part of the cockpit makes the helmsman's lot much more comfortable, and is quite easily rigged when the yacht's course is off the wind, or when extra windage can be accepted. There should be moderation in most things, and one yacht had not achieved this happy state when she had such complete cockpit protection that the helmsman was seen standing outside a canvas tent, steering most uncomfortably with his foot stuck through the look-out hole to the tiller.

Even the narrowest strip of canvas laced to the life-lines abreast the cockpit will give an amazing amount of protection from spray, or from the wave which topples over the stern to dollop into the unprotected cockpit.

Sea anchors.

The sea anchor is a useful piece of equipment for a yacht cruising in coastal waters, particularly when she is lightly manned or the crew have still to find their sea legs; then it may be a useful brake in some difficult situation. With a bag of butter muslin sewn into the apex, the sea anchor is said to be an effective means of scooping up plankton for the very hungry yachtsman; however for a reasonably planned sea voyage in a well designed modern sailing cruiser, the sea anchor does not justify the space it takes. Voss swore by the sea anchor after sailing round the world in a three masted dug-out canoe, but few would repeat his performance in that particular design of craft. Even such an experienced sea-anchor operator as Voss gained little from its use when lying to one in a gale off Japan aboard a normal shaped yacht, as she capsized and limped back again under a jury mast. More details of the value of a sea anchor is included in Chapter XIV.

Oil.

The effect of oil on rough seas in certain conditions is simply staggering, and is dealt with in more detail in Chapter XIV.

Any heavy oil can be used to effect, but paraffin is useless. Fish oil is most effective, and should be kept in cans that can easily be handled in rough weather.

Oil will not only calm the seas, but will also make an infernal mess of the boat if spilt, while ropes covered with it become very hard to handle. Canvas bags, pricked with the sewing needles to allow oil to escape, are usually recommended. In a small yacht these are difficult to fill up and secure without spilling much oil within the ship. A simpler method is to secure a rope or canvas bridle round the cans in which it is stowed, such as two-gallon petrol cans, then the can is towed astern after one or two small holes have been made with a spike. When a can is empty of oil, it is cut adrift, and another streamed without ever bringing oily ropes inboard.

Galley stoves.

Most convenient of all in a small yacht is the bottle-gas stove, even if this is only practical when cruising to places where the cylinders can be refilled; but if it is possible, then this type of cooking has much to commend it, so long as reasonable safety precautions are taken. Bottle gas is heavy, so it may collect in the bilges and explode; liquid petrol is heavier, and will explode with far greater violence. The capacity of bottle-gas cylinders depends on the standard of cooking done, but with an amply cooked diet, including two hot meals a day, one pound weight of Calor gas is sufficient for three men for one day, or the 32 pound cylinder contains cooking gas for 100 man days, with careful use. So long as the makers instructions are obeyed in fitting the equipment, and reasonable care is taken over maintenance, there is no reason why bottle gas should be any more dangerous than paraffin stoves, which can also cause damage by catching fire.

Paraffin can be obtained almost anywhere ashore, and some type of paraffin-vapourising stove is still the commonest fitted in small yachts. So long as the operation of the stove is understood, it is safe and gives a hot flame for cooking, but it is less easily adjusted than the gas flame. However in bad weather even the effort of heating the vapouriser with methylated spirit, and waiting for some time until cooking heat is available, becomes a complicated and tiresome burden.

The simple wick type paraffin stove can be readily adjusted, and is perhaps the safest. It is quite the least efficient as a stove, as its heat is limited, and it is inclined to smoke; it must always be kept level or the oil floods through the burners and flares up.

Methylated spirit stoves are popular in America, where they are called alcohol stoves. No doubt they will increase in favour for British yachts when they are more readily available.

Probably habit and feelings control the selection of cooking stoves more than logic. If a man, or woman, feels uneasy with a gas stove, it is best not to have one aboard or his feelings may emerge in some form such as short temper. For most cruises in a small yacht it is hard to escape the conclusion that bottle gas can be as safe as any other method of cooking, and is certainly far more convenient than anything other than the heat insulated coal-burning stove.

Pressure cookers.

A pressure cooker is a valuable asset as it saves time and cooking fuel. Perhaps just as important is the fact that no boiling water is spilt if a particularly heavy lurch throws everything off the stove; while it is annoying to receive a hot pressure cooker upon some unguarded portion of the body, the personal damage is far less than if struck by a saucepan

that deposits a quart of boiling water over the bare flesh, and half a
dozen boiling potatoes down the inside of the shirt. The knob that
controls the lid of the pressure cooker makes a good anchorage for a
lanyard secured to the deck head; in rough weather this is of peculiar
interest to anyone sleeping in a quarter berth that shares a compartment
with the galley stove.

As protracted boiling removes some of the value of food, particularly
fresh vegetables, pressure cooking should improve the flavour and
value.

Like almost every other piece of apparatus ever devised, the pressure
cooker can be dangerous if not correctly used. The time for possible
cooks to learn its knacks is when the yacht is steady on an even keel.

Plate 5. A jury mast, rigged for practice while at sea, rolling in a freighter. It was made of the main boom and spinnaker pole and allowed storm sails to be hoisted

Plate 6. The sloop *Drumbeat*, 58 ft. overall, under jury rig after being dismasted in a transatlantic race

Plate 7. Light, airy and dry conditions for repair work below in *Aloha of Hamble*, 51·25 ft. overall

Plate 8. Wind against sea in the Needles Channel knocked up a steep little sea that brought down the mast of an ocean racer before she reached the open sea

IV

Maintenance

WHEN a yacht is fitted out for a season's week-end sailing, perhaps with a short cruise in mid-summer, her good condition will just about last out until she is laid up some four months later. Should any of the rigging part, a sail tear, the hull leak or a minor fault occur in any of the mechanism, the defect can readily be made good before the next week-end. Even during the summer cruise, each leg away from harbour seldom exceeds 200 miles, or a couple of days with a night in between, before there is a pause in harbour to repair any defects. But if she sets forth on a deep sea cruise of any distance, the strain on every part and fitting will be far greater, and wear will accumulate in proportion to the length of the voyage, the temperature and humidity, the violence of the sea, and the speed at which the yacht is being driven. Under these conditions it is not good enough to wait until something goes wrong and put it right when next in harbour; the aim must be to prevent anything going wrong by careful maintenance.

Hull.

The hull can be strained by heavy pounding or particularly violent seas, which may open up seams. This could be a serious matter when hundreds of miles from any harbour, and the hull can only be maintained intact by realising at once that the damage has begun, and promptly easing speed or altering course in order to reduce the strain.

The essential part of hull maintenance at sea therefore is to keep the whole bilge regularly pumped out so that any leakage is quickly noticeable. It is not good enough for the pump to be sucking dry what only amounts to a small water-tight compartment bounded by the yacht's floors; if limber holes are cut through the floors, a routine clearance of these must be instituted to ensure a complete clearance

D

of water from the bilge. To overcome the difficulty of clogged limber holes Eric Hiscock had the bilge of *Wanderer III* filled with pitch to the top of the metal floors; however he reported that in warm seas anything stood on the pitch sank into its soft surface, so it became impractical to stow food tins in the bilge.

It is common enough for limber holes to become blocked by wood shavings, blanket dust or sodden tin wrappings. Then a leaking hull may not be noticed for a long time, and the crew will get quite a shock when shortly after the bilge pump sucked dry, water is found flooding into a lee bunk as she heels.

Any fitting passing through the hull of the yacht up to the heeled water-line is a possible source of leaks. Each fitting should be inspected regularly and the flange nuts tightened as soon as any trickle of water appears. Hull fittings above the upright water-line can be most troublesome, as they will only leak when the yacht is heeled on one tack. It sometimes happens that a good deal of water comes inboard when she is heeled well over, and by the time the excess water in the bilge is noticed she has gone about. Dozens of tins are removed from their carefully planned stowage in the bilges, perhaps the fixed fresh water tanks are unshipped and half the cabin joinery stripped down, but still no sign of a leak can be found, and none will show for many days. Then the mysterious leak may appear again. No one is likely to notice that it again appeared some time after she was well heeled, perhaps on the starboard tack, as by that time she may have gone about on to the port tack.

Sails.

Every sail, except perhaps a very light-weight ghoster, soon picks up enough spray to leave particles of salt spread over much of the cloth; this attracts moisture from the frequently damp sea air. Synthetic materials should not rot in such damp conditions, but certainly if the climate is hot, anything else in contact with the cloth is likely to be affected.

Apart from this, damp sails below cannot add to the habitability of the craft, so every sail in a yacht's trousseau should be aired regularly by getting them up on deck on a sunny day.

When the sails are brought up to air they should be carefully examined for any wear, loose fittings or holes and any hanks or shackles greased. The pleasant sunny day that is suitable for airing the sails is a far more pleasant occasion for simple repairs than having to do a much bigger job in the middle of a dark and stormy night, when the need may have become urgent.

When fresh water is abundant, the opportunity should always be taken to wash the sails free of this salt. Even at sea, it may be possible to joist it in heavy rain to wash off the worst of the salt; the difficulty about this treatment is that so often heavy rain is accompanied by strong wind which pushes the spray level well up the sail.

Deck equipment.

Many machines are fitted on deck, such as winches, blocks and tackles, the object of which is to make the yacht easier to handle. This they do well when in good condition, but salt water and spray soon drive out every sign of lubrication, and the resultant friction makes the machine so inefficient that the crew would be better off without it. In rough seas it is amazing how quickly the sheave of a block near the deck will jam completely with salt and corrosion.

In the early stages of a deep sea cruise, an astonished, 'But I only oiled it a day or two ago' is frequent, until the lesson of salt spray is learnt.

The view that a tall Bermudan mast, with a long track for the main sail slides, was unsuitable for open sea work, probably grew up less due to faulty design than due to the lack of knowledge of lubrication.

Regular lubrication of blocks and sail tracks, besides stripping down and greasing winches, and attending to all working parts, saves a great deal of unnecessary work at a time when it may be quite difficult enough even to remain standing on the deck.

Engine.

An engine loses much of its value if it is not always ready for use when required; careful maintenance is needed to ensure that state of readiness, in fact when an auxiliary is fitted in a deep water cruising yacht it is likely that more time must be spent in maintaining the engine than will be gained by its use. However, time is not everything in a cruise, so if an engine is fitted on board, the effort must be made to keep it in good order. Probably the main enemy of the engine on a deep sea cruise is the salt spray that impregnates the air on rough days;

it attacks any bare metal and is particularly damaging to the electrical system. The damp heat of some tropical climates is about as friendly to electrical insulation as dry rot is to wood.

Rough seas stir up the petrol tank so that any impurities such as dirt or water, which would normally sink to the bottom of the petrol, become much more likely to choke the engine's fuel supply than when the sea is calm. Another common effect of rough weather is for the sea to flood back through defective sea cocks into the exhaust system and eventually force its way into the cylinders; this should not happen, but the sea is most persistent in trying to seep into anything that floats upon it.

The diesel engine is normally less prone to interference from heat, damp and rough seas.

Petrol and gas leads.

It is not necessary to have seen a vessel burning to imagine the danger of fire in the open sea. There are many possible causes, but high up on the list of fire dangers come leaky connections in any petrol or gas leads. No joints can be guaranteed completely proof against the stresses, shocks and vibrations of a vessel at sea for a long period. It is essential for safety that such potentially dangerous systems should be regularly examined.

Plumbing.

The benefits of hygienic and efficient lavatories within the ship are obvious, even to those who have not suffered the cold discomfort of other arrangements. However, these benefits become very distant memories when the non-return valve fails in bad weather and the hull valve on the outlet pipe will not close. All hull valves should be regularly operated and normally kept closed. When a yacht is pounding into a big sea with the hull valve open, each time the outlet mounts clear of the water and then plunges deep under a wave, an open pipe experiences that alternating pressure which in time works its way through the stoutest mechanism.

Spare gear.

A good deal of spare gear must be carried if the ship is to be maintained in a fully efficient state, and the more elaborate her equipment the greater becomes the space that must be given up to this spare gear. It would be convenient if these things could be stowed right away and forgotten until they are needed, yet if this is done it will often be found that the spare sparking plugs produce no kick, the spare main sheet is half worn through in three places due to chafe in the locker with the rolling, and the glue of the spare chart pencils has melted to leave long grooved strips of wood and a length of bare pencil lead.

If at all possible before a long cruise, spare gear should be packed up and sealed after being thoroughly dried. Certainly this should be done with such vulnerable stores as sparking plugs, electric contact breakers, coils and armatures, after coating any bare metal with grease. Waxed paper and cellotape make an effective air- and damp-proof wrapping.

Maintenance routines.

Efficient maintenance in a yacht usually requires very little mechanical knowledge, a more important need being some organisation to ensure that everything is cared for properly. As well as organisation some incentive must be provided to help forward the work, and it is far better if the incentive is not provided by dire distress at the least convenient time. Thus, for instance, all six people aboard a yacht may appreciate fully the danger of loose bottle gas, all may have smelt leaking gas, and each know how to use a spanner or replace a faulty washer; but unless the crew is so organised that this is someone's responsibility, and unless that person feels that it really matters, the chances are that nothing will be done about the gas leak for some time.

It is essential that someone be responsible for the maintenance of every item of equipment on board; the bosun's job is fairly obvious, another may care for the electrics, and so on; but there must be no gap that leaves some items as nobody's pigeons. Naturally everything is eventually the responsibility of the owner, but if he retains all such details in his own control 'he will either be overwhelmed at just the time when he should be giving detached thought to a difficult situation, or the essential maintenance will go by default. When all are wet and tired after some difficult job like shifting a large sail in bad weather, the skipper may find that he just has not got the heart to tell a man to trace a gas leak when perhaps he is due to go on watch in an hour's time; yet if that same man has always felt himself responsible for the cure of gas leaks, he would feel it was a matter of personal pride that the leak was detected and put right at once. All must be encouraged to feel that a cruise without a sheet parting or a sail splitting shows far better seamanship by the yacht as a whole than some heroics up the mast by a stout-hearted individual striving to cope with an accident in foul weather that might have been a mere incident if dealt with in good time, and in fair weather.

As few deep sea yachtsmen are by nature routine minded, it is always well that some aim should be held in mind by the person responsible for each item; thus it might be the plan to start up and test the engine weekly. Even if the object is not achieved for some reason or another, having an aim at least ensures that someone is looking out for an opportunity to do the job. For example, when the bosun thinks to himself, 'I must get the storm sails and small jib on deck, as they never saw the light last week,' it acts as a far stronger personal incentive to action than such a general thought as, 'Sometime it would be a good thing if somebody got up those sails we have not used for a few days.'

Such routine work may sound unromantic, but the choice may well be between dramatic epics without getting very far, or a good deal of steady routine work in order to gain the adventure of achievement in getting where you want to go. As for being tied to routine, in fact a system of routine maintenance enables people to do a job in conditions that suit them, while the 'wait until it breaks' exponents are tied to doing the job in conditions dictated by the weather, the machine, or the fitting; weather and machines have an almost diabolical sense of humour in dealing with men who become their slaves.

Defect book.

The most infuriating defect, or lack of adjustment, can easily be forgotten in the press of other interests, until the same thing causes the same trouble the next time it is used. Thus a couple of upper hanks on a staysail may be distorted and unusable. With the sail hoisted they are out of reach, so cannot be repaired, and when the sail is next lowered, the defect is forgotten in the rush to stow away the sail before it gets wet. Once in its sail bag, no one will ever remember the trouble until the sail is being hanked on once more.

The best way to overcome this very normal human failing, unless some of the crew are superhuman and so have no need for such remedies, is to keep a defect book in which any such detail can be entered at once. Probably a small notebook, with a pencil attached firmly by a length of line, is the most convenient form of defect list; it must be kept in a standard place, that is convenient to everyone, and it is helpful, psychologically, to enter the date as well as the defect. For instance, the bosun may check through the list for any of his defects, and if he sees that the storm trisail has suffered from a worn seam for three days, it will stir him to instant action. A specimen page of such a rough defect book is shown in Fig. IV, 1.

An alternative to a book is to record the defect in chalk on a black-board in some prominent place. The disadvantage of this is that chalk is less easily secured in a sea-way, and writing on a black-board or slate is harder, when the yacht is lively, than sitting in a corner and writing in a rough notebook.

It is a common fallacy to feel that small defects can be left until the yacht reaches harbour. Usually there is more time available when at sea, and an effort should be made to have the defect list clear of all items, except those that really can only be done in shelter, by the time the yacht reaches harbour.

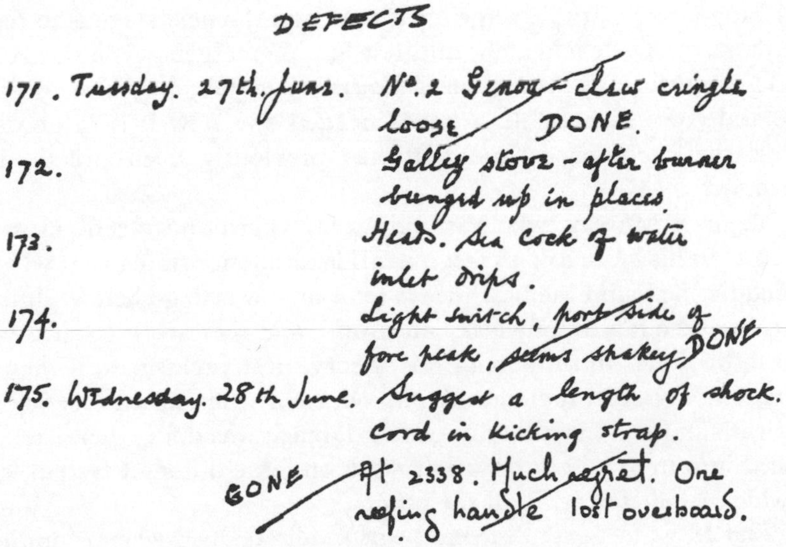
DEFECTS

171. Tuesday. 27th June. No. 2 Genoa - clew cringle loose DONE.

172. Galley stove - after burner bunged up in places.

173. Heads. Sea cock of water inlet drips.

174. Light switch, port side of fore peak, seems shakey DONE

175. Wednesday. 28th June. Suggest a length of shock cord in kicking strap.

GONE At 2338. Much regret. One reefing handle lost overboard.

Fig. IV, 1. A page from the Defect Book

V

Emergency Repairs

HOWEVER much care is taken over the preparation of a yacht for a voyage, mistakes may be made and material may fail. Emergencies will occur and the ship may suffer damage that completely or partially disables her. Repair or improvisation is then necessary by the crew with the equipment carried on board. The finest seaman is not really the one who 'instinctively' does the right thing in an emergency; he has either experienced a similar situation and recognises the similarity, or he has enough imagination to have visualised the position in advance and thought out the action to be taken.

An emergency exists so long as the ship, her crew or her gear are in danger. This requires prompt, decisive and often drastic action. Once this danger ceases, the emergency is over and the next stage is to repair the damage. The excitement and tension of emergency is a dangerous background for any strange or difficult repair job; it is best to pause first and consider carefully what is needed and how it is to be done, unless the evolution is one that has previously been practised or rehearsed.

Major J. Murray, who has cruised far at sea and raced across the Atlantic in his *Mokoia* of 38 feet overall length, once stated that when in difficulties he found the best way to save time was to go below, shut the hatch, serve out a tot of whisky all round, and then work out just what had to be done. In support of this theory most yachtsmen, if they are honest enough, can remember some occasion when an emergency was met with stunned inactivity until the damage was done, then the crew rushed into frenzied efforts, all at work on some different system, each of which conflicted with all the others.

Tavy II, 35 feet overall length, was mildly pooped when rounding a lee-shore headland off the China coast rather too close. A ton or two of water aboard need not have been dangerous if the ship had been properly secured, but this wave swept forward on deck and jammed the steering wheel with the loose end of the main sheet, whose boom had been hauled aft for a gybe, then overturned a can of paraffin to start a good blaze, and finally snarled all the halyards round the main mast into a hopeless tangle. A fire flared up under the main boom, jammed aft by its sheet in the steering wheel, and lapped up to the foot of the sail, so someone decided to douse it by lowering the spray-sodden main sail with a run; he was himself in a hot and smoky position to lee of the fire, so finding both halyards tangled, sawed at the ropes with his knife. They were the wrong ropes, and brought down both head sails. His next effort brought about a confusion of boom, sail and gaff upon the deck which effectively exterminated the fire, but nearly did the same to the rest of the crew. Someone else, seeing the yacht forging ahead towards angry breakers, hurled a sea anchor over the side, complete with its tripping line all in a tight coil; the warp stampeded out and the bight took our only engine starting handle with it, besides coming near to taking some assorted limbs of the crew as well.

Fortunately the end of the warp was secured just in time for the sea anchor to check the way of the yacht, giving a chance to clear the steering wheel, rig another fore halyard, confirm that the fire was out, and sail clear of the rocks. Little harm resulted, and at eighteen years old we considered ourselves fine seamen to have weathered such a situation, which we felt was brought about by the poor design of the yacht that became pooped so badly. Yet by the next day, we had agreed that it might be best to keep the adventure to ourselves, as we had planned further cruises and authority might view the episode in quite a different light. This was indeed likely as the incident was directly due to my misjudgement when gybing in disturbed water close to the headland, accompanied by an even more serious failure to have the ship thoroughly secured for sea, and worse still I had been unable to take charge of my crew effectively in an emergency.

The only spark of good seamanship in the story is that, protected by a span of more than twenty years that has covered a trifle more experience of sailing, one is able to admit what happened.

Emergency book.

It is an excellent plan to keep a notebook in some commanding position in the yacht recording the action to be taken for every emergency, and then a sketch plan of the possible repairs. The greatest value of the book comes from the thought that must be given to likely failures, besides their prevention. Under each heading should be written down first the immediate action to be taken and this should be well known to every member of the crew. Then should follow sketches and details of how the damage might be made good. It is unlikely in practice that an accident will fit precisely with the case assumed in the book, but at least the sample case will give some guidance to the details of equipment required and method to be employed.

When crossing the Western Ocean on one occasion I went even further, and kept under the pillow of the skipper's bunk a canvas envelope known as the 'calamity pack'. This contained the emergency book, besides a canvas-backed lifeboat chart showing the approximate position of the yacht, together with instructions so that even if one man only was left aboard, without sextant or much knowledge of navigation he would still have a good chance of reaching some harbour safely.

It might be felt that the pleasure of a cruise would be marred by the consideration of such horrors. In practice the honest facing of possible troubles produces no nightmares, yet in the loneliness of the ocean the stab in the back of an accident that has never been thought about is a horror indeed.

Hull damage.

In the open sea the most immediate and dangerous emergency to the ship is damage to the main structure of the hull. This may happen through collision with another vessel or floating object, through a heavy sea smashing in the deck or superstructure, or self-inflicted injury from damaged spars or loose equipment. The first is the most likely, and the greatest danger to a small yacht in the open sea probably comes if she is taken in tow or is closed by another vessel offering some assistance. (Even in more sheltered waters inshore the word 'tow' must figure prominently among insurance claims from yachts.)

The immediate action is to take all speed off the yacht, while down below the hole should be blocked up with the first thing that comes to hand. When *Vertue XXXV* was damaged by a particularly vicious sea in mid-Atlantic during 1950, a cushion and a blanket were pushed into an oblong cabin light of which the glass had been splintered. The large windows often fitted in the dog-house of a yacht would need a rolled up mattress, or a full sail bag, to block the hole. The inertia of habit must be overcome, as I have seen a case where a man was very reluctant to use a mattress when a boat was in real danger of sinking, on the grounds that it would wet the mattress; this is not an exaggeration as the mind is practically always slow to appreciate the gravity of a danger to which it is unaccustomed.

Damage low down on the hull is usually hard to get at owing to lockers, tanks and food storage. A sail can be draped over the damage from outside, as shown in Fig. V, 1, when the flow of water into the ship

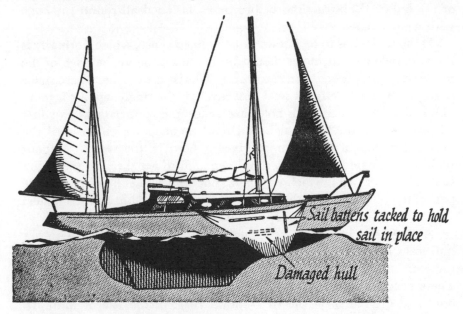

Sail battens tacked to hold sail in place

Damaged hull

Fig. V, 1. A sail used to check the flow of water through a hull leak

will tend to suck the canvas into the leak. The main difficulty comes from getting the sail into position in a rough sea, particularly if the shape of the keel hinders passing a bottom line right round the ship. This can best be overcome if some weight, such as the hand lead line, is secured to the bight of the bottom line, then lowered over the bows and worked aft to the position of the damage.

Once the leak has been temporarily stopped, or at least reduced to allow only a manageable trickle of water, the job of repair can be considered. The normal principle of the tingle will cope with almost every type of hull damage, and really only consists of nailing a patch over the leak; at the best this can be made of flexible copper sheeting with a pad of tallow-covered felt to make the joints water-tight. In the absence of the correct materials, metal can be cut from tin cans and padded with pieces of greased blanket or canvas to make quite an effective temporary repair. A tingle can be put on inside or outside the hull, and the flexibility of the sheet metal enables the patch to follow over any frame or obstruction that gets in the way; the patch is held into position over the damage, and then lightly hammered to the shape of the hull and obstructions before being fastened all round the edge with copper nails.

If the tingle has to be put on in a confined space, which normally is the case below decks, holes should be made all round the edge of the metal sheet after it has been cut to size. This is easily done, where space is ample, by hammering a steel nail through the tingle against a spare block of wood. Once these holes are made the copper tacks can first be pushed into the felt, which will hold them into position until the initial firm tap of the hammer gives a hold in the wood. Without such prefabricated holes, it is simple enough to get through the entire stock of copper tacks, which will have shot off into the most inaccessible part of the bilges, with nothing to show for the effort but bruised fingers and a face distorted with exasperation.

A crew once brought a boat safely into Douglas harbour, with her hull leaks kept within the control of vigorous bailing, by using almost the entire metal of six large biscuit tins besides half a dozen blankets. These covered a series of very bad holes and broken frames after the boat had grounded on the rock-bound coast of the Isle of Man. In this case part of the inside of the boat had been shored up with lengths cut from oars to help strengthen the structure. Some of the tingles had been secured over the bundled clothing that had first been thrust into the hole to check the inrush of water. To help in spreading the external thrust on these holes, sails had been passed under the boat and tacked into the hull as close to the damaged areas as could be reached.

Dog-houses.

The large dog-house windows that make the modern small cruiser's cabin so light and roomy are a possible cause of danger from bad seas or loose gear. Shutters of wood or metal should be carried on board, cut to the shape of these windows and with screw holes bored near the edges to coincide with the positions of the screws holding the window flanges into position; then if the glass or perspex is damaged, the shutters can fairly easily be screwed into place.

The right-angle between the deck and the coach-roof or dog-house side is likely to be a weak point in the structure. Should this joint fail, due to a really heavy blow from a wave, shores should be rigged across the inside of the structure, using such lengths of wood as the loom of an oar or the portable thwarts of the dinghy, as shown in Fig. V, 2.

Steering breakdown.

Inability to steer may well imperil the vessel, so arrangements for

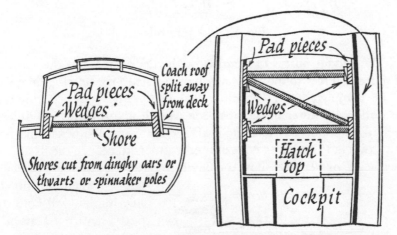

Fig. V, 2. Shoring a damaged dog-house or coach roof using dinghy oars or spinnaker poles

quick action in the event of a breakdown must be familiar to everyone who may steer the yacht. If the rudder is jammed over, and cannot be freed almost at once, it is essential to take the way off the ship, either by heaving to or lowering all sail. The direction in which the rudder is jammed will control the tack on which she can heave to.

If the rudder is free it will usually be possible to steer the yacht temporarily with an oar so long as she is reasonably well balanced. It should certainly be possible to steer by this jury rudder with the wind abaft the beam, but it becomes tedious if used for any length of time, particularly if the stern has a long overhang and the helmsman needs to be perched right aft, where he gets no shelter and may find it difficult to see the compass.

Either a spare tiller should be carried on board or a suitable strut should be earmarked for the job and made readily convertible. It may be necessary to carry a spare rudder-head, but failing that it is possible to cut flat faces or groves on either side of the rudder post and then lash a double tiller on either side as shown in Fig. V, 3.

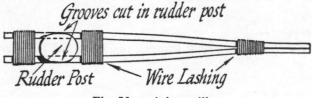

Fig. V, 3. A jury tiller

If the rudder post is broken below the deck level, but the rudder is still slung and free to move, it may be possible to rig steering lines from near the trailing edge of the rudder as shown in Fig. V, 4. Securing these lines under the water in the open sea would be a difficult job unless a hole had been bored before the craft set out; some Chinese junks have many holes in the trailing edge of their rudders to reduce the drag when under helm, or perhaps allow the devils to escape, but many yachtsmen might prefer to fill the steering lanyard hole with putty, and mark its position, so that a swimmer could gouge out the putty and pass through the line in case of need. This precaution had been taken by *Cohoe* when she won the Transatlantic race of 1950.

However, in a Transatlantic race 13 years later the crew of *Dyna* surprised everyone, including per-

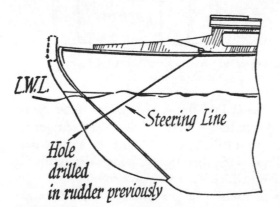

Fig. V, 4. Jury steering lines rigging with a broken rudder head

haps themselves, when she sailed the last thousand miles of the course, and correctly crossed the finishing line, with neither a rudder nor any jury rudder. She was running under spinnaker with a big sea and a near gale when knocked down, and the rudder sheared off from her aluminium hull. After various trials of jury steering arrangements, the crew eventually found they could handle her best by sail trimming alone, and even managed to do this with a spinnaker set. At much the same time as *Dyna* was knocked down, I was not far away sailing in *Bolero*, in which we split the only mainsail on board, and suffered a whole heap of other minor damages to gear; as it turned out the loss of her rudder seemed less of a handicap to *Dyna* than the accumulation of rigging failures in *Bolero*; but there can be few deep sea voyages where it would be worth going without the rudder, even if it should reduce the wetted surface!

Rigging failure.

If a shroud parts, the ship should immediately be put about on to the other tack, when the mast will not miss the support of the rigging that has failed, and there is ample time to rig another wire, or if the weather rules out going aloft, a jury shroud can be rigged with bulldog grips tying in an extra length of wire to cover the fracture.

Should the forestay part, the yacht must immediately be turned off the wind and continue running until a new forestay is set up or improvised.

In either of these situations it is wrong to start lowering sail until the yacht has turned to her safe course, as a sail partly lowered begins to flap about and bring an alternating strain on the mast.

Cross-tree failure.

Assuming that the rigging and chain plates are sound, and no skipper should take a yacht into the open sea without this assurance, the most likely trouble aloft is the failure of the cross-trees, or spreaders, as they are unlikely to be able to withstand a horizontal twisting strain and are excellent targets for any loose rigging such as the topping lift.

The immediate action in the event of a cross-tree carrying away is to tack or gybe to bring it on to the lee side. If the cross-trees carry away on both sides of the mast, sail must be lowered below the unsupported portion of the mast as soon as possible, while avoiding any extra strain from the sails flapping. This is a case where a really good helmsman may save the situation by keeping the sails neither full nor flapping until they are lowered to a safe height.

Repairing a broken cross-tree is a thoroughly difficult job even in calm weather, and damage seldom occurs under these conditions. With a tall mast it will probably prove quite impractical to repair an upper cross-tree until the weather moderates. It was done in mid-Atlantic aboard *Gulvain* of 55 feet overall length when C. Gardner and Commander King repaired the cross-tree in bad weather so that she could force on in a race, but this sort of performance needs exceptional qualities.

First-aid treatment, requiring no one aloft, can be effected by rigging a spreader within reach of the deck that will give the same support to the mast as was previously provided by the cross-tree. In order to keep the same angle between the mast and the shroud, the temporary spreader must have a far greater length than the cross-tree. I once had a jury rig with a 10-foot long spinnaker pole used to replace a 3-foot long damaged cross-tree 30 feet above the water-line on a mast 48 feet high. With the heel of the spinnaker pole well up from the foot of the mast there was little tendency for the pole to top up, but to prevent this possibility the shroud was secured to the end of the pole with binding wire; guys were rigged to hold the pole firm fore and aft, and the lower end of the shroud hauled taut with a tackle. In practice it took some ten minutes to complete this rig which gave ample support to the mast.

Repairing the cross-trees.

When the weather becomes calm enough for a man to work aloft, repairs can be made to the damaged cross-tree, or a jury rigged aloft if the whole strut has carried away. Everything possible should be

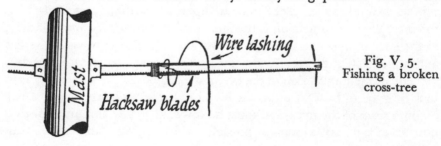

Fig. V, 5.
Fishing a broken
cross-tree

prefabricated at deck level, as the simplest job takes far longer when aloft even in the calmest sea.

If the wooden spar of a cross-tree is broken it can be fished with such items as hacksaw blades, acting as splints, very securely fastened with binding wire as shown in Fig. V, 5. The most difficult part is to improvise the fitting at the mast end, so unless a complete spare cross-tree is carried, it is best to retain any remains of the old fitting and build on to that.

However, it is this inboard end fitting that is most vulnerable due to the twisting moments it may experience, so thought must be given to its replacement. With a wooden mast it may be possible to hammer some anchorage into the mast to which the inboard end of the cross-tree may be secured. Thus when Captain J. H. Illingworth was racing his *Myth of Malham* in the Fastnet race of 1949 a lower cross-tree failed at the inboard end; spikes were hammered well into the mast around the foot of the cross-tree, which was then firmly held in position with binding wire. The yacht sailed on to win the Fastnet race for the second time in succession.

With a metal mast this would not be possible, and the best chance of success would come from cutting out a wooden strut that would key into the fittings left on the mast as shown in Fig. V, 6, and then be held in place by the tension of the shroud. The job of cutting out

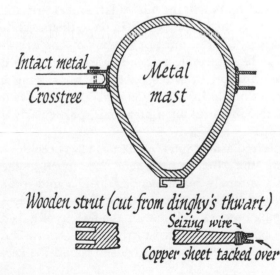

Fig. V, 6. Jury cross-tree cut from a dinghy's thwart or bunk lee board

would only be possible, except for a most expert craftsman, if a scale drawing of the fitting had been made previously, or if detailed and laborious measurements were taken aloft.

Damaged spars.

When a boom or spinnaker pole splits it will retain much of its strength if the two jagged ends are held firmly together, fitting exactly into their original shape. Often an effective repair can be made by strapping a metal sleeve round the damaged portion; even strips of metal such as copper sheeting or a stout tin can will serve if tacked to the spar and then splints, such as spare lengths of mast track, are bound over the injury with wire.

Dismasting.

The immediate danger from dismasting comes from the damage the broken spars may do to the hull of the ship when they are smashed against her by the sea. It is essential therefore to have handy some instrument that is capable of cutting the rigging. Rigging wire is tough stuff and becomes all the tougher on a dark night in a rough sea; an axe will cut through wire under the right conditions, but when masts start to fall down the axe is more likely to make a hole in the deck or remove the wielder's foot than to cut neatly through the correct wire. Wire cutters are best for the job.

The wreckage of mast and spars will inevitably fall to leeward and once they are in the water the yacht will tend to drift on to them. While one man cuts away the rigging, the rest must be fending off the wreckage from the side until it can be hauled clear ahead or astern; the yacht will then ride to it, as a sea anchor, by whatever remaining rigging is most suitable. It is important not to lose the wreckage altogether as it may contain the only suitable material for a jury mast, particularly if the yacht is a cutter or sloop.

Once the wreckage is cleared away, and if no damage has been done to the structure of the ship, the Murray treatment, mentioned at the beginning of this chapter, is strongly recommended. It is bound to be disconcerting for a crew to find themselves without any mast when far out to sea, and remaining on deck only fosters the feeling of naked helplessness. Voss had the misfortune to turn turtle in *Sea Queen* when lying to a sea anchor in a Pacific typhoon, but walked round the keel to come up the other side and find the yacht dismasted; however, he reached harbour again safely.

Jury masts.

How the jury mast is rigged will depend on where the mast has broken off, and the strength of the crew. The commonest position for a fracture is just above the deck, that leaves a broken-off spar among the wreckage not very much shorter than the original mast. Theoretically it should be possible to withdraw the stump from its step, trim the broken spar to fit, and restep it as a jury mast of excellent height. However, it is unlikely that this will prove possible in practice unless the crew is very strong, such as would be found in a yacht when racing. With careful preparation a 25-foot solid wooden spar has been hoisted single-handed at sea, but without a good deal of preliminary joinery it is about as much as four strong men can do, even in a fairly calm sea, to hoist a 30-foot hollow spar if nothing has been left standing above the superstructure. Therefore it may be necessary to trim off a portion of the broken mast so that the spar is short enough to be handled by the crew on board.

If it is decided to step the jury mast below, a temporary tabernacle

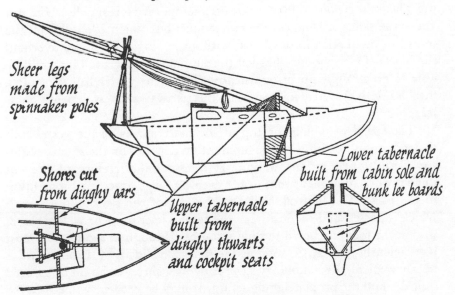

Fig. V, 7. Preparation for rigging jury mast at sea

must be built on deck to guide the heel through the deck, and another must be constructed below to guide it into the mast step. These tabernacles are the most important part in stepping a mast safely at sea, and it might well be necessary to spend two days making them from the odd woodwork fitted in the yacht. Fig. V, 7 shows a possible design of tabernacles in a small sloop, using materials that were all part of her cruising fittings; it entails no carpenter's ability beyond the use of saw, hammer and simple bosunry. All this work of preparation can continue while waiting for the weather to moderate.

When the tabernacles are completed and well greased to assist the heel of the mast to run into position, the mast is secured temporarily in position on deck with its foot resting in the upper tabernacle and supported in a crutch improvised from the two spinnaker poles, lashed together and rigged as sheer legs. In this position the jury mast can be dressed with its stays, shrouds, cross-trees and halyards.

When the time comes for hoisting, which will mostly depend on the state of the sea, the crutch is shifted forward to near the point of balance of the mast, so as to tilt the head of the mast as far up as possible. Then a temporary back-stay led from just above the point of balance and one lower shroud each side are rove to steady the mast on the way up. The mast is hoisted by a tackle on a temporary forestay led from just above the point of balance; the tackle must be of such a length that the mast can be stepped in one hoist, without having to stop and overhaul the blocks. Once the spar has left the support of the crutch it should be able to go straight up in one steady movement under full control; a mast is relatively fairly light in itself, but its awkwardness depends on its length.

The speed at which the top of the mast moves as the vessel rolls depends on its height, while its momentum depends on the square of this speed multiplied by the weight. It is essential therefore to prevent uncontrolled movement that would create a large upsetting momentum in the mast. The foot of the mast, the rim of the deck hole through which it passes, and the insides of the tabernacles must be well greased, so that the foot can begin to slide smoothly through as soon as the mast is sufficiently topped. So soon as the mast has slid right through and is nearly vertical, the temporary stays and lower shrouds should be secured quickly, and the proper rigging set up. It may be necessary to adjust the position of the heel of the mast, but that can wait until the mast is fully stayed, then the rigging can be slacked up all round and the mast lifted half an inch or so by wedges, and worked into its proper step.

Jury mast stepped on deck.

Should the mast break well above deck level leaving a considerable stump still standing, the jury mast should be stepped on deck lashed to the stump. There might be other occasions when it is considered best to step the jury mast on deck, which will sometimes be the simplest method. Less preparations will be required than when stepping the mast below, although it will almost certainly be necessary to shore up the deck or cabin top to take the strain of the mast. The stump forms a strong point on which a far simpler tabernacle can be constructed, and if it is high enough the stump will also help to steady the mast when it is being hoisted. With the heel of the mast on deck it will probably be best to step it on something soft, like a large fender, then lash the foot of the jury securely to the stump so that some of the compressive stress is passed to the stump mast.

Complete loss of mast.

Even if a single-masted vessel loses her mast altogether, there is likely to be something left on board from which to hoist a small spread of canvas. Plate 5 shows a jury mast rigged from the boom and spinnaker pole of a sloop; this particular yacht had a relatively high aspect ratio, so that the boom was comparatively short however, it still enabled her to set a trisail and small jib totalling 165 square feet compared with her normal sail area of 400 square feet. Plate 6 shows a jury rig under which *Drumbeat* sailed into a Nova Scotian harbour after dismasting.

A point to remember is that if the mast should be lost the yacht is likely to be disabled for some time, even if she has an auxiliary engine. There is usually a jumble of sails, rigging and spars in the water, and not until everything is completely clear of the propeller is it safe to start the engine. When the large ocean racing yacht *Fanfare* lost her mast off the Isle of Wight, although the sea conditions were moderate and she had a powerful racing crew onboard, they had been unable to get the wreckage clear of the water after many hours when another craft came to her assistance. In the open ocean this does not matter so much, and the classic case was the yacht *Tzu Hang*, which lost her mast and her dog-house when she turned right over while making for Cape Horn.

With a crew of only two men and a woman, a jury mast was made onboard from odd pieces of wood, and she eventually reached a South American harbour unaided; this was a brilliant piece of seamanship for which Brigadier Miles Smeeton, Beryl Smeeton and John Guzzwell were jointly awarded the Seamanship Medal of the Royal Cruising Club in 1957.

Metal masts.

When a metal mast fails it may not break right off, but might bend and possibly cripple a length of the mast. While there will then be less danger of the wreckage damaging the hull, the immediate problem will be to get the sail off as the crippled section of the mast may well jam any internal halyards. If the crippling occurs well up the mast, it is easy to visualise a situation when there is nothing left on which a man could get aloft in bad weather, and no means of freeing the head of the main sail from the rammed halyard. Probably the best that could be done then would be to brail the lower portion of the main sail and lash to the mast all the sail that could be reached.

VI

The Crew

ONCE a suitable sea-worthy craft has been found for a deep sea cruise, by far the most important consideration is the crew. Should the vessel's sea-worthiness be limited in any way, the selection of the crew becomes even more important. Many ambitious cruises have failed owing to crew difficulties; in others the destination has been reached, yet the objects of sport, pleasure and interest have been imperilled by personal relationships.

Single-handed cruising.

Some have solved the crew problem by cruising single-handed. Joshua Slocum went round the world in this fashion, and recorded that the acute pain of solitude experienced at first never returned. Single-handed cruising needs temperament and courage that is not given to everyone. Edward Allcard sailed both ways across the Atlantic single-handed, except when returning home from the Azores a stowaway disclosed her presence too late for him to beat back against the wind to land her; after his outward journey he recommended that a congenial companion is better than cruising alone, and offers the advice given him by Conor O'Brien, who sailed round the world in *Saoirse* after numerous crew difficulties, 'If you want a crew, marry one.'

As long ago as 1891 there was a single-handed race across the Atlantic Ocean, when Sid Lawlor won the race in his 15-foot *Sea Serpent* against William Andrews in his *Mermaid* of almost the same size. *Mermaid* capsized when lying to a sea anchor in heavy weather, and Andrews was in a poor state when picked up by a steamer next day.

In 1960 the cult of single-handed racing across the Atlantic began again, with races scheduled for every 4 years. These races attracted a great amount of public attention, and many competitors; in fact it seemed that the purpose of some was more concerned with the public interest, and the reward they might gain from satisfying it, than with the pleasure of sailing.

The idea of this race came from a very experienced deep sea yachtsman, H. G. Hasler, who hoped that it would foster simpler techniques and equipment in cruising yachts, and he certainly himself pioneered improvements in self-steering, besides experiments such as the Chinese schooner-rigged *Ilala* (Plate 9). However, the series soon seemed to encourage instead boats which are highly specialised and highly expensive single-handed races; very few of those who race so hard across the ocean by themselves seem to favour this crewing arrangement when the spotlights of publicity are no longer upon them.

Family Cruising.

The cruise of the 40-foot Colin Archer-built cutter *Teddy* started from Oslo with Erling Tambs and his wife; they added a first mate when a son was born at Las Palmas, before completing their voyage to New Zealand. The Fisks set out for a similar cruise in *Debonair* during 1950 with their two young children's future as the main purpose of the cruise. They were sighted in mid-Atlantic by another family party with Dr. and Mrs. Pye cruising in *Moonraker*.

Perhaps the most satisfying of all is to build a yacht oneself, designed specially to take one's family on an extensive cruise. John Guzzwell, having sailed round the world by himself in a boat he built with his own hands, later married and spent three years building the 20-ton *Treasure* for family cruising; she had to be fairly big as soon after her building started Mrs. Guzzwell gave birth to twins. *Treasure* started her first cruise from England in December, 1965, and almost inevitably ran into a winter gale in the Bay of Biscay; John Guzzwell had been three years ashore so was seasick, as was the rest of his family, but the 2-year-old twins recovered from this first, which suggests that they were to prove a valuable part of the crew in his future cruises.

Native Crews.

Allcard suggested that marrying might be too drastic a solution of the crew problem for world girdlers; perhaps also in time it might lead to too large a vessel being needed. Dwight Long discovered the ideal companion in a Tahitian boy who had no language in common with him and found aboard the 28-foot long *Idle Hour* luxuries he had not known in his Polynesian home. The fact is that two or three people living together for long periods in the close quarters of a small yacht are bound to experience far more difficult personal relationships than do people in ordinary life; they may set out hoping for adventure, freedom and enlightenment, yet find themselves psychologically constricted by bonds of incompatibility. Like Dwight's Timi, Conor O'Brien's youthful Tongan, Mullhauser's Indian boy and Robinson's Tahitian Etera all made crews and companions on such different mental planes from their masters that there was no conflict of personalities.

Personality.

Neither the close ties of family relationship, nor the widely differing idiosyncrasies of another race, will always answer the crew problem of a man wishing to go cruising in a small craft. The word 'man' is used here, as elsewhere in this book, to denote the species of mankind, whose female frequently has the same desire to go sailing, and undoubtedly has great ability in this sport. If a crew has to be found elsewhere, then the selection must be made with the greatest of care. If a man has a yacht quite unsuited to an ocean voyage, then he might do better to explore the Firth of Clyde, Long Island Sound, or wherever his home waters may be, until he has a suitable craft for a long voyage. Precisely the same applies to a suitable crew. A most important factor in the selection is the purpose of the voyage; either the crew must be found to suit the voyage, or the voyage arranged to suit the crew.

Whatever the purpose of the cruise may be, the personality of each member of the crew is more vital than his technical knowledge. It is true that it would be hazardous to set out with complete novices, yet even in such high-pressure sailing as a long distance ocean race, a boatload of enthusiastic experts might be an orchestra of discords, with the skipper struggling so hard to conduct his virtuosi in harmony, that he would have little time left to sail the ship. It may be hard ashore to recognise the qualities of adaptability, unselfishness and loyalty required in the crew of a small boat; yet it only takes a short time at sea for these to stand out. A short trial at sea will show also whether a man has courage and natural aptitude for the sea which, if added to the other qualities, will make him potentially an excellent member of the crew, however small his knowledge. If the skipper knows how to work his ship on deck and below, and has time to teach his crew their part, any experience they lack is far less important than incompatibility of temperament.

Dr. E. A. Pye tells in his book *Red Mains'l* of his problems in selecting a third member of their crew for *Moonraker*. He quotes his wife about a first-rate man, 'That's the silly part, you can't help liking him and you couldn't ask for a better crew. It is just a matter of temperament—his and mine. It's the little things . . .'

Personality is a very real factor, and some personalities, even if possessed by two quite charming people, conflict. The conflict may be only occasional, and can perhaps be avoided by organisation and strong-minded tolerance, but in the close quarters of a yacht at sea, it cannot be avoided completely, so long as the two remain on board together.

Amateur and professional.

In days gone by a man setting out for a cruise would normally employ professionals for the greater part of his crew. Now it is much more likely that the entire crew will consist of amateurs, perhaps even sharing the expenses with the owner. Once it is realised that every job on board is within their ability, and no duty is too menial to provide some interest and enjoyment, there is scope for the greatest pleasure in cruising only with those who are on board for the love of it. That does not debar the professional, if his wages and keep can be paid; many a yacht hand enjoys cruising, even if it is his livelihood, every bit as much as those who can afford to pay for the satisfaction. But the owner who employs another man as skipper, in charge of his yacht, is not gaining the greatest enjoyment from the craft.

Organisation.

Organisation is the means of parcelling out the work and responsibility to different members of the crew. Smooth organisation cuts down the cause of friction to the minimum. It is important that each member of the crew not only has his share of work, but, depending on his knowledge and ability, a reasonable share of responsibility as well. Those who volunteer for cruises in a small craft are usually strong characters and amply self-reliant; they are men of initiative, and must be given a chance to exercise their talents. Crew troubles are less likely to be fostered by excess of worthwhile work, than by ill-directed inactivity. A skipper aspiring to a race or an ambitious cruise will find more responsibility than he can undertake fully himself; unless he hands on some of this, the crew will experience gaps where either nothing is done, or ill-considered decisions are made. Nothing is more infuriating than to have a hasty decision imposed by a skipper who has no time to study the facts, when it would have been possible to delegate the whole matter to someone else who had ample time to do so on that particular point.

When a crew amounts to perhaps five or six, it is well for each to be a 'Head of department', with a clear task which is his responsibility to achieve. Organisation should ensure that there is never any doubt about the boundaries of responsibility, and the head of department must have real responsibility, enjoying enough information and time to set about the task effectively. For instance some months before setting out for a race across the Atlantic, one of the crew of a very small yacht was made responsible for all electrical, radio and mechanical matters. He needed full information about the course of the race, the yacht's plan, tactics and organisation before deciding what apparatus to recommend, a study that the skipper could not have undertaken effectively himself. Another of the crew had the same responsibility for sails and rigging, and yet another for catering. Each first made recommendations on what was needed for their departments, some compromise was found necessary and understood by all. However, once approval had been given to a recommendation, it was left to the head of the department to carry out his scheme. Some may feel that they stand to lose their authority if they hand out so much responsibility to others, yet the chairman of directors commands no less respect than the gang leader who details his men item by item.

Typical organisation and voyage instructions are shown in Tables VI*a* and VI*b*.

Discipline.
The word discipline may bring visions of a drill sergeant, or even of standing hatless on a mat in the orderly room, but in reality it covers all systems by which the efforts of several people can be directed to a common purpose. In yacht cruising, in team sport of any type, or even

'Ready for Sea' means:

Mate	All crew on board
	Fresh water and food stowed for voyage ordered
	Ship stowed below decks, with no unnecessary weights on board
Bosun	All sails ready for use, and repair gear checked
	Rigging correct and repair gear checked
	Life raft ready for immediate use
	Life buoys placed, with calcium lights, marker dyes and whistles secured
	Ship secured on deck
	Storm oil, oilbags and storm warps correct
Engineer	Batteries fully charged
	Bottle gas on board for voyage ordered
	Bilges dry and all pumps tested
	Radio apparatus ready for task ordered
	Emergency radio set in place
	Navigation lights tested
	Winches checked and greased
	Torches and spare batteries checked
Navigator	Charts and navigational publications for voyage ordered correct
	Chronometer and barometer checked
	Compasses checked
	Sextant correct
	Fog Horn, Emergency flares, radar reflector and signalling torch in position

Table VI*a*. Sample Organisation of a Small Yacht's Responsibilities

Voyage from BERMUDA to PLYMOUTH

Date	Yacht is to be ready for sea by Noon, local time, 2nd July
	Race will start off St. David's Head at 16.00, local time, 2nd July
Planned time	26 days
	Provisions for 28 days' full racing consumption, with 2 weeks' emergency stores
	Water 62 gallons
Destination	Plymouth. The race finishes at the entrance to the Sound
	Possible destinations in an emergency—Azores, Newfoundland, Ireland, Scillies or English Channel ports
Watchkeeping	Special Atlantic race organisation
Radio	Time signals each day. Distress frequencies for main set and life raft set. Shipping weather reports within soundings. Consol. B.B.C. western region news

Table VI*b*. Sample Voyage Instructions

in family life, discipline is essential for efficiency and happiness, although its type will vary in different circumstances. Where time matters little, there may be ample opportunity for all to discuss the best means of achieving a common purpose; when events move fast, or danger is imminent, decisions must be immediate. Yet whether these decisions are made in one way or the other, discipline entails that once made they are obeyed loyally and promptly.

The skipper.

Many systems of discipline have been tried out, yet all have failed unless complete and ultimate responsibility for action is vested in one man, even if he is responsible to any number of people who may act as a committee to lay down his policy. 'No man can serve two masters,' wrote Saint Matthew. At sea this one man is known as the captain, master, or in small yachts, usually the skipper. There are cases on record where two people such as twin brothers or sisters work together in such close co-operation that neither will admit that the other is skipper; yet these are rare and exceptional cases, and as triplets or quads are even rarer, it is scarcely a practicable system for manning most cruising yachts. Stanley Smith and Charles Violet claim to have co-ordinated their efforts in command of *Nova Espero*, when they were the only two aboard her for an eventful voyage across the North Atlantic; their claim seems well proved by the fact that after the voyage they wrote the book *The Wind Calls the Tune* as joint authors. They are the exceptions.

At sea therefore the skipper's responsibility is complete, and his orders are law to those aboard; yet the enthusiasm with which they are carried out will depend on his powers of leadership, which must needs increase with the quality of his crew. In times of crisis or difficulty a man's actions are controlled largely by habit and emotion, with reason playing a far smaller direct part. Thus a man may know well, due to his intelligence, that in rough weather he should wear a life-belt when working on the foredeck; yet if he has never done this before, and is feeling rather reluctant to make any extra effort, it is highly unlikely that his reasoning will overcome his habits and feeling. The skipper can achieve the greater part of his discipline, that is the working to-gether for a common purpose, by building up certain habits; example and persistency are the food and drink of habit, inconsistency is its poison.

Orders.

Of all the habits necessary for the safety of a small vessel at sea, the most vital is immediate obedience to orders; a handful of excellent seamen, each brim full of initiative and intelligence, would cause havoc if each worked to a different plan when a man went overboard on a dark, rough night. A dictator, who never tolerates any other opinion but his own, will not command the emotional instincts of a small crew intent on cruising for pleasure. The solution is for the skipper to give only sufficient orders for his crew to become accustomed to their form and intent, but beyond this whenever possible to give a direction that allows scope for discussion and individuality in the means of carrying out its purport. A command requires rigid obedience, such as, 'All hands, lower mainsail.' It must be unmistakably clear and include three essentials; first who is to obey the order, secondly what is to be done, and thirdly when it is to be done. If no time is mentioned in the command, such as 'as soon as the watch below has donned oilskins', the order must be obeyed at once.

Thus, 'Somebody get that damned sail off her, and get a move on, or the thing will split' is a thoroughly bad order; it neither specifies who is to do the job, nor makes clear which sail is to be taken off her; it is quite unnecessarily long, and as it includes an opinion about what might happen, invites an argument. If a few invectives are added to round off the order, it merely implies that the skipper is not quite certain of himself. Tone of voice is a far more powerful means of impressing urgency than any number of violent expletives and startling adjectives. A command once given must be obeyed completely before anything else is done, and should only be countermanded in exceptional circumstances. In a well-disciplined ship commands will seldom be required, and when they are given the skipper's tone of voice must make it abundantly clear that it is a command; every word should be essential to the command, which can only be confused by such attachments as 'please' or 'would you mind'.

The normal way of the skipper making known his requirement is by a direction, such as, 'Bosun, I'd like the wet headsails brought on deck to dry while the wind is still aft.' This direction hands on the responsibility for achieving a job to someone else, and should normally be used when the skipper will not personally supervise the job. The bosun in the case of this particular direction might reasonably answer that he first intended to finish the splice he was tucking in the spare genoa sheet; equally it is quite likely that the skipper will assist with the actual work of getting up the wet sail, under the control of the bosun.

Monomachia.

Such a word seems far removed from seamanship, but its meaning is not. It is a common failing among skippers in small craft, and big ones sometimes, to try to fight the battle single-handed, whether it is a battle against the elements or some racing rival.

He may either attempt to do too much himself, or try to supervise every detail personally without giving away what the object of the job is intended to be. Then individuals are deprived of responsibility, which is one of the strongest forces for work well done, and for the skipper himself essentials are obscured by a mass of detail.

A good example of this occurred in a yacht at sea in the English Channel when the skipper was engrossed in mousing a shackle at the masthead, with his mate concentrating at the halyard on which his skipper's safety depended, while two more men sat on deck waiting for the next detailed order. In the meantime the helmsman was obeying the skipper's order, 'For the love of Mike, don't let her gybe' to the exclusion of all else. No one had noticed another yacht beating up towards her. Fortunately the lee boat obeyed her obligation to avoid a collision, even when enjoying the right of way.

In a small craft the skipper will probably need to undertake some portion of the ship's duties himself, but he should never overburden himself with these to the exclusion of his main function of leading the crew and directing the sailing of the ship. In a race this primary duty can occupy practically all his efforts. Some may have undertaken the duties of cook as well as skipper, particularly where much of the pleasure of the cruise comes from the enjoyment of good food; more frequently the skipper acts as navigator, as a great deal of the detailed part of this work will have been done before the ship ever puts to sea.

The mate.

Much of the pleasure of a cruise, besides success in a long race, will depend on the smooth running of the organisation and routine down below; more personal friction can be caused by late meals, unpunctual relief on watch, and mislaid gear, than from any other cause. Traditionally at sea, the handling of this day to day life is the responsibility of the mate, and this is a system which has a great deal to commend it, even if the crew consists only of two people. Work on deck is usually pleasanter, and the need more apparent, than is some domestic chore like washing up dishes or scrubbing the galley, so the mate will have a difficult job to get the crew to take their full share. The skipper can best help him by assiduously avoiding any of the domestic arguments which are almost inevitable, stepping in only if requested by the mate, and then backing him whole-heartedly.

Obviously the more responsibility that can be given to the mate, within the degree of his knowledge and ability, the more confident he will be of his position, and the better second in command he will become. Countermanding the order of a subordinate, unless the circumstances have changed since the order was given, is no less serious an attack on discipline than if the junior member of the crew hurled his soup at the skipper. Fortunate indeed is the man who goes to sea with a perfect mate to help him; yet no one will become the perfect mate unless given ample responsibility and complete trust by his skipper.

VII

Preparing the Crew for Sea

A CREW must be prepared for the things they may encounter during a yacht's cruise. If the extent of a cruise in a well-found yacht during settled weather is from Helford River to Fowey, then the preparation can be more modest than if she aims to beat all comers in a race across the Western Ocean or Bass Straight. It is worse seamanship to attempt something with a crew unfitted to handle the ship safely, than it is to set out in a rotten old hulk with decrepit equipment.

A standard of safety at sea.

A man often claims that he cruises for pleasure, and cannot see the point of preparing for unpleasant things which might never happen. Others have no such feelings but just never 'get around' to trying their rough weather gear until the need is urgent. Yet the pleasure of any cruise is enhanced if the crew are confident in their own ability, while the anxiety in the minds of some over the more difficult evolutions is readily expelled if these evolutions are practised under simple conditions. The very thought of reefing in the open sea, storm trisails or man overboard sends a shiver down the backs of many well-travelled yachtsmen; especially if they have never experienced any of these drills, or it was carried out for the first time under really difficult conditions.

At sea in a small yacht during a gale one is in a similar predicament to a boxer whose defences are not too sound; one is hammered about until one has the reasoning power of a small child and the drive of a tired old man. It is a poor time for an untried evolution with strange gear. Training can be enjoyable and interesting, in fact it is a poor training method if this is not so. It requires some effort, but this is a far less serious matter for the most leisurely cruising man than the loss of

F

life, limb or craft due to the lack of preparation for some critical situation. An angry sea and tearing wind refuse to be leisurely; they are deadly serious.

In one yacht it was blowing near gale force when the storm trisail was first seen on deck by her crew. For half an hour or more they struggled to find which way up to hoist it, the wind or sea snarling each attempt to lay out the sail on deck to see its shape. After a further laborious battle it was found that the main halyard shackle was too small for the sail's headboard; it is a tedious task just to go below and find a shackle to a size measured roughly with numbed fingers, when a man is soaked and stupefied by rough seas. None knew the lead of the sheets, one of whose blocks was left slung over the main boom, while a ponderous trial of suitable securings for the other block continued until a stunned helmsman with blood pouring from the side of his head showed where the swinging block had hit him. Night fell; still the trisail was not hoisted; darkness added to all else to make the problem insoluble. Next day the sun was high, and the wind's violence had long departed before that yacht hoisted her original mainsail. The wind blew off-shore from the first, so the yacht was never in danger; yet during the time her crew had struggled on deck, knowing that the wind might shift to put her on a lee shore, they were continuously in peril due to half a gale combining with their ignorance. Should a man have been knocked overboard, or had the wind shifted, the situation would have been grave, although each of the crew may have been an experienced seaman. If the trisail had first been hoisted for practice on a quiet day, when the blow came the torpid brain and numbed fingers would only need to repeat actions which were already familiar.

Object of further training.

Many may feel that there is little point in preparing a crew for a standard higher than is necessary for the safety of the ship and themselves, especially as the sweat and labour necessary will only drive the ship a mere fraction of her speed faster than when cruising. Yet by nature men are competitive, and most find great satisfaction from working hard together as a team. It is physically uncomfortable, often painful, to play a bustling game of rugger, or to climb some difficult mountain face roped up as a team; yet these discomforts, besides the onerous preparations and long hours of rigorous training, become trivialities compared with the excitement of competition, the pride in achievement and the respect for one's team mates when a job has been well done in unison. All this applies even more to ocean racing, where a greater sustained effort is needed than in any other sport. The anxiety about the best sail to carry, and then the thrill of fast sailing with every inch of canvas tugging her through the waves; the loneliness of the open ocean contrasting with the warm friendship of one's shipmates; the apprehension about the wind's force and direction, and the perplexing exasperation of a calm; the intense concentration of steering, and the hectic midnight battle to smother a gale-mad spinnaker; the impetuous wave-riding as she foams ahead scarcely under control, and the heavy thud as she falls off a wave-top to lie stopped and shaken in the trough; all these are champagne-lively experiences which can only be tasted to the full by a crew whose training is fully matured.

For a crew to reach this standard the essentials are hard work, imaginative training methods and almost unlimited incentive.

Let it be quite clear for all exactly what the object of the training is to be. If a quiet cruise along a sheltered coast is planned, the object will be to train the crew as soon as possible to handle the sails and equipment needed for that trip, including the action for any possible accidents. At sea, incident can lead to accident and so to catastrophe far quicker than ashore. If the cruise extends into unsheltered water, the training must progress further to include dealing with bad weather, which can always come without warning in the Westerlies around the British Isles. If it is to be for a race, there can surely be only one object for a sportsman: that is to win the race. 'Know ye not,' wrote Saint Paul to the men of Corinth, 'that they which run in a race run all, but one receiveth the prize? So run that ye may win.'

Incentive.

Incentive comes primarily from the knowledge, even conviction, that the object is worth attaining. If the crew know that extra effort is needed to prepare them to save one of their own lives in an emergency, the incentive is clear. Although they understand that it is easier to try out the storm sails in a quiet breeze than in a westerly gale blowing over the Channel ebb-stream, incentive is weak until the gale has been experienced. In the case of the long training required to reach the highest standard, interest needs frequent stimulus, particularly in the early stages. Incitement can be produced by the encouragement and support given by others in various ways; when the proper stage is reached, a preparatory race will stir it; a visit by someone influential, who is held in some veneration, will act as a personal challenge to reach the standard the guest expects, just as the expected visit of a housewife's 'in-laws' adds burnish to her home. Enthusiasm is an expendable asset, as well as being contagious; if a crew are training hard for some important race, the consumption of this enthusiasm is very heavy, so fresh contacts with outside enthusiasm are frequently needed. All progress should be rewarded with praise, so that it can be recognised as progress; any stage not fully mastered must be repeated until the standard required has been gained; any relapse must be pointed out, and the loss regained.

Elementary lessons for safety.

As the training is intended to meet situations at sea, it must be carried out at sea, so far as is possible. The first steps must be to make the ship safe for crew even in fully sheltered waters, where the immediate danger is for a man to fall overboard or a fire to break out. Each man who will be mate of a watch should take the tiller in turn and pick up a buoy representing a body in the water, using the exact procedure which the skipper wants carried out in his own yacht. Next, the fire extinguishers are provided as though a fire had occurred in the most vulnerable positions below. Should the galley be between the main hatch and any portion of the accommodation, this is a place of danger; a petrol engine is another. Only after these exercises, even if each of the crew starts off a good seaman, is the ship safe for simple cruising.

Learning the ship.

The next stage is to hoist in succession, without any attempt at sail shifting drill, every sail carried on board. Each should be carefully set and trimmed so that the whole crew is familiar with the appearance, feel, fittings and sheeting positions of every sail. It is probable that during this parade of the yacht's trousseau some defects will be noticed; it may be that a missing hank from the staysail's luff has been replaced by one of a different type from the remainder, which could cost three seconds and a broken finger nail on a dark night; perhaps the marking on a sail's tack no longer shows clearly; or the second genoa sheets are too short for their purpose. All these points must be recorded at once in the defect book which is kept handy, complete with a sharpened pencil secured to it by a length of string.

After the sails, each item of her sea-going gear must be tried out. The log should be streamed, storm warps paid out astern secured as they might be towed, sea anchor streamed, if one is carried, and the oil bag or can tried.

During all this time it is best to remain at sea, certainly throughout a full night, cruising quietly between the periods when trying the gear. There is a great deal that can only be learnt by living in a boat at sea under simple conditions, since when it comes to rough weather the slightest unfamiliar action requires extra effort that may be too much for a numbed mind. It needs experiment and practice even to find the best sleeping positions in each bunk under different conditions of sailing; it may later be important that every hour of rest is well used. All the time experience is being gained of the cooking apparatus and the exact positions of everything connected with the preparation of food, so that balance and security below are more rapidly achieved later on. There is ample opportunity too for each of the crew to become really familiar with the steering of that particular boat, essential even to the best of helmsmen.

During training never must any of the crew feel bored; every moment that all hands or the watch are on duty, they must have some definite object that is worth attaining. Should the yacht be quietly cruising, having finished a heavy period of exercise, then the watch can still be given some object to strive for, perhaps a lighthouse to be passed, or a distance to be completed on the log; if there is no need to make good any distance, a definite task can be set such as noting the speeds with varying sail trims under different conditions of sailing.

Once the yacht has been at sea for twenty-four hours, and all her sailing equipment has been seen in use, the crew should be competent to deal in slow time with any situation, and be fit to enjoy cruising without any anxiety about being caught out by bad weather. If a really high standard of eventual training is expected, this preliminary phase must be completed before advancing the training, so that in future phases full use can be made of any time available, whatever the weather. Probably this period at sea will be enough to show the skipper if he has the right crew to achieve the purpose of his cruise; it will also enable him to decide on the composition of the watches, in particular who will make the best mates of watches.

As time is usually an important factor, this preliminary stage can well be achieved in one week-end. At any rate it will have brought about a good many entries in the defect book, so a pause in harbour would be valuable.

Basic sail drill.

The next stage marks the beginning of training for a racing standard, but no attempt should be made to enter a race until the crew is ready for this, particularly if a really polished performance is the eventual aim. In a race there is no time to stop and correct errors or difficulties due to different members of the crew having varying methods; each time a thing is done it is turning more and more into a habit. If a wrong habit is developed, forceful negative training is essential to eradicate it. 'Don'ts' merely discourage, and are no basis at all for training a keen crew. Yet on the other hand 'Stop', followed by a clear description on the spot of what is required, will discourage no one.

When training is being carried out there is no room for a debating society. The sailing master, who may well be the skipper, must know what drill he intends to teach, and no other methods are of any interest at all at that stage. This does not mean that the drill can never be modified; some of it certainly will be altered to suit personal idiosyncrasies. But first of all a sound drill must be thoroughly mastered by the team carrying it out, so as to have a basis to which adjustments can be made, or against which quite different methods can be judged. The essential point is that each member of the team understands what the others are doing.

First the ship is tacked in slow time, giving instructions for the exact drill that is to be carried out in that ship. Tacking is a simple enough matter in a modern yacht, yet it is the basic evolution on which many others depend. In a long race the boat will probably tack so often that even two or three seconds wasted each time will add up to an important waste of time. Worse than that, any casual departure from the drill will eventually, and probably it will be on a dark rough night, lead to some jam which may throw the yacht into irons, or cause a long delay. How often has one heard a crew bemoaning their luck when they tell of leading in a race until something snarled up to ruin their hopes. On a nasty wet night it is an irksome bore to shift from the slight shelter of the cockpit, risking more drops of water down one's neck, just to tack the ship in any old slap-happy fashion; yet if the ship is tacked smartly, with each man doing his piece with the timing of a trapeze artist, a warm glow of satisfaction will counter the night damp.

Tacking will normally be a watch manœuvre, so each watch in turn must be thoroughly proficient. Then follows gybing, which is slightly more difficult to get the timing right, and definitely more dangerous than tacking if the drill is casual.

The finest crew will need to practise even these simple manœuvres many times to achieve perfection, but they must never be allowed to get bored. As soon as any signs of less than an 'all out' effort appear, some other evolution must be carried out as a change, or the exercise stopped. Man overboard can be exercised as a complete change, and if the climate is suitable the best way is to invite one of the crew, unknown to the others, to fall overboard deliberately. It must be a firm habit, when training for racing, that everything is done 'all out', as soon as the drill has been taught. The perfect way to finish up any series of exercises is to stop after the best effort has just been achieved.

Sail Shifting.

When the crew can tack, gybe and pick up a man overboard with real *élan*, the next stage is sail shifting. Again the precise stations and drill for each sail shift is first taught, and then carried out in quick time. When training for ocean racing it is best to have one drill for each evolution, which is suitable for all weather conditions; it is possible to cut off seconds by a separate calm weather drill, yet this may involve the loss of minutes in bad weather, due to that drill being practised less often. While practising sail shifting, care should be taken to ring the changes through the whole outfit of sails; some shifts are far simpler than others, such as changing a working staysail for a spitfire jib, so that will need less practice than shifting from spinnaker to largest genoa; yet unless the simple ones are tried occasionally the lead of the sheets will be forgotten, and much time lost. Even when the drill is being carried out at full speed, if any serious mistake occurs, the order

'Stop' should be given, and the mistakes sorted out; then the whole evolution should be done again. Bad drill must never be overlooked, as it usually leaves a feeling of uncertainty about what went wrong; it may lead to loss of mutual confidence, and perhaps even an argument which festers for weeks afterwards between two or three of the crew who saw the situation differently; each will have a different solution, which will probably cause even greater chaos if the evolution is next carried out when racing.

Timing and competition.

Once all the sail drills have been taught, they should always be carried out with a stopwatch if possible. With a 'scratch' time established for each evolution, not only can any falling off be noticed with certainty, but also there is a standard against which any modifications can be judged. Competition provides incentive, even if it is against the clock.

Set pieces or short races.

It may well be that a full week-end of sail shifting, or a similar period given to exercises when cruising, will have brought the crew up to a standard where an inshore race would be a great advantage to stir up incentive. But it must be stressed that if the skipper, or sailing master, is to retain real control of his crew as a team, no race should be attempted until the drill is thoroughly mastered; racing with an untrained crew gives good sport at the time, but it is like setting a retriever puppy to chase rabbits and then expecting him to turn into a field-trial champion later on. However, if the right stage has been reached, it is best to start with a short race, and immediately after finishing repeat any evolution that went wrong.

Sometimes an actual race against other yachts cannot be arranged, then the next best is to plan a set piece course, such as shown in Table VII*a*. This was made out when the wind's direction was known, and shown to the crew in advance. The notes were filled in as each evolution was completed.

By this time all should be getting full enjoyment out of sailing together as a crew, and can pride themselves that they are showing their ship to good advantage, which always brings satisfaction to a seaman.

'*All out*' *trial.*

The next stage is more difficult to achieve as it depends on the weather and needs several days at sea. The yacht should go out and deliberately search for bad weather, which alone can test the yacht and her crew to the full. However, if no strong blows will oblige, a good deal of experience can be achieved with the help of the steep seas that readily build up in the tidal races off many headlands. The crew must become thoroughly accustomed to the ship's movement in bad weather, and learn how the yacht steers and behaves; they must

	Mark	*Evolution*	*Notes*
Start	Mooring buoy head of harbour	Practice begins	
1	Second mooring buoy	Hoist spinnaker	*Repeat*
2	Pearl Island buoy	Gybe spinnaker	*Repeat*
3	Grace Island buoy	Turn on to wind	*Good*
4	103 buoy	Shift to 2A	*52 secs*
5	40 buoy	Up second spinnaker	*4 mins*
6	100 buoy	Hoist snarl net	*Repeat*
7	102 buoy	Gybe spinnaker	*Fair*
8	Near Watford Bridge	Turn on to wind with big genoa	*1 min. 14 secs*
9	DunDonald channel	Close tacking	*Good*
10	Last channel buoy	Reef mainsail	*52 secs*
11	Grassy Bay mooring buoy	Set full main	*33 secs*
12	Yacht will then anchor	Down main sail, set trisail	*1 min. 5 secs*

Table VIIa. Set piece Sail Drills

get used to working in oilskins and lifebelts, by day and by night (see Plate 13). Sail drill will be more limited than in light weather and sheltered waters, as some of the bigger sails cannot be used, yet it would be perfect if each were kept hoisted up to near the strongest wind in which it can be used. Each evolution becomes much harder work with heavy clothing and the ever present 'index error' of inertia to start any movement in rough conditions, so an over-ambitious programme should not be attempted or the crew will be overtired and discouraged. The aim should be to do enough to demonstrate to everyone's satisfaction that the ship and crew are well under control when it is rough (see Plate 14).

Very few people are likely to enjoy a full gale when afloat in a small craft, and undoubtedly many hardy seamen will be slightly frightened (see Plate 22), yet it is far better to experience a gale under these controlled conditions, perhaps not so very far from assistance, than to meet one for the first time in that craft far out in the middle of an ocean, when perhaps the crew are already exhausted by a hard race. More important even than that, many of us would be very reluctant to set out for a really long ocean passage without having first seen the ship and crew extended by bad weather, knowing full well that a gale at some time or another was almost inevitable.

Even if no strong blow is experienced on this extended trial, while she remains at sea for several days, it is almost certain that there will be enough wind to make reefing realistic, and enough sea to experience sail shifting when the fore deck is dipping under water and spray is flying through the air. This period is not only valuable on deck; the result of a long race depends just as much on the organisation below. Without sleep and sustaining meals, no crew can do well. There is only one way to learn cooking in a sea-way, and that is to practise it under these conditions; there is a great deal to be learnt about how best to sleep when the ship is smacking into a steep head sea; one of the most strenuous jobs aboard is donning oilskins when the ship is well heeled and bouncing too. In quiet conditions much depends on the ability to talk and hear, when it is rough talking allows too much salt water into the mouth, and listening gets little beyond the shriek and roar of the elements. Then there is the greatest menace a skipper has to face in rough weather with an untried crew; that is seasickness, against which immunity is almost unknown if the yacht is really driven hard. Even when a man claims that he has never been seasick, the skipper cannot be quite content with the statement until he sees what happens when the bilge pump suctions choke while she is driving to windward through a Gulf Stream gale. Seasickness is dealt with later on, but skipper and crew must know where they stand in this matter, and this can only be discovered by trial.

After the crew and gear have been tried out under 'full power' conditions, a reasonable period in harbour is important, as there will be repairs and adjustments to make good, and probably changes in drill or organisation to be considered and worked out. If things have gone well, skipper and crew will know that they are well trained for an ocean race.

Final tuning.

Even with a crew fully trained for ocean racing, final tuning will still be necessary to achieve the best result in any particular race. This should be directed at the needs of that particular race, as no two seas are alike. Thus if the aim should be the Bermuda race, which is probably the hardest to win of any sailing contest, then the place for tuning-up is the Gulf Stream. Here the sea is nearly always restless and squalls come unexpectedly; some squalls bring only heavy rain; some shatter the atmosphere with the battle noises of thunder, while flash after flash of lightning does more to blind the eyes than light the scene; others bring fierce gusts of ever-changing wind; all bring uncertainty. Squalls in the Gulf Stream appear as though from nowhere then dissolve. The only way to tune men and gear to such conditions is to experience them, so this training must be carried out within the Gulf Stream's turbulence.

When preparing for a race across the North Atlantic, such Gulf Stream conditions will be experienced too; so will long periods of fog. However, in this race, the main feature is the long period of isolation from the rest of the world when the ship must be self-dependent, not only in stores and apparatus, but in the minds of the crew. The training for this should aim at convincing them that the race goes on, come what may. Drill should be organised to deal with some really serious breakdown, to show that it can be overcome; thus rigging a jury mast leads to a feeling of confidence that the crew need never be at a loss. In such a long race, the ability to speak with any ships sighted has a powerful influence on morale, so the training should perfect visual signalling. It may be that in some race, various aids to navigation will be of special value, such as radio beacons, or *Consol*; then their use should be practised, not only to ensure accurate results, but to enable these to be achieved without unnecessary effort during the actual race.

Training programme.

Only by long, enthusiastic and arduous training by her crew can a yacht be sailing at her very best in a long ocean race. Obviously such a full course of preparation cannot be undertaken before all races; yet if a yacht goes abroad flying her national colours and enters any race of international standard, she is taken to represent her country and is received with honour for that reason. It would be a cause of lasting shame for her crew if they failed to put up a performance worthy of their craft, besides the men who designed and built her.

Yet there are many races where the standard is more modest, and any crew doing their best with the time at their disposal should be honoured. Once I began an ocean race with skipper and crew scrambling aboard her for the first time under full sail, to relieve a cruising crew who were bundled into a motor launch alongside, from which they passed over the racing gear and food while the yacht manœuvred in readiness for the starting gun. She finished her race reasonably well, mostly due to the fortunes of calm weather, which lost the ship little time while the crew hoisted each sail and tried out the gear; yet we would have enjoyed ourselves far more had we started really fit to make use of the yacht's qualities.

In another race it was reported that a lady owner set out in bad weather for an ocean race, soon to realize that once they reached open waters her crew were not sufficiently trained to race the yacht to windward in a gale. Instead of abandoning the race, as many others did, she anchored while still in sheltered waters and spent six hours training her crew to the high standard required; then she went on with the race, and actually caught up time on some of her rivals. Such an action combined real sportsmanship with splendid seamanship.

A training programme must therefore be devised to suit every situation, whether it is an important international race, when time training the crew should rank equal with the need for time to fit out and prepare the yacht, or whether it consists of a last minute gathering of two or three friends for a modest cruise. However little time is available, the ship cannot be considered seaworthy until the crew have completed the first two stages of training; in some cases that may be done readily in half an hour on the way out to sea, but it must be done as soon as possible when the ship is under way. It is just when everything is unfamiliar that a man is most likely to go overboard, or a fire to blaze forth. One often hears the expression 'caught out', as though that meant a ship was caught at sea when the weather turned bad; it really means that her crew were caught out, because the elementary stage of learning the ship had been neglected.

VIII

Watchkeeping and Routine

WHEN a yacht is to be at sea for more than a few hours some system of watchkeeping must be organised. The object is to keep the ship sailing safely without needless exhaustion of the crew, who will also have to maintain the ship, repair damage, prepare food, eat, rest and enjoy recreation.

Frequency of watches.

Traditionally the crews of ships were divided into two watches, with half the crew on deck at any one time. Men accustomed to this life learnt at an early age to sleep for short periods, which added up to a reasonable amount of rest throughout the whole day. This is the system that enables the ship to be handled with the least man-power, and to be sailing at her fastest with a given size of crew. It is the normal system used when ocean racing with a crew of four or more, and is usually used when cruising with a crew of only two; the alternative with such a crew being to heave-to without a watchkeeper part of the time. When not racing it means altogether too much effort to work in two watches, as there will always be situations when it is necessary to call all hands on deck for some major evolution.

In practice, not only have the time and effort when actually on watch to be considered, but also the preparations for going on deck, besides those on coming below. Especially in a small yacht, the need for oilskins on watch is frequent in most seas. The operation of putting on scarves, jerseys, oilskins and perhaps lifebelts, is one of the most strenuous of all when the vessel is well heeled and pounding into a steep sea; after a watch it also takes time and hard work to remove wet clothing with cold hands and change into dry clothes before settling down to a meal or sleep. Twelve hours on watch each day only allows some eight or less hours below in bad weather for this purpose, and these eight hours must be split up into short periods, as there is a limit to the time the watch on deck can remain fully efficient.

When cruising therefore it is always best to aim at two watches below for every watch on deck, which allows ample time for sleep in the longer periods that we are accustomed to in shore life; it also allows ample time to maintain the ship in good condition.

Length of watches.

The time continuously on watch depends chiefly on the period in which men can remain efficient at their duties; this varies with the exposure of the man and ease of handling of the ship. What is possible in the Trade Wind zones with a ship that nearly sails herself, is no guide to the organisation in a blizzard. When racing, the crew will always aspire to the highest standards of efficiency; when cruising there can be a comfortable compromise between speed and comfort. The number of men in the watch will also affect the time it can remain efficient; if the crew is so small that only one man is on watch at a time, the situation differs from a ship where three or four men are on watch and can take turns with the steering. People, ships and conditions vary, but generally four hours is about the limiting time for steering a yacht continuously with any efficiency as a matter of routine. Often this will prove too long; it is usually harder to concentrate for such a time with a wheel than with a tiller; steering on a reach is easier than hard on the wind or running before a big sea; ample food is essential for good steering during long periods, just as George Eliot recorded that no man can be wise on an empty stomach. Therefore if only one man can be on watch at a time, his length of duty should not exceed four hours; if the ship is in three watches, that is two watches below and one on deck, then the four hours on deck allows a convenient eight hours below, which becomes cut to a maximum effective sleeping time of seven hours at a stretch, every third night.

The perfect cruising yacht would have such simple gear in proportion to her size and habitability that one watch was sufficient to keep the ship sailing safely and efficiently without ever having to call for help from the hands below. With a well-designed rig this can almost be achieved when cruising, particularly when good judgement and weather forecasting keeps the amount of canvas set such that any shift of sails can await the change of watches, a time when double the number of men will be on deck. Success in ocean racing, on the other hand, depends upon always carrying the canvas that will drive the ship at the best speed, so that sail shifting is much more frequent, and must be effected as soon as the weather changes; this offers a delicate problem of watch organisation, especially as work such as sail sewing for the men off watch is more frequent when racing.

Excused watchkeeping.

Normally certain of the crew are excused keeping watches so as to carry out special duties; this is particularly so with larger crews, where the crew organisation becomes easier. If it is at all possible the skipper should not keep a watch as his complete responsibility for the ship means that he must be continuously on call. The more a ship is being pressed, the more essential is it that the skipper be available at all times; should he also keep a watch it will handicap the ship when racing as there are bound to be occasions when the mate of another watch would be reluctant to call him at perhaps 2.30 a.m., when he is due to come on deck at 4 a.m., yet would not feel entitled to take risks without consulting the skipper. How often has one heard, 'Perhaps she'd take the full mainsail now, but the skipper's going to be called in an hour, so we can leave it until then.' It is also a racing advantage to have someone free of routine watchkeeping who can see things with a more detached point of view; a relatively fresh crew will be depressed by a tired skipper, yet a rested and vigorous skipper can inspire the more jaded crew to great efforts. The same applies to cruising should long periods of bad weather or difficult conditions be experienced.

The cook.

In larger yachts' crews the cook may be excused watchkeeping, and certainly good food is essential whatever the object of the cruise. Yet unless the crew consists of five or more it is scarcely justifiable to have one person cooking continuously, besides which few people will want to cook all the time. Variety is important for all. Probably the best solution is for different watchkeepers to take turns as cook, which allows each a change from his watches, and produces variety in the presentation of the food. While the chef's art is not given to all, any reasonably intelligent man or woman can make a passable attempt at cooking after some simple instruction, and many can occasionally be inspired to produce near masterpieces of cuisine.

Cruising watchkeeping systems.

An interesting watchkeeping routine for four men cruising was used in *Iolaire* by Robert Somerset, whose experience of yacht sailing is exceptionally wide. This system divided the day into three watches of four hours, and the night into four watches of three hours. Each of the four men was cook every fourth day and had each of the day and night watches only once in every four-day cycle. As will be seen by following the fortunes of say A in Table VIII*a*, he enjoys an easy day and a quiet night of watchkeeping on the first day, which stores up his energies for the duties of cook on the second day; then he celebrates his return to the deck on the third day with ample fresh air and daylight followed by three hours' duty in the depth of the night. Such a watchkeeping system as this expels any chance of monotony, even in a long passage under steady conditions such as might be found with the Trade Winds.

Day	Cook	0700–1100	1100–1500	1500–1900	1900–2200	2200–0100	0100–0400	0400–0700
1st	D	A	B	C	A	B	C	D
2nd	A	B	C	D	B	C	D	A
3rd	B	C	D	A	C	D	A	B
4th	C	D	A	B	D	A	B	C

Table VIII*a*. IOLAIRE SYSTEM. Cruising Watches for Four Men

Another interesting compromise for cruising comes from Robin Kilroy's voyage from Singapore to England in *Boleh*, with a total crew of five. Chinese Chang came as cook, three others kept watch and the skipper helped out with a very ample share of watchkeeping at fixed times. Again the night watches lasted three hours but day watches varied from one hour to four and a quarter to suit meal-times. This system, shown in Table VIII*b*, worked well with most of the cruise in a warm climate but in colder climates the shorter watches would entail a great deal of work wasted in dressing and undressing.

Plate 9. Cruising in the open sea a yacht should often look after herself. This is *Ilala* of 36 ft. overall, rigged as a Chinese schooner, with Hasler self-steering gear

Plate 10. Racing speeds up the tempo and demands more of the crew, as shown in *Griffin II* of 48·5 ft. overall, a one-time Fastnet winner

Plate 11. Coming up to the Fastnet rock in *Belmore II* of 37·6 ft. overall. The yacht to the left of the rock is *Rabbit*, which proved to be the Fastnet winner

Work of the watch.

The amount of work put into the actual sailing of the ship will not only depend upon the number of men in a watch, but also upon what those on watch are required to do. The easiest conditions are when the sails have been adjusted so that the ship sails herself; then the watchkeeper keeps a look-out and may occasionally need to adjust the sails and tiller, and perhaps cooks.

If the vessel must be steered continuously, the duty of helmsman can be divided up amongst the members of the watch, perhaps doing tricks of an hour or two hours at a time. In some hard-raced vessels only selected men are allowed to steer, yet it would seem unfortunate if the great satisfaction of steering the ship is denied to any of those who work

Day	0200–0500	0500–0700	0700–0800	0800–1215	1215–1530	1530–1800	1800–2000	2000–2300	2300–0200
1st	A	SKIPPER	B	SKIPPER	C	A	B	C	A
2nd	B	SKIPPER	C	SKIPPER	A	B	C	A	B
3rd	C	SKIPPER	A	SKIPPER	B	C	A	B	C

Table VIII*b*. BOLEH SYSTEM. Cruising Watches for Five Men with a Permanent Cook

her. When ocean racing the rest of the watch, apart from the helmsman, will frequently be busy changing and trimming sails, besides making regular examinations so that any suspicion of chafe is stopped before damage occurs to sails or rigging; the time spent on these anti-chafe measures is repaid very many times in the work saved on repairs.

When there is nothing else to be done those on watch often get some rest when not actually steering, so long as they are dressed and instantly ready for anything; the danger in allowing part of the watch to sleep until needed is that most mates of watches are slightly reluctant to wake a sleeping man for some trivial job, although it is only by an accumulation of small things that the yacht can be trimmed to go her very fastest.

With more than one man in a watch, with the consequent shifts of helmsmen, it is often best to increase the length of the duty on watch, so as to allow longer periods of sleep for those off watch. When *Cohoe* won the Transatlantic race of 1950 her crew of four men were in two

G

watches, each taking six hours on deck, and relieving at two o'clock and eight o'clock, a.m. and p.m.

Racing watches with a small crew.

Racing with a very small crew requires careful and slightly flexible organisation to get the fastest speed. The minimum effective number for an open sea race taking more than a few days seems to be four men; this is the least crew allowed by the rules of the Cruising Club of America for their classic ocean race to Bermuda. Even with this small racing crew it is probably best for the skipper to stand out of the regular watchkeeping, to give flexibility necessary to meet different conditions and so that he can lead his crew most effectively throughout, resting when things are easy and making extra efforts when they are hard. This will leave three men, yet much of the time two are necessary on deck to drive the ship. The best system then is for the helmsman to keep watch for periods of four hours, while the next man is the stand-by watch-keeper, who is dressed and ready to go on deck at short notice either to work the sails or to relieve the helmsman for short periods at the tiller. The third man, who is off watch, becomes cook for whatever meal is next due. The dogwatch is split into two, so that each man has different watches through the three-day cycle.

However, this scheme as it stands allows for very little sleep indeed and so, depending upon the conditions and urgency, can be modified by the skipper carrying out the functions of the stand-by watch-keeper throughout the hours of darkness, which is always the most difficult time to keep a vessel driving fast; if in such a small crew the skipper is also navigator, he will in any case want to be dressed for the deck at dusk and dawn to take star sights.

A further relaxation is to make the stand-by watchkeeper cook, so that during the hour or two of daylight required for cooking each day either the ship will not be sailing at her utmost, or the skipper can again become stand-by watchkeeper. In practice the only time when this relaxation of alertness really loses much is when the stand-by is preparing breakfast, as that is the time when the middle watchkeeper and skipper will be deepest in sleep; at the times the other meals are being cooked someone is likely to be alert and probably working on deck. With this modification it means that each man in turn should get about seven hours' continuous sleep every third night, yet two men are either on deck or in immediate readiness for the deck at all times except about half an hour each day. This system is illustrated in Table VIIIc.

Day	Duty	0800–Noon	Noon–1600	1600–1800	1800–2000	2000–Midt.	Midt–0400	0400–0800
1	Mate of Watch	A	B	C	A	B	C	A
	Stand by	B	C	A	B	Skipper	Skipper	Skipper to 0700
	Cook	C (lunch)			C (supper)			C (breakfast)
2	Mate of watch	B	C	A	B	C	A	B
	Stand by	C	A	B	C	Skipper	Skipper	Skipper to 0700
	Cook	A			A			A
3	Mate of Watch	C	A	B	C	A	B	C
	Stand by	A	B	C	A	Skipper	Skipper	Skipper to 0700
	Cook	B			B			B

Table VIIIc. SAMUEL PEPYS SYSTEM. Racing Watches with Four Men

Each of the watchkeeping systems mentioned has been designed for a specific purpose and no system is adaptable enough to suit all conditions and situations, but it is important to have some system arranged, and understood by the crew, before the yacht goes to sea. There is one system, often enough used for short cruises, that has little to commend it. That is for the whole crew to remain on deck when the ship leaves harbour, all helping valiantly with any evolution on deck for ten, twenty or perhaps even more hours, then just when the skipper begins to realise that the voyage is taking longer than he estimated, he also realises that everyone is too tired to keep a watch, so for some hours the ship is virtually not under command. As soon as the ship is under way, and everything is secured for the open sea, the skipper should give the order 'Watch cruising', or 'Watch racing', particularly if sea-sickness is apparent, as often happens in the early stages of a cruise, and he should insist on those off watch going below to rest.

Mate of the watch.

As the skipper cannot be continuously on deck, he must delegate the immediate responsibility for the safety of the vessel to the mate of the watch. There should never be any doubt as to who is mate of the watch, whether he is in immediate charge, or the skipper has taken over, and exactly what his responsibility entails. Many vessels have been imperilled due to uncertainty on this point. The skipper must specifically tell the mate of the watch when he hands over authority to him, and again say so if he has taken immediate charge of the ship.

It is so important that the mate of the watch knows exactly where he stands with his skipper, that his orders should be written down on the front page of the log, or somewhere readily seen and referred to when on watch, as shown in Table VIIId. The alternative to such positive orders is for the skipper to wait until something has been done wrong and then correct it with a negative order; this may be less trouble for the skipper, but is far less pleasant for those on watch.

In an emergency the mate of the watch should use his discretion about taking any action he considers necessary, but tell me as soon as possible.

If I am required on deck in a hurry the hail is 'Skipper on deck.'

Please tell me at once if:

(a) The weather changes or shows signs of change.
(b) If the visibility falls below one mile.
(c) On sighting any ship, when beyond the hundred fathom line.
(d) If any ship is likely to pass within one mile, at any time.
(e) On sighting land or lights.
(f) If any sail change seems necessary.
(g) If any damage occurs to sails, rigging, equipment or hull.

Never fail to call me, whatever the circumstances, if help or advice is needed.

Table VIIId. Typical instructions for mate of the watch written on the cover of the ship's log

The decision to shift sails, reef or alter course will normally be for the skipper to make, although he will probably ask for the opinion of the mate of the watch. Often the skipper will take over the ship while an evolution is being undertaken, and in the case of an 'All hands' evolution this is inevitable. However, for a watch evolution it is often advisable for the mate of the watch to remain in charge, sometimes perhaps with the skipper assisting with the sail change. In this case the skipper should give a direction such as, 'Mr. Mate, I would like you to shift to the second genoa,' then it is up to the mate of the watch to complete the job as best he can; when racing, all sail shifts should be competitive against time.

Routine.

In Chapter II it was stated that the amount of living space within a ship depends partly upon the habits of her crew. Some rhythm of life is essential when several people have to fit into a small space, and this is achieved by organising a routine that fits in with the purpose of the cruise. It seems a paradox, but nevertheless is soon apparent, that only with a fairly rigid routine will the crew have any freedom to arrange their own affairs on board, as otherwise they will spend much of their time waiting for somebody else, or standing on each other's toes. 'Without routine,' wrote E. G. Martin, 'life aboard ship is unbearable.'

The framework round which the routine must be built is the time of meals. Times must be found which fit in best and these times adhered to rigidly while at sea, with nothing but 'All hands' evolutions on deck interfering. If a meal is not ready until ten minutes late, that ten minutes' worth for the cook has cost in recreational or working time ten minutes multiplied by the number of people eating the meal; not only that but the losses tend to be cumulative, so that after a time everyone is continuously trying to catch up with the greatest output for the least result.

Closely connected with meal-times is the organisation of the watches. The racing watches for a crew of four shown in Table VIII*c* allows for the meals to be shortly before changes of watches, so that one man goes on duty well fed and another comes off watch to find a meal ready. It is important to keep the changes of watches punctual, as a late relief on watch ranks about equal with a late meal as a cause of dissension. A four-hour watch always seems long enough, but every minute beyond that time seems like an hour, unless there is some very good reason for the delay. The man who really wants to be a perfect shipmate in a small yacht can commit almost any blunder so long as he always arrives on deck a minute or two before the time he is due to take over his watch, and if as cook he always sees to it that the meal is ready to be eaten at the exact time arranged in the routine; it is even worth going without a meal once in a cruise to get the reputation for punctuality that is nearly always rewarded by punctual relief in return.

Those who cruise in small craft tend to love independence, and may perhaps feel that any routine would bind them too tightly. A badly planned routine will certainly prove irksome, yet at its best it is no more a tie than the band which beats out the rhythm so that dancers can keep time with one another. If the music is out of harmony with the dancers' moods, or the rhythm is erratic, no one will get the full enjoyment from the dance, but if there is no music at all, they will tread on each other's toes. If more than one person is aboard a yacht, there can be no harmony without a carefully planned routine. A simple daily sea routine is shown in Table VIII*e*.

07.30	Breakfast
09.00	Clear up ship below
11.30	Lunch
15.30	Tea
19.20	Dinner
20.20	Clear up ship below

Table VIII*e*. Typical Daily Sea Routine when Racing
(This fits in with *Samuel Pepys* Watchkeeping, shown in Table VIII*c*)

Ship's time.

The skipper at sea has a great advantage over people ashore in that he can do whatever he likes with the clock. When a man feels that it is very early to rise at five in the morning, his feelings are controlled more by the hands of the clock than the altitude of the sun. It would be over complicated to change the clock's hands so frequently that whenever anyone was called for a night watch the clock showed half past seven, and each meal started at a conventional hour as well; yet judicious use of zone time, local time and the sun's behaviour can certainly lighten the load of watchkeeping, besides making meals more acceptable.

Thus the slow moving hours of darkness may perhaps be split equally between the watches, so that during some summer cruises no watch need be kept in total darkness. Again if breakfast be ordered at six in the morning, wherever the sun may be, many will remain in their bunks and go without the meal; yet if breakfast be arranged at seven thirty, even if the summer sun has hardly topped the horizon, all will eat the better for it. If the mate is to be in charge of the domestic arrangements and routine, as suggested in Chapter VI, he should be the man to recommend when the period of darkness is to come, and the skipper order the ship's time accordingly.

Any such juggling with the clocks does not make the slightest difference to navigation, or to anyone else outside the ship. The clocks should always be retarded in the dog watches, so that no long watch exceeds its normal length; the clocks are normally advanced at midnight, or at the change of watches nearest to this, so that the night watchkeepers may share a bonus of reduced time on watch. However, this also deprives the watch below of a portion of their sleep, so if they are hard worked it is best to keep all changes of the clocks to the dog watches.

IX

Food and Water

FOOD is the most important factor of all those that affect the enjoyment of a cruise exceeding a few hours, while water is the most vital factor in determining whether the objective can be reached. In any race exceeding twelve hours the ability of the crew to eat limits the speed of the yacht, and eating in turn is controlled by the consumption of water.

It is not just that an enjoyable cruise consists merely of good eating, although this is certainly one of the pleasures of life at all times, but simply that no one except the odd Yogi can gain the full benefit of life unless sustained by an ample diet. Racing requires exceptionally hard work over long hours, so that a very full diet is required to sustain the output of physical energy, and it must be interesting enough to help support that enthusiasm which drives the body to this effort.

Crew energy.

The fuel problem for a machine is simple mathematics; the quantity of energy required for a certain voyage is readily calculated, the efficiency of the machine is found by experiment, so it is easy enough to work out the fuel needed when its calorific value is well known. Yet the fuel problem for the motive power of a sailing vessel, her crew, exercises an art with infinitely greater scope and variations. The great difference is that in the human being both input of calories of food and output of calorics of energy are controlled by feelings; the first can be affected by tempting flavours or unsavoury appearance, while the other is largely dependent on some form of inspiration. Inspiration can be a most powerful force and at times will drive the body to an output far exceeding the calorific value of its intake, but there is a limit to the human reserves of energy and eventually the body must absorb a certain quantity of food to achieve the work required.

Food value is measured in calories, which are merely units of energy; a certain amount of heavy work may mean an essential food input of 3,500 calories a day, but that is not the whole story; within this quantity the diet must be balanced to contain the right proportions of protein, fat and carbohydrates, besides minute quantities of certain mineral salts and vitamins. It is simple enough to stuff a crew with food until they are half-dazed with excess bulk, yet lack the vital force to hoist the mid-night spinnaker.

Balanced diets.

A balanced diet must contain the right proportion of:

Proteins (from meat, fish, eggs, cheese and milk) which build and repair muscles and tissue.

Fats (from butter, cooking fats, milk-chocolate, suet, fish, meat and bacon) which are slow heat and energy producers in the body. Although fats have a high calorific value they are not easy to assimilate. For instance a pound of butter has sufficient calories for a heavy day's work, but would not be very welcome as a hot day's diet.

Carbohydrates (from bread, cakes, sugar, chocolate and cocoa) which produce heat and energy quickly, and help the body to assimilate proteins and fats.

The normal ratio for a balanced diet is about one part each of protein and fat to four parts of carbohydrates, but where calories have to be concentrated into a small weight the balance may reach two units of protein to three of fat and four of carbohydrates, particularly when the weather is very cold. For planning, the diet should be based on the protein, which can most easily fall short of the requirements; a twelve stone man needs nearly three ounces of good quality animal protein every day, with the requirement increasing or decreasing according to the size of the man at the rate of one thousandth of the man's weight.

Mineral salts and vitamins (from fruit and vegetables) which protect the body against diseases. Fresh fruit and vegetables should be eaten as far as possible, as canning or bottling removes some of these essential qualities. The important anti-scorbutic vitamin C is destroyed by almost any form of cooking; it is found in citrus fruits and green salads, but curiously enough the traditional lime-juice is a much poorer source than lemons, oranges and grapefruit, of which the juices retain the vitamin when the fruit is preserved by special processes, as does blackcurrant juice and rose-hip syrup, which are both easy to obtain. Vitamin D is often insufficient in a normal fresh diet, as little is found in ordinary foods except egg-yolk. However cod-liver oil is a strong source, and is easily consumed in sufficient quantities in a small vitamin pill; some special chocolates and margarines are enriched with this vitamin.

Individual idiosyncrasies.

Different people vary greatly in the foods they like, their habits of eating and the quantity they need to consume. Dislikes may be due to some ridiculous chance like being slapped by a nanny at the age of two while eating porridge, for throwing a cup of milk at the cat, since when the distaste for porridge has persisted; eating faster or slower than the normal may be due to well-established habit and the variety of quantity needed may be due to some minor metabolism. Whatever the causes, this variety in human need exists and must be allowed for when planning the food requirements, particularly in a long race when it is the caterer's problem to ensure that all the crew eat enough to sustain them for the powerful effort required.

Quantity.

A sedentary worker requires some 2,400 calories a day, with an additional supply of some 200 to 300 calories (equivalent to a two-ounce bar of fruit and nut chocolate) for every hour of hard work, so that a crew ocean racing might need over 4,000 calories a day to maintain their physical condition. Particularly in hot weather it is hard enough to offer enough variety to get the ordinary person to eat as much as this; in cold weather the greater fat tolerance encourages a higher calorie intake, as fat has about twice the calorific value of carbohydrates. Explorers have devised a highly concentrated food giving a balanced diet of some 5,000 calories a day and weighing less than two pounds a man, but this assumes that ample supplies of drinking water can be found on the way. As a yacht has to carry all her water, whether in pure form or as a constituent of some of the food, there is little advantage in dehydrated foods, as it merely means carrying more water to reconstitute the food to the same extent as it was removed in the process of dehydration.

It is of rather doubtful value to give a general figure of the weight needed to provide a day's rations for a man, as this depends on his size, the amount of work he has to do, the climate, the skill of caterer and cook, and some sort of index error for each member of the crew. However, as a mean figure for planning purposes eight pounds weight of food and water together is needed for the sustenance of a man working hard at sea.

Preparation of food.

It is simple enough to reach the stage in a small crew where half their effort is spent in preparing and cooking food, besides cleaning the apparatus used in its consumption. If to this is added the time spent in actual eating, it may well be that little time or effort is left to sail and maintain the ship. A great deal can be done to reduce the effort of food preparation by careful planning of the galley and domestic apparatus; as already suggested in Chapter II, food preparation deserves the best position of all below decks in a deep sea cruising yacht. The stowage of galley utensils is sometimes arranged on the 'one tack' lay out, so that on the wrong tack everything manages to reach the bilges long before the meal is ready for serving; similar to this is the fore and aft cupboard with fiddle-less shelves for cooking gear, which is excellent until the cupboard door is opened on the wrong tack, when the contents stampede to leeward; even refrigerators are sometimes fitted this way, then the anger which smoulders as one crouches in the lee bilge collecting the relics, is not cooled at all as the open door releases the box of ice cubes down one's neck.

One of the most important requirements for the cook at sea, as with the jockey ashore, is a really good seat so that he can retain control of his body whatever his mount is doing. The cook must be able to wedge himself into a comfortable position, even when cooking uphill (i.e. with the stove heeled above him), so that he has both hands to spare. In a broad beamed ship this may require a rail built at a comfortable distance back from the stove, but in a small narrow cruiser a tiny ledge on the quarter berth lee board may serve the purpose. When *Dorade* raced over the Grand Banks to win the Transatlantic race of 1931 her cook found trouble in maintaining his stand at the galley, so rigged himself a harness that could be hooked into eyebolts in the deck head; unfortunately one day the harness held him up to the job when

an unusually violent lurch dislodged the boiling kettle, which poured
its contents down his front to scald him. A shelf or preparing table
within easy reach of the cook should have a ledge at least three inches
high to catch the run-away mugs, carving knife, salt pot and other
numerous weapons of the good cook. Every square inch of gymballed
stove top below is worth about a square foot of canvas on deck even in
the hard test of ocean racing; there is no routine work on board which
requires anything like the number of tools needed for cooking.

A great deal of time and effort in food preparation can also be saved
by an efficient stowage plan and well-planned menus.

Stowage.

Fresh food, and that not packed in water-tight tins, must be stowed
well above any likely encroachment by bilge water, with some allow-
ance for the fact that bilge water does some very unlikely things at
times. Usually the caterer must be content with the cans being stowed
deep in the bilges to retain the yacht's stability, and perhaps because
there is not enough room elsewhere. First the labels must be removed
to prevent the soggy paper choking the bilge pump suctions; as soon
as the label is removed, before the beef steak (protein) can be muddled
with the margarine (fat with vitamin D added), or even the bottom
paint (racing topcoat), the naked tins should be marked with their
contents, using a special crayon which grocers employ for writing
on tins; a far less satisfactory method is to scratch on a symbol with the
point of a knife; this loses its effect when the key to the symbol of a
little-used store is forgotten. For a long voyage it is well worth dipping
the tins in special transparent coloured varnish to prevent them from
rusting; this costs money, but in hot climates tins can rust right through
in quite a short time, which is not only much more expensive than the
varnish but also embarrassing if it happens in mid-ocean, with no grocer
round the corner.

Storekeeping.

The system of storekeeping will depend on what space is available,
and the length of the cruise. Some favour keeping together all the stores
of the same or a similar type, while others keep together all the main
stores required for a week's use. A most satisfactory compromise is to
group the stores together in their varieties, and have a ready-use

locker handy to the cook that is filled up every few days with all the stores for current use. The longitudinal trim of the ship is important to her speed, and the stowage plan must ensure that all the stores are not first eaten from aft so that for the last few days at sea the yacht is struggling along bows down; generally it is best to use first the weights furthest from the centre, which will also be the highest above the keel.

It is quite essential to be able to discover readily where every item is stowed and also to know what has been consumed and what remains. Anxiety about food supplies happens often enough at some stage in a long voyage. There are two frequent causes; one is that the accounting has gone all wrong, and some forgotten locker discloses that the shortage is really only muddle; the other happens when the crew are getting heartily tired of the vast amount of excellent tinned meat during the first three quarters of the voyage, but then find that the stock of tins remaining contain condensed milk, diced turnips and half a dozen are table salt.

Aboard *Iolaire*, Robert Somerset gave a number to every locker in the ship, and the location was shown in a master plan in his 'Brown Book', which was always handy to the cook; this book also listed all stores in alphabetical order, showing where each was located and the number on board; this was kept up to date every time any item was used. The book was also very useful when re-stocking in harbour; and finally the back of a finished page on dried fruit was used to write the introduction to this book. Aboard *Samuel Pepys* in 1950 a similar system was used, except that the list of stores was posted on the inside of the coach-roof, before the cook's eyes; even then it was possible to forget the paper-work of crossing out the tick representing an item, so this method was abandoned on her next Atlantic crossing in favour of the ready-use locker which was periodically refilled under careful stock-taking conditions.

One fine yacht which raced across the Atlantic in 1960 went even further in detailed planning, as before the voyage a book was prepared giving not only where everything was stored, but details of every meal that was to be served throughout the race, and also full instructions on how to cook each item. The yacht also carried the most elaborate equipment, including a powerful radio transmitter. However, even the best of plans can have some little weakness, and it was said that one day the radio receivers had been switched on aboard several of her rivals, and they were delighted to hear an angry voice going over the air to a secretary in New York explaining, 'It's all very well referring me to page 217, plan 19 (b). I still can't find the pepper.'

Menus.

One of the hardest tasks of a cook is to plan an interesting meal on a rough day with limited time at his disposal. If he could do this, maintaining a balanced diet, ample calorific value, economy of fuel and all the other considerations so necessary for a consistent high standard of menus, he would obviously be an artist such as is seldom met except in the kitchens of the most splendid hotel. The ordinary mortal, under these severe conditions, tends to snatch at the nearest few tins and serve up whatever the tin opener discloses inside them.

The only sure way to obtain a balanced diet that is really interesting as well, is to work out a series of menus before going to sea, when there is ample opportunity to get advice on this technical subject. It is usually sufficient to make up the menus for a week, and use this as a master plan from which slight modifications can be made.

Table IX*a* shows specimen menus for a crew racing in a moderate climate. It is assumed that only such fresh foods are on board as would be left after fourteen days at sea, so during the earlier days fresh vegetables and fruit would be used to replace the tinned varieties, and the midday meal would often be in the form of sandwiches to use the bread. The days are lettered from A to F, each one being a complete balanced diet, so they are interchangeable to suit the whims of the cook for the day, but obviously day E, for instance, cannot be used twice in one week. This menu is expensive to buy and is designed to require very little labour during the actual race.

An important feature of the week's menus is the X day. This is designed to be different from other days, both in the arrangement of the meals and the type of food; it requires a little more labour in producing the midday meal, although it simplifies the evening meal. It is a most valuable weapon in the hands of the caterer and skipper, as it can be used under the right physical and psychological conditions to give a gastronomical and mental fillip to the crew. It is suitable for fair weather, and would probably be used to celebrate some event or achievement, such as the return of calm weather after a gale, or the completion of a thousand miles in good time. The X day is not intended

	A	B	C	D	E	F	X
Breakfast ..	Cornflakes	All bran	Shredded wheat	Grape nuts	Rice Crispies	Weetabix	Canned Fruit Juice
	Bacon and scrambled egg	Sausage and bacon	Bacon and tomato	Sausage and fried egg	Bacon and baked beans	Sausage and tomato	Bacon and egg
			Biscuit and butter with Marmalade Coffee or Nescafé				
Mid Forenoon			Fresh lemon or lime juice with sugar Sweet biscuits				
Lunch	Tomato soup	Celery Soup	Mulligatawny Soup Sardines Vegetable salad	Scotch Broth	Chicken noodle Soup Pressed beef Beetroot	Ox tail Soup	Gin or Sherry Fruit Juice Roast chicken Peas Potatoes Burgundy Xmas pudding Brandy sauce Coffee Liqueur
	Ox tongue Pickles	Pork Luncheon meat Beetroot		Ham Pickles		Salmon Vegetable salad	
	Peaches and cream	Pears and cream	Apricots and cream	Pineapple and cream	Plums and cream	Raspberries and cream	
Tea			Tea and milk or lime, biscuit, butter and jam. Cake				
Supper	Stewed steak Onions	Irish stew Carrots	Rabbit Peas	Steak and kidney Carrots	Hamburger Onions	Corned beef Peas	Tomato Soup
	Sultana pudding Coffee	Welsh rarebit Coffee	Date pudding Coffee	Herring roe Coffee	Fig pudding Coffee	Cheese savoury Coffee	Cold Ham Pickles Peaches and cream
Night Watches ..			Bars of chocolate, sweet biscuits and dried fruit				

Table IXa. Sample 7 day Racing Menus allowing for no fresh food except lemons, onions, potatoes and eggs. These menus are calculated for use with a simple two-burner galley stove, and aim at a good varied diet using the least amount of preparation and cooking fuel.

to turn the six-day cycle into a seven-day cycle, although these special days might be used about every week. Generally towards the start of a long passage no such device will be needed, and later on the prospect of land not so very far away will provide ample incentive; yet in the ocean wastes, far from anywhere both in time and distance, the X day might be used more frequently than once a week.

The effect of weather on diet.

In hot climates cooking becomes intolerable in the middle of the day, owing to the heat below decks, so tropical climate menus should assume that no cooking takes place for the midday meal. Yet however burning the noonday sun, a hot meal is always welcome before nightfall, which is normally the main meal of the day and provides sustenance for the night. The advantages of completing this main meal in daylight are such that it is often convenient to base the daily routine on this meal; thus dinner is usually most acceptable at 7.30 p.m., with those coming off watch, when relieved, eating half an hour later. Then the ship's time can be so arranged that the sun does not set until 8.30 p.m., as explained in Chapter VII.

In heavy weather it may be necessary to batten down the ship for a long period when all cooking will have to stop due to the fugginess it causes; the conditions when battened down in any case make eating little pleasure, yet the heavy motion of the vessel uses up much bodily energy, apart from any needed for work on deck. Highly concentrated nourishment can then be taken, such as barley sugar, toffee, raisins, dates, chocolate and Horlicks malted milk tablets and even raw eggs, which are excellent with a dash of Worcester sauce.

Fresh foods.

The importance of fresh foods for vitamins and mineral salts is obvious, and just as vital is the extra enjoyment they provide. In practice there are few convenient rules about how long various foods will keep fresh, as so much depends on the climate, the means of stowage, and the condition of the food when bought. Climate is not just a matter of latitude; for instance things keep worse in the Gulf Stream current of 40 degrees north than at times off Singapore, on the equator. Fresh meat scarcely enters the menu for a long voyage, if no refrigerator is fitted, as it must be eaten within a day of sailing; fish is much more

Plate 12. Three thousand miles of ocean ahead for *Samuel Pepys* of 30·5 ft. overall, as she sets out from Bermuda to win a transatlantic race to Plymouth

Plate 13. Setting storm canvas on board *Wyvern* of 43 ft. overall,
during a gale off Start Point

important as it may get aboard at any time. Vegetables depend very largely on different samples, so they must be marketed with great care, and an attempt made to buy them direct from the grower. Thus aboard one yacht it was found that carrots bought at Bermuda were still good when eaten raw fourteen days later, so a bigger supply was bought at the next visit to the same port, but that time they went soft and mouldy within a week. Onions are the most consistent keeping vegetables, coupled with potatoes, both of which should remain good for over a tropical month. After these two, no vegetable will keep with any certainty beyond ten days in the tropics.

Bread keeps longer than normal if it is baked with a little extra salt, then wrapped as soon as it is cool, when it will last well over two weeks, although towards the end of that time the crust must be cut off.

The value of eggs is obvious, with their high protein value white and yolk contain fat, vitamins A and D, besides mineral salts. The egg is one of the simplest items of food to cook in a great variety of ways, or it can be eaten in a few seconds with no preparation at all. There are many ways of helping eggs to keep fresh longer, but all depend on the eggs being really fresh when treated; without any treatment except a cool place with fresh air circulation, a new-laid egg will last out a normal Atlantic crossing. It must be remembered that in shops the expression 'fresh egg' merely means that it has not been preserved; it will often be ten days old or more when bought. The expression 'new laid' has a higher standard, but once an egg has gone through a shop it is usually beyond preservation.

The main supply of fresh food for the later part of a long voyage therefore comes from eggs and fruit. Of this the most consistent good keeping fruit are limes (which have little vitamin C content) and coconuts, both of which can last a month in the tropics if well chosen. Oranges, lemons, grapefruit and apples come next with two to three weeks' reliability; however, the lemon is well worth risking for many days more, as it probably makes the most welcome and valuable fresh drink of all. A mid-forenoon daily drink of lemon-juice is worth planning for three weeks, as it uses also a good quantity of sugar (116 calories to the ounce). A convenient tropical fruit is the papaw, which bought green should ripen after a week or so, and if it fails to do so can be cooked as an excellent vegetable. In tropical climates one of the most welcome gifts for a small yacht about to sail is a stalk of green bananas;

H

if all goes well they should start to ripen about a dozen a day when a week out of harbour; sometimes they practically all ripen at once, but they still seem to get eaten none the less.

After writing the last few paragraphs, in which the importance of fresh food is stressed, it seems unforgivable that I should make the mistake of finishing a race across the Atlantic in *Belmore*, of 36 ft. overall, with what a Swedish doctor described laughingly as scurvy among my crew. He probably did not mean this in its strict medical sense, but the fact is that some of them had unhealed sores and cuts, besides complaining that their teeth felt loose. This was due to my failure to supervise this important department, so we set out for a 25-day race, in which there was scarcely any sun after the first week, carrying practically no fresh fruit, besides eggs which had clearly waited long enough to be eaten. We had plenty of fruit in tins, but this lacked the necessary vitamins; we also had a large bottle of vitamin pills, but the doctor pointed out the simple truth that pills still in the bottle made poor medicine.

Someone suggested rather cruelly that I had done this on purpose to ensure that my crew would be all the more eager to reach the finishing line, and in fact we did win the first place in our class against far better fed crews. However, overall winner in that race was the American yacht *Figaro*, whose owner had perhaps gone further to insure his crew would lose no time, as about the same day that I noticed our shortage of fresh food, he found that by error he had onboard only half the fresh water he had considered necessary.

Fish is in a category by itself on a long cruise, as it is liable to come at the most valuable time, when all other fresh food has been finished. Even racing, when the drag of a fishing line cannot be accepted, flying-fish may come aboard to provide an excellent meal. When *Bloodhound* sailed across the Atlantic in 1952, the accomplished wife of her owner, M. D. N. Wyatt, served up flying-fish cooked in white wine for a company of eight, as the ship rolled down the trades.

Refrigeration.

If a refrigerator is fitted on board, the diet problem becomes much simpler, at any rate for the first few days until the fresh meat and butter give out. However, it needs to be a large yacht to have aboard refrigeration sufficient for fresh provisions on any really long passage, and for a small yacht its advantages have to be balanced against the large amount of space it occupies for a comparatively small cool stowage. It is certainly not essential to have refrigeration to cruise anywhere in the world and enjoy excellent food, and unless the refrigerator or ice box is mounted well clear of the yacht's structure, the fresh water condensation on it is a likely cause of rot.

Snacks.

A considerable amount of the total intake of calories can be consumed at other than regular meals and however large a dinner has been eaten the middle watch men will be very hungry after a few vigorous sail shifts. For some people no night watch is tolerable until they have first a cup of hot cocoa and enough such cups represent a good intake of food, although it is expensive in fuel and also effort of preparation. For sheer efficiency few such foods can beat a bar of chocolate as a night sustainer, as it is liked by most, contains concentrated nourishment, cannot be spilled (as happens to so many cups of cocoa), and can be eaten by the helmsman without the 'cocoa-zig-zag' which so often wakes a racing skipper for a quarter of an hour after each watch shift. Oddly enough it is not unusual for people to declare in advance that they don't eat chocolate, yet it is unwise to plan on their retaining this particular dislike for more than two or three days at sea. Biscuits are also valuable as snacks, the most nourishing being fat varieties such as Peak Frean's shortcake. Another useful food on watch is dried fruit, such as raisins, which have the advantage over biscuits that they are still quite edible even if the ready-use tin in the cockpit is flooded with salt water unexpectedly. When the yacht's motion tends to make all food distasteful on the first day or two of a voyage, dried fruit is one of the most readily eaten of foods and the sugar content provides the body with an almost immediate supply of energy.

As sweet foods contain much carbohydrates, they appease the appetite quickly and at the same time reduce the appetite for other foods that complete the balance, so the caterer determined to keep the crew fit for really big efforts will arrange that the snacks are completed or removed two hours before any normal meal.

Cooking fuel.

Whether oil or gas is used there is likely to be a limit to the amount that can be carried on board, so for a long voyage consideration of fuel economy must affect the menus. Frequent hot drinks use a large amount of fuel, as each time the stove and surroundings must be heated up as well as the comparatively small amount of liquid for the drink. It is surprising how often shortage of fuel is experienced on a long voyage, and it is a frequent event to read in logs of the last day of the passage how the oil navigation lights were emptied of their oil to cook a hot meal.

Water.

Heavy diets entail a large consumption of water, as a thirsty man cannot eat well. It has also been noticed that in rough weather, with salt spray impregnating the air, water consumption increases more than it does in hot weather. In average conditions a man will need nearly three pints of water a day, and it is normal to use half a gallon for calculations, assuming that a small amount is used to clean the teeth and so on. If fresh water is to be used regularly for washing, the supply will need to be many gallons a day, but there is no need for this with the various soapless detergents, such as Tide, that lather in salt water.

The most important thing about the fresh water supply is an exact knowledge of the amount on board at any time. It seems amazing that any skipper would set out to cross an ocean without a certain knowledge of the capacity of his water tanks; yet this has happened even when the tank was being sounded daily, but the interpretation of the sounding was incorrect. For any long voyage the water must be stowed in several tanks, whose capacities have been accurately measured, so that a check can be kept on the water remaining.

A convenient way is to arrange that all water used comes from one tank, perhaps holding a four days' or a week's supply, which acts as a water meter. Each time the ready-use tank is emptied a certain check on consumption is obtained. Even with this safety precaution, a routine sounding of all full tanks is important in case any one becomes damaged and leaks away into the bilges unnoticed. Due to the cumbersome nature of metal tanks for a small yacht, plastic bags have been tried as they are so much lighter and can easily take up the shape of a small space; however their flexibility allows movement and the continuous movement of a small craft on a long voyage will rub through the plastic in time unless it is protected against every hard surface.

If a leak occurs in the fresh water supply, a prompt adjustment of water consumption will be necessary, which may entail a reduction in diet also; then every opportunity should be seized to collect rain water. The simplest way with roller reefing gear is to take a roll in the mainsail, top up the boom a few inches, and then run or reach during the rainfall. If roller reefing is not fitted the halyard is lowered until the foot of the sail forms something of a trough. In either case the rain water will pour out of the tack of the sail where it can be collected in buckets. The first few bucketfuls should be tasted before pouring into tanks in case they are too salty, but in a good downpour the sail soon washes clean so long as the yacht is not going to windward or the wind is not strong enough to raise the spray level above the foot of the sail.

Large ships make their own water from the sea by the process of distillation, but this cannot be done economically on a small scale. The weight of the apparatus added to the weight of the fuel needed to produce say fifty gallons of water is greater than the weight of embarking fifty gallons of water in the first place. Small stills come under the heading of life-saving equipment, and will eke out a little water. Certain chemicals can extract the salt from the sea, such as the permutit process, but they are expensive and require a great deal of effort to make the water.

In recent Transatlantic sailing races the rules required a certain minimum quantity of fresh water to be on board at the start, depending on the numbers in the crew. In 1952 this water requirement was fifteen gallons per man, and although it was a slow race due to head winds, this quantity was found ample except in the case of one yacht which lost part of her supply due to leaks in the plastic water bags.

Reduced rations.

If a voyage is likely to be prolonged well beyond the time planned, due to exceptionally adverse weather or an accident, it will be necessary to reduce the rations. So long as the amount of food on board and previous consumption are accurately known, this is not difficult to arrange. For instance if the ship was dismantled twelve days out on a voyage planned to take twenty-four days, it may be estimated that with jury mast rigged the voyage will take a total of thirty-six days; then the rations intended for twelve days must last out for twenty-four. If a heavy work diet in the order of 3,500 calories a day had been provided for, then 1,750 calories will be satisfactory if work and exposure to the elements are reduced to the minimum necessary to keep the ship sailing with a small sail area. The most convenient way of rearranging the reduced ration is to make one day's planned diet last for two days.

Survival diet.

It might happen that the crew are cut off from all the normal food supply, either due to abandoning the ship or some gross miscalculation or misfortune.

Experience of lifeboats during the wars showed that it is possible to survive for many weeks without food, but only a few days without water. Stowage of emergency food and water is dealt with on page 131, but the aim for a survival diet should be one pint of water per day per man, with four ounces each of boiled sweets, sweetened condensed milk and caramel toffee. If less than a pint of water is available, the diet must be reduced further. In *The Kon-Tiki Expedition* Thor Heyerdahl states that on very hot days his crew added twenty to forty per cent of salt water to their fresh water rations, and found this mixture quenched their thirst better than pure water, besides increasing the ration. In hot climates the pangs of thirst can be mitigated by immersing the body in water to reduce evaporation besides absorbing a small amount of water through the pores of the skin. Every opportunity must be taken to collect even the tiniest amount of rain water; a solar still might be used.

The sea carries a rich harvest of food, if only it can be gleaned. Fish are much more likely to come near a floating dinghy or derelict yacht than to a fast moving vessel; the deeper living fish tend to swim near the surface at night, and will often come close enough out of curiosity to be stabbed or caught by hand, as was done in the Kon-Tiki expedition. All salt water fish are safe to eat so long as they have no spines or beaks like a parrot (although the limbs of an octopus are fit to eat), or puff themselves up like a balloon. C. O. Jennings describes in *An Ocean Without Shores* how he and his companion, after many days without food, caught seagulls by hand when they perched on the boat. If phosphorescence shows in the sea there must be plankton, which forms the complete diet of whales; it smells unpleasant but can be eaten raw and imagined as shrimp paste. The connoisseurs sort out the shrimp-like objects and the ova, discarding the jelly substances and vegetable matter which are usually bitter; the really hungry eat the lot, and perhaps wish that they were whales.

Dr. Bombard sailed a 15-foot raft *L'Hérétique* from the Canaries to Barbados at the end of 1952, without taking any fresh water on board at all. He claimed that he persisted on sea food alone for the sixty-five days of the passage, and it is stated that he drank liquid from crushed fish to quench his thirst, besides eating plankton and some sea birds. During the voyage he is said to have lost fifty-five pounds of weight besides his liking for a fish diet.

In spite of the views of Dr. Bombard, many other doctors who have studied survival at sea are quite convinced that the liquid from crushed fish cannot replace water, as it is so full of protein that it needs a great deal of extra water for the body to absorb it. After examining his evidence carefully, they also still feel that drinking salt water will definitely reduce the chance of survival. However, Dr. Bombard proved that a man with enough faith can survive on the sea without taking any food or water with him, even if it is as much a miracle as walking on the sea.

He was awarded the Seamanship Medal of the Royal Cruising Club, having achieved his voyage across the ocean with the simplest possible equipment; this can be an encouragement to any seafarer, but I hope it does not suggest to them that they need not bother too much over victuals and fresh water.

x

Safety at Sea

SAFETY at sea depends primarily on thought and preparation before the vessel leaves harbour; the smaller the vessel and the fewer her crew, the more is the need for care in these preparations. It is significant that in modern ocean racing, even with testing courses and large entries, fatal accidents have been very rare indeed. Considering the very large number of people who have been at sea in small sailing craft under all weather conditions, the clubs organising these fixtures have done a great service in fostering seamanlike safety precautions.

The first essential of safety in a small vessel at sea is that the crew should remain aboard. No crew should ever doubt that once overboard and left astern, a man has but a poor chance of survival; loss of life even in partly sheltered waters forces home this lesson every season.

Life-lines and pulpit.

A sailing vessel is often heeled to a steep angle, its decks are frequently swept by waves and spray, while the turbulent motion of a small yacht in a steep sea is something beyond the designed stability of a land animal. Yet many small yachts are seen with absolutely nothing between the narrow decks on which the crew must work and the sea. This is folly.

A boat without bulwarks, yet intended for the open sea, should have fixed wire life-lines along both sides of the craft. The wires, with the stanchions supporting them, must be strong enough to support the weight of a man hurled across the deck. If the stanchions are fitted to stand vertically, then with the boat heeled they may act merely as a ramp to direct a helpless body into the sea; the stanchions should accordingly be fixed tilted slightly inwards. The upper wire needs to be high enough to come well above the knee of a man standing on deck, say twenty-four inches; as this allows ample space for a man to be washed under, a second wire should be fitted half-way up the stanchion (see Plate 4). A pulpit, consisting of a frame of metal tubing mounted on the stem, can be fitted even to such small vessels as the 25-foot overall length *Vertue*, without being unsightly or over-heavy; it adds greatly to the feeling of security when working in the eyes of the ship, and may often provide an anchorage for the fore ends of the life-lines.

Safety belts.

In very bad weather the protection of the ship's life-lines is not enough for those working on deck, unless sheltered by a deep cockpit coming above their waists. A violent lurch has been known to catapult a man well above the height of the life-lines; the yacht's stem may dig two feet deep into a wave, or it may be necessary for a man to clamber some distance above the deck. In the spring of 1952, *Marabu* was hove-to under a single staysail off Cape Finisterre. It was daylight with a heavy confused sea when the strop of the sheet leading block parted; one of the crew went forward at once to secure it, and as the ship rolled he stepped straight into the sea just abaft the rigging. He was exceptionally fortunate to be recovered twenty minutes later.

A high degree of safety can be given by a personal safety belt carrying a lanyard with a spring hook which can hank on to the life-lines or rigging. Fig. X, 1 shows a combined safety belt and buoyancy bag, with a hemp lanyard leading to a lifting strop under the man's chin. Should a man go into the sea when the yacht is moving fast, he will be towed head first, with his face above water. The lifting strop is important for, if a man becomes detached from his ship, it provides a simple and apparent point of attachment for hoisting him over the side. Men have been drowned, when actually alongside a rescuing ship, because there was no effective means of getting hold of them in bad weather. Plate 3 shows how a man can be hauled inboard with the lifting strop.

While the mechanics of an efficient safety belt are simple enough, the device is no use if stowed below when the man goes overboard. In the open sea it is seldom that the conditions throughout the watch ahead can be foretold, so the only effective solution is for the crew to bring their safety belts on watch with them always and stow them within immediate reach; a rigid routine must be enforced for the belts to be

donned if the weather deteriorates, and always at night. It may take
half a minute to secure the safety belt over the top of oilskins or warm
clothing, yet once something goes wrong on deck no one will waste
thirty seconds on his own safety before rushing forward to lower the
flapping headsail, save the spinnaker boom from washing over the

Fig. X, 1. A safety
belt combined with a
life belt. The life-lines
can be hooked to any
rigging and takes the
strain from a lifting
strop under the chin

side, or even rescue his trousers hung up to dry. The best seaman is not
the man who claims that a threatening sea is a trifle, but the man who is
quick to notice any change, and fits himself to deal with some incident
before it occurs.

These safety belts will cause some restriction to movement when
worn, which will be the chief reason why their use may be neglected.
Yet with practice the body becomes accustomed to their use, just as it
has learnt to tolerate some grotesque articles of clothing ordained by
convention. During a long ocean race, after the wearing of safety belts
had been enforced for a few days, each member of *Samuel Pepys'* crew
felt as uncomfortable without them as might a *débutante* feel on a
steaming hot day at Ascot without her gloves.

Lifebuoys.

Two lifebuoys should be placed within reach of the helmsman at sea, so secured that with one hand he can readily cast them over the side. (See Frontispiece.) Hard cork rings, white enamelled and with the ship's name in gold leaf, are often seen prominently secured, perhaps in a yacht's mizzen rigging. They make a fine decoration, and would undoubtedly float. Yet experience shows that a white buoy in a sea trimmed with white horses is rather like a khaki-clad soldier stalking through good cover, it can only be seen by sheer chance. The ring is hard to get into, even in calm water; in the rough sea which is likely to be the cause of the accident, only a marine contortionist of exceptional ability could get his head and shoulders through the ring when wearing oilskins.

A buoy for life saving, as opposed to a frame for the painter's art, should be horseshoe shaped, so that a man can get into it. It should be painted bright orange, so that it may be seen by the man in the water, besides those trying to rescue him. With near calm sea flecked with occasional white horses in the Indian ocean during 1946, an indifferent swimmer fell overboard from a vessel moving at speed, to be followed quickly by a white life ring hurled at his receding head by a quick-witted friend. I picked up the man waterlogged and in need of artificial respiration. He was within ten yards of the white life ring, which he had never seen.

Often enough a towed dinghy, the painter parted, has been lost in daylight when the waves were a few feet high. Yet the dinghy has a freeboard measured in feet, while a lifebuoy or drowning man show no more than an inch or so above the water. When a man fell overboard from *L'Apache* during the Pacific ocean race to Honolulu in 1951, the sky was clear, wind moderate and waves five feet high. Destroyers and aircraft combed the area and only chanced on him during the last sweep of the search, when he had been adrift for thirty hours, and they had criss-crossed his position. The white life ring into which he had squirmed, as fortunately he was of slender build and wearing no oilskins, was fitted with an automatic electrical water light; yet as he fell overboard at breakfast time, the light was ineffective by daylight, and the battery exhausted by nightfall. Salt spray is no friend of electrics, and dry batteries gradually lose their power during the wait until a crisis occurs.

For the best chance of sighting a lifebuoy, day or night, calm sea or rough, two attachments should be secured to it; one contains a dye sea-marker and the other a bright flashing light, and both are activated by the lifebuoy being thrown into the sea. The dye-marker spreads a coloured film over an area of water, some portion of which is likely to be on the wave top at the time the rescuing vessel rises to her wave crest. Neither of these fittings is permanently trouble free in practice; the seams of the dye's package work loose with the normal rough treatment in rough weather, and it is unsightly to see the trickle of dye on deck, which in some unaccountable way may get on to the nylon spinnaker. However, these are clear signs that the fitting needs renewal for safety. The electrical device does not signal when the battery is low or the contacts corroded.

The experience of *Figaro*, see page 126, suggests that a drogue might also be fitted to the lifebuoy.

Man overboard.

Should a man fall overboard at sea, in spite of guard rails, safety belts, and seamanlike care in moving about the ship, his survival depends even more on the actions of the crew than on the efficiency of the life-saving apparatus. The best means of handling the ship to recover the man in the water will depend on many variable factors, but certain immediate actions must be so well known by each member of the crew that he can carry out his part habitually, even if it is dark and rough, he is tired, wet or seasick.

The immediate needs are to mark the man's position in the water, and to get the ship under full control for manoeuvring. A yacht sailing in the open sea may well have her spinnaker set, a boom preventer set up, scotsman rigged on the forestay and running rigging; should it be on a long run such as a Trade Wind passage, there may be numerous semi-permanent lashings to check chafe. If under these con-ditions the helmsman reacts to the cry of 'man overboard' with an immediate gybe, the resulting chaos can almost guarantee the man's death. It may well be that the ship is laid over flat on her side, due to the boom preventer remaining taut; water pouring down the hatch will at the least handicap the crew coming up from below to help. Even if the preventer parts before the hatches are awash, the resulting *Chinese gybe* putting the upper part of the mainsail on one tack, while the lower part is held on the other, may split the mainsail, break the boom, or carry away the spreaders. At the same time the spinnaker taken aback might snarl round the rigging so thoroughly, especially if it be made of nylon, that it would be impossible to lower the sail. Far from a smart recovery of the man from the water, the yacht would find herself drifting to leeward disorganised, with too much sail fouled in the forestay to enable the engine to turn her into the wind, and perhaps half an hour's acrobatics aloft needed before the sail is cut away.

The first action of the helmsman should be to hurl overboard a lifebuoy, announcing stridently 'man overboard' at the same time. He should keep the ship firmly on her course, keeping his eye on the man astern as well as the compass. After ten seconds he should throw overboard the second lifebuoy, which doubles the chance of one or the other being sighted, besides giving a line leading back to the man's position, should there have been considerable delay in dropping the first buoy, such as when a man falls over unseen in the dark. Meanwhile the emergency order 'man overboard' will have brought the entire crew to gather in at the rush. Depending on the size of the crew the procedure will vary as to whether the helmsman keeps his eye on the man or buoy, probably being relieved at the tiller by the skipper, or whether someone else is detailed to watch. Whoever it is, looking out is a full time job immediately the yacht begins to alter course. 'Gathering in' means that without any further order the boom guy is cast off, the spinnaker lowered and the various scotsmen to check chafe are cut.

At seven knots, which would be fast going for any yacht less than thirty feet on the water-line, she will have travelled 120 yards in the half minute which should be ample to get the ship in hand if reasonably well manned. If there is any delay, the helmsman should continue at regular intervals to throw overboard objects that will float to form a path back to the man; anything that floats for a few minutes will serve, such as a cockpit cushion, a piece of wood or even clothing. If the ship is on the wind at the time of the accident, it will only take a second or two to gather her in, by casting off the kicking strap and manning the runners.

Once the ship is in hand, the decision whether to gybe or go about will depend on many factors. In general if the wind is on or before the beam, it is best to gybe the ship; if the wind is well abaft the beam, she should go about head to wind. Much depends on her turning circle, whether she is slow in stays, her rig and her crew, the important thing is that the skipper should have thought out the problem for his particular ship beforehand, and know at once what action is needed. As skippers are not themselves immune from accident at sea, it is always well if the entire crew are familiar with his intentions. If the procedure for man overboard is actually practised by each man who may be left in charge on deck, owner and crew will feel confident that all reasonable precautions have been taken against a man being drowned.

The American yacht *Figaro*, owned by the outstandingly experienced yachtsman William Snaith, successfully recovered a man who went overboard in just about the most difficult conditions of all. *Figaro* was racing towards the Fastnet rock when the wind blew up to about 35 knots, making it too much for her to carry her spinnaker. When struggling to lower it, a man was thrown overboard as the spinnaker boom lifted with the sail out of control. A lifebuoy was thrown overboard, and the helmsman at once put the yacht on a course roughly at right angles to the wind as he noted both the compass course and the log reading.

As soon as the spinnaker had been brought under control and doused, he again read the log and put her about on a reciprocal course, calculating that the yacht would come up with the man in the water after sailing back the same distance. The man was saved, but an interesting point was that, driven by the strong wind, the lifebuoy had drifted faster than the man could swim. After that, *Figaro*'s lifebuoys were fitted with drogues.

Going aloft in bad weather.

If it is essential to go aloft in bad weather, the evolution must be treated with careful preparation, as the violent motion even thirty feet above the deck makes it very hard to keep a grip on the mast when sitting in a bosun's chair. Once the grip is lost the man may swing far out from the mast, then crash back into it to be badly damaged or thrown out of the chair. The man must first be so secured into the bosun's chair that he cannot fall out even if unconscious, then a line should be secured round his waist so that he may lash himself to the mast when working; a convenient form is the safety belt. He should be hoisted aloft by the halyard whose block is closest above the point where the work is to be done to reduce the scope of the free swinging should he become detached from the mast.

All these precautions may seem ridiculous when compared with the crew's antics 150 feet from the water above the sailing ships of old; however, the ten ton yacht's motion in a sea-way is as different from a thousand ton sailing ship's as the terrier shaking a rat differs from the dignified movements of an elephant; besides this the sailing ship's mast was intended to be climbed, while the mast of a modern small sailing cruiser is a highly efficient strut in compression, stripped of every vestige of unnecessary windage. In a yacht definitely intended for deep sea cruising it might be wise to have climbing steps welded to a metal mast, as was done aboard *Beyond* before starting on a cruise round the world.

Domestic hazards.

Fire and explosion have taken a heavy toll of life in yachts, with the danger just as imminent in harbour as at sea. Some of these accidents can be traced to bad equipment, but far more are due to ignorance or carelessness in its use. Almost inevitably every vessel will have someone aboard at one time or another who is ignorant of the gear, and equally the most careful man or woman will have an occasional lapse into carelessness, perhaps due to exhaustion or seasickness. The ship's organisation must be designed to cope with these possible failings. Against the risk of fire, at least two extinguishers should be carried in even the smallest boat cruising off-shore, stowed in brackets at carefully considered positions; if they are just left loose in a corner or locker, someone will invariably have moved them elsewhere when the emergency comes. Almost certainly one should be kept near the main hatch where it can be reached from inside or out, and the other should normally be near the fore hatch, if there is one. Burning bedding, furniture, packaging and so forth make so much smoke that they can only be safely attacked from fairly close to a hatch, so that a quick retreat is possible when the lungs are full of smoke. At the same time it is useless to aim an extinguisher down into the smoke without knowing the position of the seat of the fire.

The powder type extinguisher is very effective, and does no harm other than leaving an awful mess. For a boat of some 30 ft. in length,

I would recommend two, each with a capacity of 3 lb. Powder ex-tinguishers have proved effective against bad petrol fires onboard, but some people prefer carbon dioxide or foam extinguishers, when space is no problem. It needs a 5 lb. carbon dioxide extinguisher, or a 2 gallon foam one, to match the 3 lb. powder type, which is therefore very much smaller.

A further valuable aid against galley fires, or the results of careless smokers, is an asbestos blanket, which can be kept in a small cylindrical container in the galley ready to be pulled out and spread over a fire. Another aid to the domestic fire is a canvas bucket readily available in the cockpit, where it can be filled up over the side when needed. How-ever, water from a bucket only spreads burning petrol, and if it is chucked at blazing hot cooking fat, it will probably cause an explosion.

Carbon-tetra-chloride (C.T.C.) or methyl bromide extinguishers are unsuited to yachts as they give off poisonous fumes, which could be dangerous in the confined space of a yacht's cabin. Another danger from some chemical extinguishers is that on use they may attack and destroy the resin of a glass-fibre hull.

Explosion can be fought only by the elimination of its causes. Fumes from petrol or bottle gas will explode when mixed with certain quantities of oxygen in the air and ignited; although the proportion of air to gas has to be correct within fairly narrow limits, before an explosion can occur. If large quantities of fumes escape into the yacht, it is likely that there will be an explosive mixture somewhere aboard her and it only needs a match, cigarette, or electric spark in that position to set off the explosion. The cure is an effective organisation to stop leaks of petrol or bottle gas, and dispose of the fumes should any leak occur. Some member of the crew should be made responsible for domestic safety in every vessel, and he must make it his concern to inspect all apparatus for leaky joints, loose connexions or worn fittings regularly. This will not stop gas and petrol taps from being left on carelessly, so a regular check on these should be instituted by someone independent of the actual user at the time, who will obviously know the importance of shutting off at the cylinder, yet still sometimes forget. Thus the mate of the watch coming below at 8 p.m. might make it his concern to check any such dangers before turning into his bunk.

Collision.

It is a fact of unceasing amazement to most seamen that a vessel may sail for days in the open ocean without sighting another, yet when eventually she does, its track leads so close that one of the vessels has to alter course to avoid a collision. Correct navigation lights and an alert look-out should be able to cope with this nearly always, but the good seaman is not content with what ought to happen, and will have an extra precaution at hand. With the low freeboard of a small yacht and difficulty of keeping the beam clear of the sails when heeled, her lights will not be visible continuously in rough seas; lights have been known to fail, and look-outs to doze or be distracted; fog sometimes falls suddenly, and may be unnoticed at night. Ready for immediate use there should always be a flare, a powerful torch and a fog horn. In very small vessels with perhaps one man only on deck at night, these are best kept in the shelter of the cabin stowed in a rack made to fit them, which will make their absence just as obvious at any time as is their presence when needed.

The development of radar enables ships fitted with it to continue at their normal speed in a fog, confident that they will be warned of other ships in time to avoid a collision. Yet experience shows that the radar sets normally fitted probably will not detect a small wooden vessel such as a yacht, which lacks reflecting surface. This can be overcome by hoisting in bad visibility a radar reflector made of thin sheet metal or aluminium painted fabric on a light frame. It is easy to make an effective reflector made of thin aluminium sheets, which can be taken apart and stowed flat.

Lightning.

The violence of thunderstorms has awed mankind since his creation on earth; when he first went to sea they frightened him even more. In a small craft, perhaps hundreds of miles from land, with the tall mast seeming to reach up into the midst of the lightning which is splitting the air all round it, a man would need amazing self-sufficiency not to feel impelled to say some prayer to his Maker. Such thunder squalls are frequent in areas like the Gulf Stream. Yet yachts are seldom struck, and when they are the danger to life is probably no greater than when in a house; the risk is least if well away from objects like a metal mast, the bulk of an engine, or a large water tank. A simple precaution

I

which at least brings reassurance is to convert a shroud each side and a backstay or runner into lightning conductors by shackling to their lower ends wire pendants long enough to reach the water however much she heels. The rigging can be earthed by throwing overboard the wire pendants when a thunderstorm comes close. On one occasion when *Samuel Pepys* appeared to have been struck, such was the concussion the yacht received, one of the crew had an earthing pendant in his hand in the act of throwing it overboard, yet he was undamaged. People struck by lightning are sometimes not burnt but paralysed by shock; artificial respiration applied at once may save their lives.

Life saving raft.

It is most unlikely that any sea-going yacht will float if flooded. The possibility of sinking is always present; it may be due to collision with another vessel, floating debris, or ice; it can come from fire or explosion; and it might be caused from swamping by the waves or failure of the hull.

The dinghy normally carried by cruising yachts is intended to take the crew ashore when anchored in sheltered waters; it is seldom big enough to carry all the crew at once; it is very unlikely to be a safe sea-boat, and is probably secured at sea in a way which would require many minutes to launch it even in simple conditions. Ships seldom sink in calm seas and broad daylight, with their crews unhurried by fire or unshaken by explosion.

If any degree of security is to be provided for the crew should the yacht sink, the minimum requirement is something seaworthy, big enough to keep all the crew out of the water and sheltered from the elements, yet able to be launched within a few seconds. This is best achieved by an inflatable raft carried permanently on deck. When fitted with a canopy the occupants will be protected from the cold which so often is the greatest hazard for castaways. A raft big enough to carry eight people under cover, with an emergency radio transmitter, survival food and means of making fresh water, fireworks, fishing lines and a drogue, can weigh less than a hundred pounds complete with the cylinders of compressed gas that inflate it. It need be no bigger than the sail bag containing a 250 square foot main sail for a six tonner. A point to remember is that an automatically inflated raft needs regular inspection to be effective at all times; but when it comes to it, so does any other item of equipment for use at sea.

The best means of carrying water for taking to the raft in an emergency is to keep some two-gallon water cans, with lanyards attached, in a handy position on deck or in the cockpit; if these are stoppered when not quite full, they will just float in salt water. They should be painted bright orange which, quite literally, is the most obvious colour for all life saving apparatus at sea. Should the ship sink far from help, a sun still will be valuable to produce the few ounces of fresh water essential for life; each stows in a packet the size of a large postage envelope, and inflates in use to a ball about two feet in diameter. In hot weather thirst can be reduced in the sea, which lessens evaporation from the body.

Survival diets are considered in Chapter IX, and radio distress messages in Chapter XVI.

XI

Navigation

NAVIGATION is the art of getting from one place to another. With no more apparatus than a carved coco-nut shell half filled with water, the forerunner of the airman's bubble sextant, Polynesian navigators found their way to tiny islands hundreds of miles distant in the Pacific. They did not go straight, they had to wait for exactly the right season, and no record was kept of those that failed to get there.

Sextant.

An improvement on the coco-nut is offered today in the form of the sextant which is a simple but expensive instrument for measuring the angle between two objects. The deep sea sailor uses it to measure the angle between the horizon and the sun, moon or stars. From the observations he takes, the vessel's latitude can easily be worked out, and if the time is accurately known, the longitude can also be calculated by a process which needs no more learning than the ability to look up figures in a book, add, subtract and write. Observations of several stars, taken within a few minutes of each other, give the most certain position, but stars can only be observed when it is dark enough for them to be visible, yet still light enough for the horizon to show. In practice this works out to short periods at dawn and dusk, which may be reduced, or lost altogether, if the sky is cloudy. Seamen warmly welcomed the idea of the airman's bubble sextant, which needed no visible horizon, and they were even more pleased when these very expensive instruments could be bought for a tiny fraction of their cost price as surplus war stores. However, once bought, these soon became surplus yacht stores, as a small craft at sea is too unsteady a platform from which to get even reasonably accurate results with this instrument.

So the ordinary hand sextant is still the main instrument for finding the position of a small vessel out of sight of land. The operation of the sextant takes a few seconds to understand, but as with a shot-gun, much practice is needed before consistent accuracy is achieved. The first difficulty to be overcome, again like the shot-gun, is holding the instrument level. Although the sextant has a handle which leads almost inevitably to the correct grip, the exact balance of the various muscles will only come when the sextant has frequently been held in this grip. There is no need to wait for the open seas to practise this; it is easy to find a few minutes in harbour, or on a coastal passage, when the right hand can be spared just to hold the sextant. This practice not only assists with taking sights later on but reduces the chance of the instrument being dropped when the sea is rough.

Bad weather sights.

Once this grip becomes habitual there is no difficulty in taking sights well when the sea is calm. In a sea-way, accuracy is more difficult and needs much practice. The first essential is to anchor the body from the waist down. When the feet are not sufficient for this, it may be possible to wedge the hips in an open hatch or lash the lower part of the body to the mast; sitting on the deck with feet stressed against the life-lines is another position. The upper part of the body is left free to move, acting as a gimbal to counter the movement of the vessel.

The next trouble is that the true horizon must be used and not the top of the nearest wave. This limits the time for taking the sight to the short period when the boat is herself on the top of a wave. In a typical North Atlantic sea, with the waves 12 feet high and 400 feet long, the navigator with his eye 5 feet above the surface will only be able to see the horizon for flashes of about four seconds in every nine. It often helps him if someone else watches the sea to say when the true horizon is in sight, as the view through the sextant mirror may not differentiate between wave and horizon, particularly in the dim light when stars peep through.

Another difficulty is spray, as the smallest amount of moisture on the mirrors will make the reflection of a star invisible; worse even than spray is a film of mist which forms on the mirrors if their temperature is different from the air around the sextant. For this reason it is always best to take the sextant from its box some time before the time for star sights and hold it well sheltered from spray in the outside air. If the navigator can get someone to help by noting and writing down the times, he should take four or five observations of each star and add them up to get the mean. One of the commonest sources of errors in the calculations comes in this averaging of the times and observed altitudes, as these both require the use of simple division, which is harder than addition. Another common source of error is for the watch to be read one minute wrong, a particularly unfortunate error in that it is too small to be obvious, yet big enough to cause a bad landfall.

Sextant practice.

All these difficulties may seem overpowering; but practice overcomes them. As an example of the accuracy that may be achieved even in very small craft experiencing rough weather, *Cohoe* 32 feet length overall, *Samuel Pepys* 30 feet overall length, and *Mokoia* 38 feet raced each other across the Atlantic in 1950 in under three weeks, each to make her landfall within a mile of reckoning after a day and night of gale. In such conditions as those, the navigators could not wait for the sun to shine before observing its altitude. Even when the cloud seems thick, if the navigator waits patiently with sextant in hand, set to an estimated altitude, he will usually get a glimpse of the outline of the sun at top or bottom.

Time.

Slocum was content with a dollar clock, bought cheap because the face was smashed, for his navigation. Later it was further damaged, but after being boiled in oil it continued its duties, although by then with only the hour hand left. Joshua Slocum was a fine lunarian and he told a good story too. For the normal amateur navigator, fixing the longitude will depend on the accuracy with which he knows the time, four seconds of time being the equivalent of one mile.

However, a good wireless receiver costs no more than a good chronometer, so there is no need to buy the latter instrument. If someone is fortunate enough to have a battery operated electric wrist-watch, he can rely on accurate time from this; even a reasonably priced spring wrist-watch, so long as it is regularly wound up, is likely to be ample for navigational purposes, if it is supported by a radio receiver which can tune to one of the world-wide continuous time signals.

Calculations.

After taking the observations and the time, some calculations must be made to find the position of the vessel. There are many different methods and tables to do this, with varying degrees of accuracy, at the expense of corresponding amounts of work. Working sights is not difficult when the habit is established, and most yachtsmen now choose the U.S. Hydrographic Office H.O. Publication No. 214, which in Britain is published as H.D. 486.

Personally I prefer to stick to a standard method of working a sun sight, with the slight modifications necessary for stars and moon. The mathematically minded may delight in all the varieties of meridian altitudes, ex-meridian altitudes and other complications; however, these enthusiasts can follow the example of Joshua Slocum and after boiling their watch and radio set in oil, have the more intriguing scope as lunarians. For the possibly tired, often wet, and perhaps slightly seasick small boat navigator, who has many other functions to perform as well as working out sights, the glorious simplicity of one set method of calculations is a luxury.

Finding the stars.

One of the keys to good evening star sights is seeing the stars in ample time while a really clear horizon is visible. When at a young age I first assisted a navigator by taking the times of his sights, it seemed to me that I must have been blind or he had amazing eyesight, as absolutely no glimmer of a star would be visible to me some minutes after he had finished. The answer was partly that he had trained his eyes what to look for, but also he set the altitude of the star on to the sextant, estimated to within a degree, and then picked up its faint glow in the sextant telescope long before it was visible with the naked eye.

It is always valuable to work out in advance the approximate azimuth and altitude of the stars it is intended to take, remembering which tack the yacht is likely to be on at the time, so the selected stars are clear of the sails. This is done by taking a time about fifteen minutes after sunset when the yacht is near the sun's declination, or rather later relative to sunset when in high latitudes, and based on that time the same calculations are made as will eventually be done at the exact time of the observations. For convenience it is often useful to draw a star diagram as shown in Fig. XI, 1. The position of the stars

can also be found by a star globe, or some publication such as *What Star is it?*; however, in a
small craft it will inevitably take time to get out
some special instrument, and in the end the
task of the navigator is simplified by using as
few books and tools as will serve his purpose.

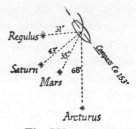

    In practice from a small yacht in poor
weather conditions, I have found that four
observations taken at the very earliest moment
gave position lines that cut in quite closely.
Another set started some fifteen minutes

Fig. XI, 1. Typical
navigator's star dia-
gram prepared for
evening star sights

later when the stars were bright, and the horizon still looked
reasonable, gave a cocked hat that enclosed a big enough sea area in
which to play hide-and-seek with a small island. Morning star sights
should be left as late as possible to get the greatest accuracy.

Compasses.

    Basically there has been little change in the compass for many
hundreds of years, as it still consists of something that points in a known
direction due to magnetic attraction. However, there have been
changes in the steadiness of the needle or card that points, and the ease
with which its direction can be read. For a long time the compass course
was assessed in such a complicated manner that its comprehension
marked the difference between a seaman and a landlubber. This complex system of points and quarter points then had to be corrected
for variation and deviation before using a chart, so the whole thing
needed some of the best brains among seafarers to devise machines or
formulae that could solve this artificial complication. Not only does
the point system take time to learn, and far more time to learn how to
correct it, but the thoroughly clumsy nomenclature often needs many
words to describe one course or bearing, thus adding to the danger of a
mistake. 'South-south-east three quarters east' seems a long and
confusing name for a simple direction, but the coasting navigator who
could memorise three such bearings to fix the position must be almost a
superman.

    A system that developed from this was to divide the compass sectors
into degrees and order a course with two cardinal points and two
figures, such as 'North seventy-five east'. This is simpler to say, and

slightly easier for the navigator, but it is still necessary to add westerly variation in one sector and subtract it in another. Also in practice it has been found the 'North fifty West' has been confused by sound or brain with 'North fifty East', and both tend to get abbreviated to 'North fifty', so that accidents have been caused.

The system now coming into general use divides the compass card into 360 degrees, so that any course or bearing can be described in three figures, while corrections for variation and deviation are quite simply applied. Some people, perhaps due to habit, prefer the system venerated by long custom, and having learnt something as complicated as boxing the compass, I too felt some grievance at dispensing with the need for such toil. One compass card I saw achieved real simplicity in all essentials; there was a blue splodge on one side of the card, and a red one on the other. 'But you've got to remember,' said the boat's owner, 'that red's for out and blue's for 'ome.'

Steering compasses.

It is important to site the compass where it can be readily seen by the helmsman. In a small yacht some compromise may be necessary between putting it where it can be seen on either tack, and putting it where it will avoid unknown deviation due to cooking tools in the galley nearby, or perhaps where an iron keel immediately below will cause large errors when heeled.

An effective solution is two compasses, as in the open ocean there can be no compromise over steering, and a duplicate for such an important fitting is in any case wise. One is the standard compass that should be mounted far away from any unfixed ferrous metal, but need not be continuously visible to the helmsman, so long as he can check the course when needed. The other is the steering compass whose sole object is to be easily seen by the helmsman; the Sestrel yacht compass is particularly suitable as it is fitted so that it can be shipped in a second on to simple brackets that do not project far enough from the side of the cockpit to foul ropes or even be uncomfortable to the back. The steering compass can be moved around from one bracket to another as the yacht tracks, or even to suit the shape of individual helmsmen, and it does not matter what deviation errors are included, nor where the lubber's line is pointing, as the course is set by the standard compass and the helmsman merely keeps her going in the same direction with occasional checks on the standard. When beating into a wind variable in direction, he still assesses the course steered from the steering compass, but occasional checks on the standard will be needed for the navigator to interpret this.

The grid compass is also often used successfully for steering, but it is more difficult to read the ship's head when steering a variable course on the wind. In one yacht on a long cruise I had a grid compass and a Sestrel both placed with equal convenience to the helmsman, but after a time it was found that the grid was not used.

Compass lighting.

Compass lighting must be carefully considered, particularly if the helmsman has to keep a look-out as well. An amber light is more restful for the eyes than a white one, and is less harmful to night vision. Only a small area of the compass card around the lubber's line need be lit, and this can be achieved with a tiny electric bulb in a rubber sticker that clings to the outside of the glass face in the position that suits the particular helmsman; the bulb can be fed from a single cell dry battery, and quite a small battery will last for weeks of night sailing. Another alternative which lasts for many years is a Beta light, set inside the compass where it glows continuously with sufficient brilliance to read the compass when it gets dark.

Charts.

For any long distance passage it is essential to plan on a small scale chart that covers the whole scope of the passage. This seems obvious enough yet there have been occasions where the navigator, planning a passage piecemeal on various sheets, has mistaken a figure of latitude or longitude to find himself aiming at the wrong destination. This small scale chart will not be suitable for plotting the mechanics of navigation, the observed position lines, the estimated set from currents and leeway, and the everyday details. For this purpose the perfect plotting sheet is just the right size to fit the chart table, has a scale such that two or three normal days' run will cross the sheet, and has a compass rose and convenient scale of latitude and longitude, with a line for degrees going right across the sheet. Such printed plotting charts can be bought, but they are expensive, may not fit the chart table in a very small vessel, and either a different one is required for each strip of latitude, or a complicated variable scale is used, which is a potent cause of mistakes.

A good way to deal with this problem is to use portions of local area charts, whose scale is convenient and whose latitude is the same as that of the yacht. The longitude can be altered to fit in with the requirement, and the conventions referring to sea and land must just be ignored. Thus a navigator in mid-Atlantic might use part of the chart of the English Channel, adding 50 degrees to each longitude marking merely by writing in the extra digit 5; he will soon grow accustomed to ignoring the railway line from Rouen to Paris and be able to treat the markings for rocks, shoals and mountains with equal disrespect.

If no chart with the right scale, or latitude, is available, then the backs of charts, or blank sheets of paper can be used. A compass rose can be stuck on from another chart, and a convenient scale of longitude created. From this the latitude scale can be calculated from the cosine of the longitude, and plotted along the side of the chart. The latitude must have fixed figures on the scale, but the degrees of longitude can be pencilled in as required; should the passage be approximately in an east and west direction the same plotting sheet will serve for a long distance with the help of an India rubber. For instance a passage from the Cape Verde Islands to Antigua would only need one plotting sheet, while the lesser distance from the Cape Verde Islands to the Scillies would need several. The work of preparing these plotting sheets would need to be completed before the voyage, when ample space and a steady platform are available. No very great accuracy is needed for these plotting charts in the open ocean, so long as a proper chart is used for plotting on approaching the landfall.

Plotting.

The basis of navigation should depend on a conscientiously kept plot of compass course steered and distance run, modified by every scrap of information the navigator can glean, whether from sun, stars, radio, knowledge of currents and his vessel, movement of birds, aircraft and ships, behaviour of the sea, or even a sight of the land. Skill in the art of navigation consists in the ability to assess the accuracy of information which comes from these different sources; the best navigator may be no mathematician and have no steadier eye than anyone else but he will have learnt how much trust he can put in a hazy horizon, in his radio devices and in his knowledge of the sea. This art comes from experience. Slocum, on finding himself less than five miles out in his dead-reckoning after crossing the Pacific, wrote that he kept his longitude by intuition; yet he kept a careful track chart.

Many ingenious instruments have been invented to help the process of plotting. In a very small vessel, whose motion at times may be vehement, the greatest need is simplicity. A pencil is essential, probably many pencils as one after another is hurled into the bilges in rough weather; an India rubber, pair of dividers and parallel rulers are all necessary, but in rough weather are about as much as can be handled. Nothing else is essential for accuracy or speed of working, so it is best to stick to these few simple instruments and become thoroughly accustomed to their manipulation.

The question of the best type of parallel ruler is largely a matter of taste. Where space is ample and the motion not too violent, the brass roller type takes a great deal of beating and is the quickest in use. In a small craft there are times when it needs more than the navigator's available number of hands to prevent this heavy instrument from digging its sharp corner into his feet as it falls off the chart table. Then there is much to be said for a perspex or other plastic instrument.

It is in racing across the oceans that the navigator's skill in plotting is tested to the utmost. Then, as he approaches the landfall, the vessel cannot afford to wait for visibility to clear, or the sun to peer through the clouds. An error in position of only a couple of miles might mean half an hour lost to an opponent. In a race such as the Transatlantic victory of *Cohoe*, which she won in 1950 by two hours after 3,000 miles of sailing, navigation needs great accuracy.

Distance recorders.

In a sailing vessel, whose speed is constantly altering, the estimation of distance run through the water becomes very difficult. There are various instruments that will measure this with reasonable accuracy. From the point of view of the navigator the best is the bottom log in which a small tube or impellor protrudes through the bottom of the ship, giving a recording of distance and speed on a dial placed conveniently within the ship. This is expensive, requires an underwater opening in the hull, and cannot be repaired with the ship afloat if it is damaged. The patent log, which consists of a metal rotator towed astern on a length of untwistable log-line, records the distance travelled on a simple counting device; it is slightly less convenient for reading, but is less liable to any trouble; the worst that can happen is for the rotator to be lost, when the cure is to stream another. An additional fitting to the speed recorder of the patent log is a relative speed indicator, which measures the drag of the towed rotator. This instrument is particularly valuable when racing, as the sheets can be trimmed, or the sails shifted, until the highest speed is recorded for the particular conditions of wind and sea at the time.

Over a long distance the drag of the rotator through the water might retard the vessel as much as several miles. Yet in a long race this loss is easily accounted for by the extra incentive given to the crew, perhaps without sight of ship or land for weeks on end, in trying to achieve the best run in their watch. When speed is unimportant, there can be no doubt of the value of the patent log; although Slocum could only afford a dollar for his timepiece when setting out on a voyage round the world, he bought a 'rotator-log'.

Logbook.

Everything affecting the navigation of the ship is recorded in the logbook. It is often known as the log, as is the speed measuring instrument; this is confusing, so it is best to give each a title that defines it with certainty. The two have this in common, that each is vital to accurate navigation. When racing, or approaching a landfall at any time, the three factors most important to accurate navigation are a reliable compass, a reliable helmsman, and a reliable logbook. The importance of the logbook does not stop there; in any cruise for pleasure, much of the joy comes after a voyage when concise and accurate information is invaluable for years afterwards. The logbook is worthless unless it really is accurate; if the wind direction is estimated from a glance at the compass, without any consideration for variation, it might just as well not be written down at all. If the wave height is guessed casually, the barometer read incorrectly, and the course actually steered not faithfully recorded, the logbook has no purpose.

Many varieties of logbook are printed, yet the most vital points for a small sailing craft are usually overlooked; the covers should be waterproof, and a pencil should be secured to the book on a string. The form of book will depend on the type of vessel and purpose of the voyage, so it is best to buy a rough notebook, attach stiff covers with waterproof adhesive tape, secure a short length of sharpened pencil, and then rule it out as needed. A sample logbook page is shown in Fig. XI, 2.

Windward work.

Many a long distance cruising man claims that windward work can be ignored completely, as the strategy of the seaman should prevent the need of sailing on the wind. Yet even in the Trade Wind zones, a contrary wind may sometimes be met, and in such areas as the Westerlies in north or south hemisphere, long periods of Easterlies may persist. If time is a factor, there will then be no alternative to windward work; it is the hardest point of sailing for crew, sailing-master and navigator. The navigator needs to estimate the leeway, a factor which

DATE   *Saturday 26th. July 1952*
           25th. day of passage from Bermuda to Plymouth

TIME	COURSE STEERED		LOG	RUN	BARO-METER	WIND	SEA HEIGHT	WEATHER & REMARKS
	Steering	Standard						
0100								
0200								
0300								*Sailing fast under full main & cca genoa, sheets*
0400	*112°*	*095°*	*2689.2*	*26.8*	*1024.2*	*NNE 5*	*6'*	*just started. Ship pounding occasionally, lee rail awash*
0500								
0600								
0700								*0710 Entered soundings (100 fathoms)*
0800	*112°*	*095°*	*2710.6*	*26.4*	*1024.2*	*NNE 4*	*6'*	*Sailing nearly as fast with less wind & easier sea*
2000	*114°*	*097°*	*2790.0*	*12.8*	*1020.8*	*NNE 5*	*7'*	*Sailing under full main & small genoa. Ship pounding & taking water into cockpit*
2100								*2100 Shifted to cca genoa before dark*
2200								*2230 Unknown steam ship passed ½ ml. to South*
2300								*on parallel course but would not answer signals*
Midt	*114°*	*097°*	*2805.7*	*15.7*	*1020.1*	*NNE 5*	*7'*	*0 Lee rail well awash, very wet but sailing fast*

NOON { 49° 21' N   Run to noon { By sights *135'*   Total run   *2894°*
        { 10° 10' W   { By log   *136.4'*   Distance to go *241*

Fresh Water Left   *32 Gals*   Zone Time at Noon *G.M.T +30 mins*
Mean Daily Run   *119'*
Forecast for Next 24 hours *B.B.C. Wind fresh to strong veering to E*

Plan for Next 24 hours *Aim for position 1' South of Lizard. If headed come hard on wm.*
                           Critical course for Port Tack 150° by steering compass
                           Estimated 2 day 5 hr. 02 min. in hand on Carristore at noon

Fig. XI, 2. Sample page of a logbook for deep sea sailing yachts

varies enormously with different conditions of sea, besides calculating what distance the ship will make to windward under different points relative to the wind. There is absolutely no rule for calculating leeway, which can only be assessed by experience of the ship; some idea can sometimes be gained by noting the angle between the ship's head and the line of her wake, but this will be a gross approximation. In the case of a fast modern sailing cruiser, leeway is very small so long as the ship is moving easily to windward; when she becomes sluggish, due to a steep sea or perhaps a set of the sails that makes her uncomfortable, leeway will amount to more and more, until in the hove-to position, leeway will exceed headway. With enough experience the amount of leeway can almost be felt.

When planning the course it is necessary to know how far the yacht must sail through the water to make a position to windward. Often in a head sea she will not get moving when close on the wind, so Table XI*a* also shows what increase of speed through the water is necessary to compensate for paying off. This table is based on the assumption that when close hauled in calm water the yacht sails within 45 degrees of the wind. The first column refers to course made good, after allowing for leeway, and not the course on which her head is pointing; there are often occasions when pinching the yacht into a head sea that her leeway will be considerable, but as soon as she is freed to romp ahead there is practically no leeway.

Course made good relative to wind	Distance to be sailed to reach a point 100 miles to windward	Percentage increase of speed to compensate for running off	Example
45 degrees	143 miles	0 per cent	4 knots
48 ,,	150 ,,	5 ,, ,,	4.2 ,,
50 ,,	156 ,,	9 ,, ,,	4.4 ,,
55 ,,	173 ,,	21 ,, ,,	4.8 ,,
60 ,,	200 ,,	40 ,, ,,	5.6 ,,

Table XI*a*. Distance to be sailed to reach a point dead to windward, and speed increase
to compensate for running off

Great circle sailing.

A great circle is the shortest distance between two places on the earth's surface. Unless these two places are both on the equator, or in the same longitude, a great circle line between them will require a variety of courses to be sailed. There is no navigational difficulty at all about plotting a great circle course; the only requirement is a special chart, called the Gnomic chart. This is so drawn that a great circle appears as a straight line between two places. The chart cannot conveniently be used for plotting the ship's position, but at regular intervals along the great circle track the longitude and latitude are taken off and transferred to a normal chart, on Mercator's projection, and these points joined together by a rhumb line.

Wind relative to direction of destination	Distance to be sailed to make good 100 miles when sailing at different angles from the wind				
	45°	48°	50°	55°	60°
o Degrees	143 miles	150	156	173	200 miles
10 ,,	141 ,,	147	154	171	197 ,,
20 ,,	134 ,,	142	145	162	188 ,,
30 ,,	122 ,,	129	135	149	174 ,,
40 ,,	108 ,,	115	129	133	152 ,,
50 ,,			100	112	128 ,,
60 ,,					100 ,,

Table XI*b*. Distance to be sailed to reach positions at varying directions to windward

Radio aids.

The assistance radio can give to the small yacht navigator is so valuable that the cost of the apparatus and amount of space required are well justified in even the smallest vessel. The apparatus costs little more than a good chronometer, which it can replace, without the need for daily winding. The main essential of the yacht's radio is that it should work reliably under the severe conditions experienced in small sailing craft. Many sets are designed for this purpose but little reliance should be put on the normal domestic set, which is not so designed.

Marine radio sets suitable for yachts are made which will transmit as well as receive. Except for some special purpose, such as two vessels cruising in close company with pre-arranged operating times or broadcasting, there is little advantage to be gained from the ability to transmit until the yacht is of such a size that more elaborate apparatus and a really competent operator can be carried.

For a yacht cruising in the open sea the main navigational objective of radio reception is the time signal. The best of these are transmitted on high frequency, such as Washington's on 12,630 kcs., and the various overseas frequencies of the B.B.C., ranging from 6,050 kcs. to 26,100 kcs., which are nearly world wide. The medium or low frequency bands, such as the B.B.C.'s light programme transmissions on 200 kcs., have a far lesser range of distance, although this is much increased when there is darkness all the way from the transmitter to the receiver, as the rising of the Heaviside layer at night affects the reflection of the radio waves back to the earth's surface.

Some sets designed for marine use do not cover the whole high frequency band, although they can be used on the 'Marine High Frequency Band' of the order of 1,500 to 4,000 kcs. This is the band used by small vessels for short range communication with the shore. It does not cover the Washington time signal, nor the B.B.C. overseas services, but will receive many useful stations, particularly in American waters. With a set limited to the 'Marine High Frequency Band' it is still possible to get time signals each night when, for instance, crossing the North Atlantic, as there are valuable continuous time signals from Beltsville on 2,500 kcs. and Ottawa on 3,330 kcs.

Most marine sets are marked in kilocycles (kcs.) instead of metres, and all stations are shown in the *Admiralty List of Radio Signals* by their frequencies in kcs. It is likely that frequency in kcs. will eventually oust the wavelength in metres, although this marking is still used for many domestic receivers. For those accustomed to wavelengths in radio it must be remembered that high frequency equals short wave, and vice versa. Wavelength can be converted to frequency by the formula:

$$kcs. = \frac{300,000}{metres}.$$ For example 100 metres = 3,000 kcs., 2,000 metres = 150 kcs.

Megacycles (mgs.) are sometimes used, 1 mg. being 1,000 kgs.

When within soundings it is often helpful to be able to take the bearing of a radio beacon. Most good sets can be modified to do this approximately but navigators will always yearn for a set whose direction finding is accurate. Some parts of the world are very well supplied with radio beacons, such as both seaboards of the North Atlantic ocean, mostly operating on frequencies between 200 and 350 kcs. Some of

K

these have working ranges of 200 miles, for instance Nantucket (314 kcs.) and Cape Cod (302 kcs.) on the American side, and Round Island (308.0 kcs.) on the European side. There are also numerous lower powered beacons, with ranges of some twenty miles, which transmit in fog only.

Approaching the European freeboard, the *Consol* system of radio aid to navigation is helpful to small vessels and on the American side there is *Consolan*; both can be received on many good marine sets. This system depends on various stations, such as Bushmills (266 kcs.) in Ireland, Stavanger (319 kcs.) in Norway, Ploneis (257 kcs.) near Brest, and Lugo (285 kcs.) in Spain. Each transmits a signal that alters with the position of the receiver relative to the transmitter. The receiver picks up a group of dots and a group of dashes, whose number added together should make up sixty symbols. Simply by counting the number of dots and dashes, a position line is obtained. By doing this with two different stations, two position lines are quickly achieved, to give a fix. In practice the untrained ear does not find it easy to get the correct number of dots or dashes and, as other errors arise as well, an error of ten miles in one position line would not be exceptional. As radio signals travel in a great circle line, the user of *Consol* needs to buy a special chart, with the various position lines traced in, unless he is a sufficiently able mathematician to plot all these himself. Ploneis and Bushmills operate continuously, and can readily be picked up on a good receiver at 1,200 miles; the station at Lugo works all night on Wednesdays, but then tails off to long rests and siestas at the week-end.

The value of radio weather reports in the open sea is very limited indeed, unless there be an operator who can read morse and plot synoptic charts. The spoken shipping weather reports cover areas each so large that for instance area 'Finisterre' is big enough to include such variety of weather as might be experienced simultaneously in London and Copenhagen. The reports can therefore do no more than give a very general idea of the weather, which would be of even less value in the open ocean beyond the scope of these coastal shipping reports, of which no spoken report is made. Therefore short range reception is ample for weather reports, such as can be obtained from the medium frequency stations at New York (2,522 kcs.) or the B.B.C. home services.

Radio weather reports become important should the vessel be

sailing within the area and season of tropical storms or icebergs. Neither of these situations is at all desirable for a sailing yacht.

Full details of the radio stations affecting navigation throughout the world are given in the *Admiralty List of Radio Signals*.

Further Electronic aids.

The sport of offshore racing in the tricky tidal waters around Britain has put such a high premium on navigational accuracy that really excellent electronic equipment has been developed, designed and produced especially for yachts; so the modern offshore racing navigator whose owner can afford the cost, may be blessed with a navigatorium blinking and buzzing with precision instruments. They still need skill in operation; yet if this is combined with almost full-time work for the navigator, they can produce amazing accuracy.

Denied to the offshore racer by the rules of the sport are further superbly accurate navigational aids, such as radar; even with the means of producing sufficient electric power which must be included, they can be fitted in a relatively large sailing cruiser; but are normally only seen in powered craft, which already have ample supplies of electric power.

However, all these beautifully designed and manufactured instruments are bound to be expensive; indeed utility versions are cheaper only because they go without those important points which make the equipment effective and reliable in the difficult conditions faced by small craft in the open sea. Their purpose is mostly in coastal waters, so when it is remembered that even world-wide cruises have been achieved in craft whose total cost was no more than, for instance, the simplest yacht radar set, their cost-effectiveness must be assessed in relation to the particular requirements of a voyage, and a compromise struck somewhere between the Polynesian coco-nut shell and the electronic navigational computer.

XII

Cruise Strategy, Weather and Currents

STRATEGY is defined as the art of conducting a campaign, which is a series of organised operations. In cruising terms, therefore, strategy is the art of conducting the whole cruise, and the two main factors that influence sailing cruise strategy are weather and currents.

It is clear from reading accounts of cruises that some yachtsmen have set forth with very hazy notions of the general world climate and weather. Often they appear surprised and almost indignant that the weather behaved differently from their expectations, when it might be that their expectations were at fault. Perhaps the Trade Winds are expected to blow true without ceasing, or the Westerlies to blow from the west, except for a regular cyclonic circulation of winds round a depression, while currents are expected to move with the steadiness of an escalator. A seaman should no more blame the weather that blows against his hopes than he should blame a shroud that parts; had he studied the climate or the shroud more carefully, perhaps he would have been less surprised.

Climate.

The simplest factor of the world's climate is that it is hot on the equator and cold at the poles. In the southern hemisphere, where ocean predominates so abundantly, the variation between these extremes is very regular; for instance in mid-Pacific longitudes the 'heat equator' of sea-level air is around the geographical equator throughout the year; travelling due south the temperature falls in a well-ordered seamanlike fashion until at a latitude of 60 degrees it has dropped 40 degrees Fahrenheit in January and 50 degrees in July.

Wherever land masses protrude through the sea's surface, the whole simple picture of uniformity is upset, as land tends to become excruciatingly cold in winter and abominably hot in summer. This does not greatly affect the world climate in the southern hemisphere, as Africa does not stick her nose so far below the equator as Algiers rises above it; Australia goes little further south than this, and even its enormous expanse is as a mere island compared with the vast oceans which surround it; so only the strip of South America's finger-point forms any break to the endless waves of the Roaring Forties and the Southern Ocean, which stretches right down to the Antarctic Continent. The finger of South America is too narrow to cause anything more than local variations to the maritime climate, so the southern hemisphere is as though there were no land masses north of Lisbon, Washington or San Francisco.

The northern hemisphere is influenced to a far greater extent by the land masses. Thus in January the Faroes, at the leeward side of the North Atlantic ocean, are nearly a hundred degrees warmer than parts of Siberia in the same latitude but at the leeward side of the Asiatic land mass; similarly the Faroes are some 70 degrees warmer than parts of Canada in the same latitude.

Air pressure.

The general plan of the world air pressure distribution is shown in Fig. XII, 1. Among the main features of the pattern are the areas of semi-permanent high pressure in the centre of the ocean masses at about 30 degrees north and south latitude. Those in the southern hemisphere scarcely shift latitude with the seasons, but the 'highs' of the North Pacific and the North Atlantic, always tending to the leeward side of their oceans, move north in their summer.

It is these semi-permanent ocean anti-cyclones, or 'highs', that cause the persistent sea winds such as the Trade Winds. In the northern summer an intense low pressure area develops over the baking hot land mass of Asia, and this counters any Trade Wind tendency in the north Indian Ocean and China seas, giving instead the south-west monsoon which blows strongest in the Gulf of Arabia and more modestly off China. In winter the same land mass becomes very cold causing the highest air pressure of all; this causes the north-east monsoon, which blows strongest in the China seas as they are closest to the pressure centre. The prevailing winds throughout the world in Feb-

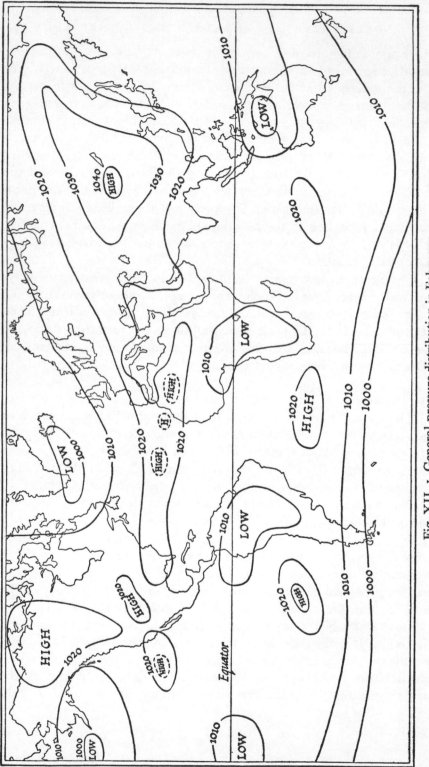

Fig. XII, 1. General pressure distribution in February

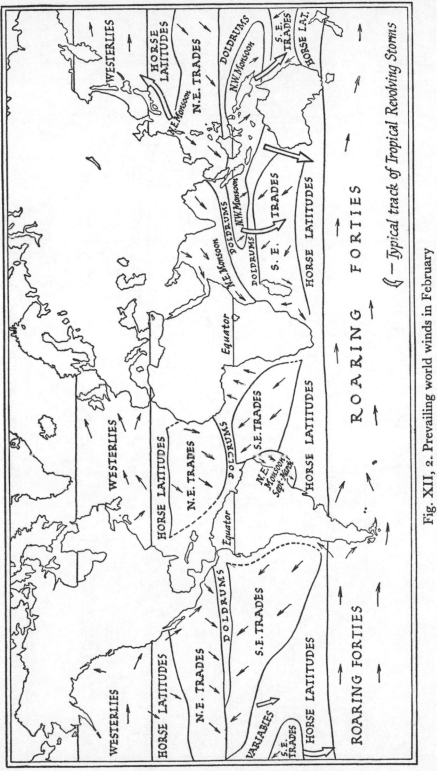

Fig. XII, 2. Prevailing world winds in February

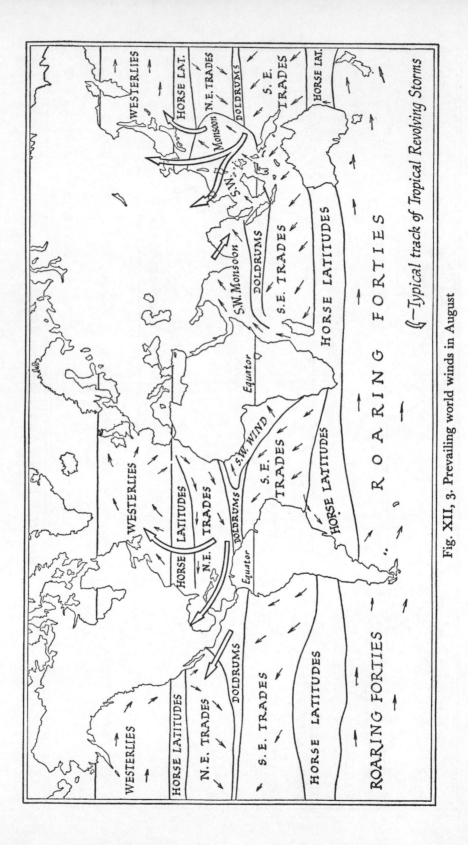

Fig. XII, 3. Prevailing world winds in August

⟨—Typical track of Tropical Revolving Storms

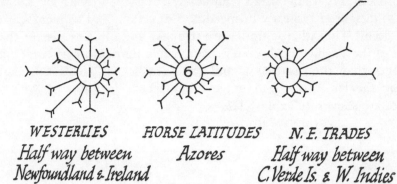

WESTERLIES
*Half way between
Newfoundland & Ireland*

HORSE LATITUDES
Azores

N. E. TRADES
*Half way between
C. Verde Is. & W. Indies*

Fig.XII, 4. Typical daily winds in North Atlantic areas during July

ruary and August are shown in Figs. XII, 2 and XII, 3, while actual day by day winds in typical North Atlantic positions are shown in Fig. XII, 4.

Trade Winds.

The trades are probably the most important passage winds for any sailing vessel on an extensive ocean cruise. Their boundaries depend on the position of the semi-permanent ocean 'highs', but the approximate limits in the different seasons are shown in Table XIIa.

Ocean	Trade Wind	January	July
North Atlantic	North-East	2°N–25°N	10°N–28°N
North Pacific	North-East	8°N–25°N	12°N–29°N
South Atlantic	South-East	Equator–30°S	5°N–25°S
South Pacific	South-East	4°N–30°S	8°N–25°S
Indian	South-East	15°S–30°S	Equator–25°S

Table XIIa. Normal boundaries of Trade Winds

The trades follow round the area of high pressure, tending to blow more towards the equator on the eastern sides, and more towards the poles at the western sides. They are remarkable for their steadiness, often blowing from the main direction on as many as twenty-four days a month in the summer and twenty days a month in the winter of that hemisphere. Where the winds tend polewards at the western sides of the oceans they are less steady in speed and direction, and tropical storms may occur. The Atlantic trades are stronger and more persistent than those of the Pacific and Indian oceans, while the south-east trades are stronger than the north-east, and each reaches its greatest strength during the local spring. Average wind speeds in knots of Atlantic trades are shown in Table XII*b*.

Wind	January	April	July	October
North-East	9	11	8	5
South-East	12	11	11	13

Table XII*b*. Average wind speeds of Atlantic trades

Westerlies.

Westerly winds predominate in the zones bounded by latitude 40 degrees and 65 degrees in the northern hemisphere, and between 35 degrees and 65 degrees in the southern hemisphere. In the northern hemisphere depressions abound in these areas so that Westerlies are very variable in strength and direction, blowing mainly between north-west and south-west. In the southern hemisphere the Westerlies are more persistent and are known as the Roaring Forties yet, even for instance off Cape Horn, a northerly wind is just as frequent as a true westerly wind.

Position and Latitude		Gale Frequency		Frequency of S.W.–N.W. winds	
		January	July	January	July
		(Percentages of observations)			
Off Cape Horn	58°S	11	20	80	65
Off Cape of Good Hope	40°S	8	22	84	70
Mid-Atlantic	50°N	30	5	75	67
Off Alaska	50°N	12	1	60	72
As a comparison					
Portland Bill	50°N	5	0.5	54	65

Table XII*c*. Horse Latitudes: Frequencies of gales and west winds in the Westerlies

Horse latitudes.

Most things pleasant are protected by something annoying to make the object the more worth-while, so that the trades, or Mecca of the sailing cruiser, are bounded by the variables of Cancer and Capricorn, known as the Horse Latitudes. These areas of high atmospheric pressure have light winds, cloudless skies and clear dry atmosphere. On land they are marked by the Sahara, Californian, Calahari and Australian deserts, in the North Atlantic by the Sargasso Sea. Although tropical storms usually form near the equator in the Trade Wind zone, they often re-curve, with greater danger, in the Horse Latitudes.

Doldrums or Intertropical Convergence Zone

These are the areas which separate the north-east and the south-east trades on their respective sides of the equator. The Doldrums tend to follow the sun's declination; they extend through about three degrees of latitude. The hot damp air in these regions causes vigorous convection with frequent rainfall and particularly violent thunderstorms. Winds generally are very light, except in the squalls, and vessels often remain becalmed for long periods. An auxiliary motor with even a very modest range of endurance might well be justified merely to cross from one hemisphere to the other, although some cruising yachtsmen might prefer to rely on patience, an oilskin that does not become tacky in heat, and provisions for a few more days at sea.

Tropical revolving storms.

Tropical revolving storms are so violent that no yachtsman should willingly risk his ship within the areas and seasons in which they normally occur. The tactics for avoiding a tropical revolving storm are simple on paper, but far more difficult in practice, so cruise strategy should rely on evasion, not just of the storm itself but of the risk of encountering one. The formation of such storms is shown in Fig. XII, 5; in the southern hemisphere the wind directions are reversed. A typical hurricane track is shown in Fig. XII, 6.

Tropical revolving storms occur mostly on the western side of the oceans, though they are also experienced in the Bay of Bengal, off the west coast of America and the north-west coast of Australia. They are most frequent in the late summer of their hemisphere, except in the Arabian Sea which has two seasons at the changes of the monsoon.

Out-of-season tropical revolving storms occur
occasionally during any month, particularly
in the western North Pacific and the Indian
Ocean. Only the South Atlantic, of the
tropical oceans, is quite free from these
storms. Some years bring a whole string of
storms and others have comparatively few.
Table XII*d* shows the average annual
frequency, and the most dangerous months
in each area with the local names of these
storms.

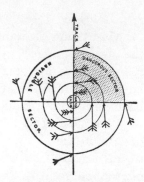

Fig. XII, 5. Tropical
revolving storm in Nor-
thern Hemisphere at
point of recurvature

Air masses.

The earth's atmosphere consists of large
masses, in each of which the air has an approximately uniform character throughout. To reach this state of uniformity the air forming
the mass must spend several days in the same locality and the whole
of it must be in contact with the same type of earth's surface. The

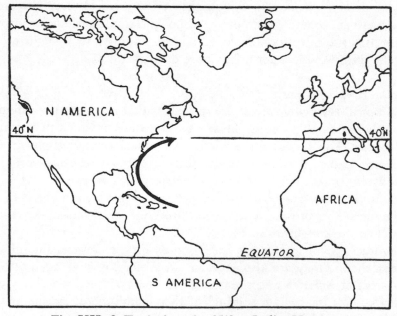

Fig. XII, 6. Typical track of West Indies Hurricane

Area	Name	Worst Months	Average Annual Occurrence
(Northern Hemisphere)			
West Indies	Hurricane	Aug.–Oct.	5
Bay of Bengal	Cyclone	May and Oct.–Nov.	2
Arabian Sea	Cyclone	May–June and Oct.–Nov.	1
China Sea and west North Pacific	Typhoon	July–October (Occur in all months)	25
East North Pacific	Hurricane	September	3
(Southern Hemisphere)			
Indian Ocean	Cyclone	Jan.–March	6
West Australia	Willy-willies	January	1
Pacific	Hurricane	Jan.–March	3

Table XII*d*. Names, seasons and frequencies of Tropical Revolving Storms

normal condition for this to take place is a stationary area of high pressure such as the semi-permanent ocean 'highs' of the Horse Latitudes, and those over the great land masses. The most familiar in England are the anti-cyclones over the Azores which influence our climate particularly in the late summer, and over Siberia which sends us cold, clear air in the spring.

Most of the weather at sea is characteristic of the air mass present except when in the 'front' between two air masses, where conditions are always unsettled. There are six main types of air mass which affect the seaman, and knowledge of their character helps understanding of the weather.

(a) *Polar continental air* originates over land in high latitudes such as Canada and Siberia. It starts as dry and stable air, whose temperature is well below that of any sea over which it travels. Conditions at sea are fine and visibility good, but the relatively warm sea evaporates quickly into the air and soon forms cloud in increasing quantity until after a couple of days at sea the air mass has turned to polar maritime air.

When the sea is particularly warm, such as the Gulf Stream off the North American coast or the Oya Siwo off Japan, evaporation is very rapid and rain or snow showers are likely. Polar continental air is seldom found in the southern hemisphere as the only land suitable to form it is South America, which is a comparatively narrow strip in the colder latitudes.

It is more common on the eastern sides of oceans than on the western sides. England, for instance, gets comparatively few visits from the Siberian air mass and the North American Continent's polar air has become thoroughly salty and damp before it is half-way across the Atlantic (a common condition too among people crossing in close contact with the ocean).

(b) *Arctic air* is formed over snow and ice, being similar to polar continental air but much colder, so that a front occurs where they meet. Over the sea it soon becomes modified by heat and evaporation to become polar maritime air.

It is this very cold air passing over the far warmer sea water that causes the sea smoke of very high latitudes, when the whole sea appears to be boiling. This arctic phenomenon is also sometimes seen in the Gulf Stream off New England and the Oya Siwo, the two sea areas of all the oceans which seem to revel in every known type of weather peculiarity.

(c) *Polar maritime air* is the most common type of air mass within the Westerlies of both hemispheres, except within a few hundred miles to the eastward of the continents of North America and Asia, where polar continental air predominates. Polar maritime air is caused by the warming and moistening of polar continental and arctic airs, and generally its temperature is still a little lower than the sea so that visibility remains good, and there is often little cloud. However, if this air is warmed rapidly when moving fast to the south, or encountering particularly hot sea like the Gulf Stream, there will be much convection forming a great deal of cloud with heavy showers and squalls.

(d) *Tropical continental air* is formed in the anti-cyclones over the hot land masses such as the Sahara and Californian deserts. At sea this air is hot, cloudless but hazy owing to the dust it has picked up ashore. As more and more sea water is evaporated it becomes oppressively hot, such as the particularly unpleasant southerly wind of the Mediterranean summer, known as Sirocco.

(e) *Tropical maritime air* provides the main atmosphere at sea in the tropics and sub-tropics. It forms in the Horse Latitude 'highs' centred over each of the oceans, north and south of the equator. In the higher latitudes this air is warmer than the sea beneath it, but this is not so at the equator, so its character varies with its position relative to the centre of the 'high', and therefore whether its movement is towards colder or warmer water. When bound for colder water on the western side of the 'highs', visibility is excellent with fair weather cumulus clouds and only occasional showers; on the eastern sides of the oceans, when tropical maritime air moves towards warmer water, visibility is poor, with much stratus cloud and more showers.

(f) *Equatorial air* is formed particularly at the leeward ends of the trades. It is very hot and carries moisture up to great heights, so there is much high cloud and frequent heavy showers. Thunderstorms, heavy rain and fog are typical.

Fronts.

The greater the difference in character between two adjacent air masses, the worse is the weather along the boundary or front. In the area of the Westerlies there are frequent changes of air masses, so the frontal system between them is often very complicated and the weather extremely fickle, but in the trades there is little change in air mass, so that an occasional front will do little more than modify the wind strength and perhaps bring some rain. There are certain regions where highly dissimilar air masses come into conflict; the most outstanding in the northern hemisphere are the polar fronts a few hundred miles to the east of the North American and Asiatic coasts and roughly parallel to them. The general position of fronts and air masses are shown in Fig. XII, 7 and Fig. XII, 8.

In the southern hemisphere the most pronounced zone of air mass conflict forms a circle surrounding the Antarctic Continent. Knowledge of the Antarctic frontal zones is still very sketchy, and they embrace an area which would concern few yachtsmen, but it seems likely that a prolific source of Antarctic gales is the area around the Weddell Sea current, just as main depression forming areas of the North Atlantic and Pacific coincide with the Gulf Stream and Oya Siwo.

In these conflict zones the weather is notoriously bad and along the line of the polar fronts are formed frontal waves, on whose crests depressions are born, which may develop in intensity as they move off to the westward. Generally the contrast between conflicting air masses is less in summer than in winter, so frontal weather is less bad, and the depressions formed by the frontal waves are less intense.

In the tropics the meeting line of the tropical maritime air masses generated in the north and south hemispheres tends to move north and south with the sun, but never goes south of the equator in the Atlantic

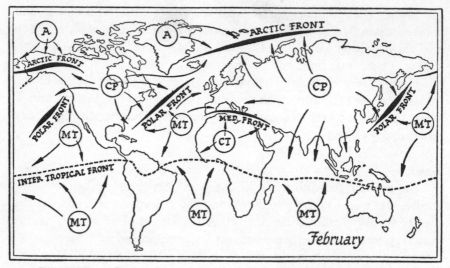

Fig. XII, 7. General positions of air masses and founts in February

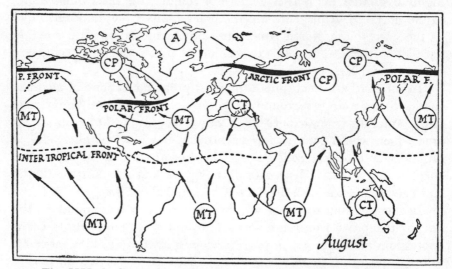

Fig. XII, 8. General positions of air masses and fronts in August

A Arctic Source
CP Continental Polar Source
CT Continental Tropical Source
MT Maritime Tropical Source

Plate 14. The big cutter *Lisoletta V* racing to windward against hard conditions in the Skagerrak. Nearby a much smaller yacht in the same race was turned right over and sunk where the waves steepened in the shoaling waters approaching the Swedish coast

Plate 15. With spinnaker set over the genoa, the kicking strap being hauled taut, a main boom fore guy about to be rigged, and further gear set up to keep her running fast. It would take many minutes at the best before the yacht could be rounded up under full control if a man went over the side

Plate 16. The helmsman must always have immediately ready in his mind the action he would take should a man fall over the side, a shroud or a back stay let go

and eastern Pacific. As these two air masses are so nearly similar they do not strictly form a front, but the area of their meeting is known as the intertropical convergence zone or intertropical front, which is the Doldrum area.

Barometer.

Modern weather forecasting depends very largely upon the knowledge of the atmospheric pressure at many places, and this is measured by the barometer. Yet a single barometer can do no more than give a general impression of the weather. A barograph is far better as it shows the barometric tendency up to the moment of the forecast. It must never be assumed that there will always be a fall of pressure before a blow, any more than that a falling glass inevitably means foul weather. A typical barograph trace was examined in which the pressure was practically steady until the time when then a steep trough passed the position, and the wind increased rapidly to Force 11, gusting to 74 knots in dense snow. The barograph began to dip at the time of the first fierce squall, and although the pressure fell very fast for twenty minutes, the total fall was no more than 4 millibars or 0.1 of an inch. Had the barometer been read every hour, no warning would have been given of the storm, and there would be no readings afterwards to suggest that anything untoward had happened.

Another trace was examined carefully when the pressure fell 16 millibars or half an inch in six hours, with a total fall of an inch in one day; then it rose just as steeply to a point 45 millibars higher. Yet during the whole of that time the wind never exceeded Force 6.

Both these traces were made in 60 degrees North latitude, where a steeper pressure gradient is needed to give the same wind force as that which would be required nearer to the equator.

Line squalls.

Line squalls may be dangerous to sailing craft as they bring a sudden increase of wind speed, and a drastic change of wind direction. The line squall is a very well marked cold front, that is, the region where warm air is succeeded by cold air; they may occur in any of the temperate regions of the westerlies, and often penetrate into the tropical zones of the Horse Latitudes. They are frequent in the Mediterranean winter; here the warm air mass from the Sahara is often quite dry, so a white

L

squall, or cloudless front, results. In the southern hemisphere line squalls are frequent off South Africa; off South America they are known as the Pampero, and off South Australia as the Southern Buster.

The barometer gives little warning of the approach of a line squall, but the appearance of the sky gives a good indication except in the case of white squalls. With a clear sky overhead a long line of low black cloud is seen approaching from the west or north-west, with beyond it a light grey uniform sky. The black line of cloud often appears roll-shaped, and is obviously threatening. In the northern hemisphere the wind falls light from the south, until the edge of the dark cloud line is nearly overhead, when a violent squall blows from the north-west; in the southern hemisphere the wind falls light from the north, and the squall usually strikes from the south-west. Boisterous conditions with a sudden drop in temperature and perhaps thunderstorms occur while the black cloud roll is overhead. As this gives way to the light grey cloud cover heavy rain falls, the barometer rises steeply and the wind eases.

Line squalls occur often in British waters during the spring and very early summer. A typical one passed over Tor Bay in late April 1951 when several early-season dinghy sailors were afloat on a Sunday afternoon. Within a few seconds many dinghies had capsized in the cold water, and from a rescue launch I could only see one still afloat the right way up; the man in charge of her must have been a fine seaman, as he had recognised the line squall coming, lowered his sails, and lay-to single handed in his dinghy not far from a lee shore with his main sail and boom streamed out ahead as a sea anchor.

Ocean Currents. (Fig. XII, 9)

Currents are caused mainly by prevailing winds, making it more fruitless than ever to attempt to sail against them. The main currents make a complete circulation round the semi-permanent ocean 'highs' of the Horse Latitudes; they tend to be cool currents on the eastern sides of this circulation, such as the Canaries current bringing cold water from the Portuguese coast down to the Cape Verde Islands or the Humbolt current setting from the coast of Chile up to the Galapagos Islands. On the western sides of the oceans they are normally warm currents, such as the Gulf Stream bringing water from the Gulf of

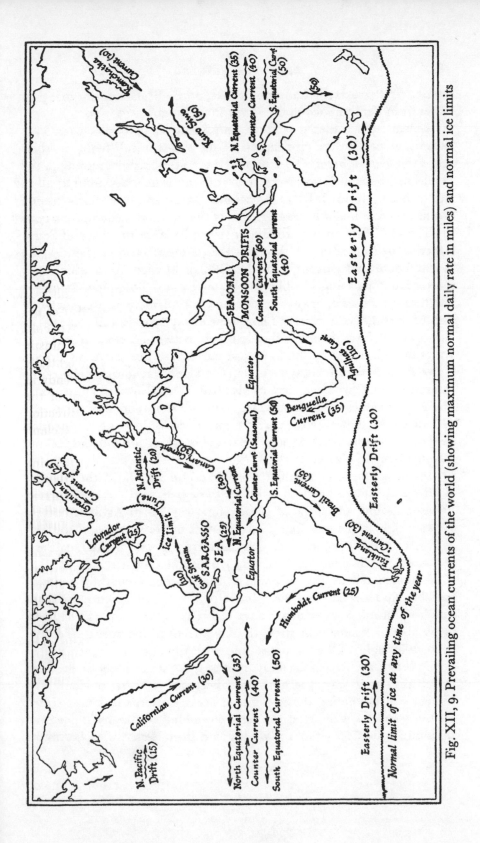

Fig. XII, 9. Prevailing ocean currents of the world (showing maximum normal daily rate in miles) and normal ice limits

Mexico up towards the Labrador banks, or the Brazil current bringing water from Pernambuco to the River Plate estuary.

Beneath the trades the North and South Equatorial currents set easterly as part of the circulations of the sub-tropical 'highs' in their respective hemispheres. Often there is a counter-current running in the Doldrums, but this is not very persistent, and is only apparent at all in the Atlantic from July to December, although the non-seasonal Guinea current might be an extension of the equatorial counter-current.

The Gulf Stream is particularly strong because the shape of South America deflects some of the South Equatorial current, besides the North Equatorial current, into the Gulf of Mexico, from which it is directed out past Florida like the water from a hose-pipe. It moves north and then east, always restive and turbulent, with frequent side and back eddies; the current's hose-pipe effect takes it well clear of the east coast of North America, thus letting in between them a strip of cold water brought south by the Labrador current, so that there is a drastic water front between the two currents, making navigation delightfully interesting and weather deplorably bad. The Gulf Stream ends in about 40 degrees West longitude, soon after passing the tail of the Grand Banks; however the current continues in an easterly direction as the North Atlantic Drift, which passes between Scotland and Iceland into the North Polar Sea.

In the southern hemisphere the westerly drift follows the Roaring Forties and extends north to less than 30 degrees south in the Atlantic; however, round the Cape of Good Hope the warm Agulhas current runs strongly to the west for a short distance out to seaward. A westerly gale against this current, and such gales are frequent in July, causes a sea which reminds me of an easterly gale in the Gulf Stream.

All currents can give valuable assistance, but their rates are very variable and depend on the wind strength or persistence, perhaps hundreds of miles away many days beforehand. It is therefore almost impossible to estimate the strength of a current in the open sea, except by regular sights. Often when sailing with the current, it seems to be giving very little help to the daily positions, but if the vessel turns round to sail the other way, the hindrance becomes only too obvious. The difficulty of estimating the strength of ocean currents is demonstrated by the wreck of a liner on the reefs stretching out many miles from Bermuda; this ship was on a weekly run from America to Bermuda,

each time crossing a belt of the Gulf Stream some 200 miles wide.
From her regular voyages she must have had exceptional knowledge
of the behaviour of the Gulf Stream, yet this did not protect her from
over-estimating its set on the occasion which brought about her total
loss.

Ice.

It is in the North Atlantic that ice is the greatest menace to normal
navigation; in the southern hemisphere one must go far south of the
normal cruising tracks to find it, as ice keeps well away from the three
continents that project into the Roaring Forties, except the Horn.

In the North Atlantic the ice danger is greatest in mid-summer, a
time when the yacht cruising season is at its height. This is due to icebergs that have 'calved' from glaciers in the early summer and drifted
well south by June and July. Glacier bergs do not exceed 450 feet in
height above the sea surface, while those that reach the North Atlantic
trade routes have never been measured as much as 300 feet high and
a couple of liner's lengths in above-water extent; however, they look
far bigger than this under any conditions, particularly in low visibility;
and as much as 75 to 90 per cent of their mass may be submerged.
The effects of hitting an iceberg would be precisely the same as striking
a rocky coast fully exposed to the open ocean; except that the after-
effects would be colder.

An international ice patrol searches for bergs near the trade routes
and reports their movements by radio, details of which signals can
be found in the *Admiralty List of Radio Signals.* In addition the U.S.
Hydrographic office prepare a weekly chartlet showing graphically
the ice conditions; this can be obtained from the Branch Hydrographic
offices at Boston, New York or Norfolk, as can the *Hydrographic Daily
Memorandum* which shows the latest ice information.

The area up to 400 miles south and east of Cape Race in Newfoundland is all within the July limit of drifting icebergs, and in addition coincides with very high fog frequency in that month. The main
Atlantic Lane shipping route is diverted south of this in the early summer, and adds over a hundred miles to the voyage from New York to
the Channel, so giving some indication of the risk even for a ship fitted
with modern aids to navigation. It is surprising that the great circle
route from say Nassau in the West Indies to the Scilly Islands at the

entrance to the English Channel takes a vessel well within this summer
ice zone to the south-east of Newfoundland.

Stray bergs have been known to drift well beyond these limits; one
has been sighted close to Flores in the Azores, and others as far south as
the latitude of Bermuda. However, anyone sunk by an iceberg in these
fog-free, relatively calm waters would be about as unlucky as if he were
mauled by a tiger in Piccadilly or on Fifth Avenue.

There is no simple way of detecting the presence of an isolated
iceberg in fog or darkness, except with the help of a radar set or the
cruder method of hitting it. No change of temperature can be detected
in time to avoid a collision and the North Atlantic icebergs are too
small to give a noticeable lee, unlike the southern hemisphere ice islands
which around South Georgia have been seen three times the length of
the Isle of Wight and with ice mountains rising 1,700 feet above the
water.

In the North Atlantic ice evasion can be strategical, by avoiding the
ice zone, which is the normal cruising method; or it can be tactical,
as when Rod Stephens deliberately took *Stormy Weather* through an
area known to be glittering with icebergs to win the Transatlantic
race of 1935, after he had plotted every report by radio and sought
advice from two continents. Finally one could use the method of
Commander Graham, single-handed aboard *Emanuel* in 1934, who
kept a good look-out as long as he could, photographed any icebergs
that happened to show up if the fog cleared, and hoped for the best
the rest of the time with the mathematical assurance that the ocean is
very large and drifting icebergs are very small.

Steamship routes.

Steamship routes seldom coincide with the best course for a sailing
vessel, and it may be worth while to plan a voyage definitely to avoid
busy shipping routes in areas where visibility is doubtful, such as the
Gulf Stream south of Nova Scotia. If it is essential to be in these areas,
the Atlantic lane routes in force at that date should be traced on the
chart. In these lanes the eastbound and westbound traffic have their
own tracks; this separation vastly reduces the risk of collision between
steamships, but the situation of a yachtsman is rather similar to a
pedestrian crossing a dual carriage way by-pass; by plotting the tracks
at least he can discover which way to look for oncoming traffic.

Shipping routes for the different oceans are shown on special Admiralty charts; that for the North Atlantic is Misc. 48.

It is a never-ceasing cause of amazement to the open ocean seaman that he will sail for days without sighting a thing, but when a ship does appear its track passes so close that one or the other must alter course. It must be remembered that the rule of the road at sea is only effective if the giving-way ship sights the other in time; under certain conditions light small yachts do not show up clearly to the eye from the height of a liner's bridge, and perhaps show not at all on her radar, particularly as the officer of the watch will not be expecting such things. In 1950 *Cohoe* was lying under bare pole in bad weather about as far from land as it is possible to be in the North Atlantic, when a liner passed unwittingly within a quarter of a mile of her before sighting this tiny craft; the liner's high-speed wash pounding against the waves from a westerly gale pooped *Cohoe*, which then broached-to and the voyage might have finished completely but for the pertinacious seamanship of Adlard Coles, her owner.

Ocean station ships.

In the North Atlantic an international weather and safety patrol has been established in certain fixed positions, which are nearly always occupied, as shown in Table XII*e*.

The ships on these stations are continuously under way, but normally steam around within ten miles of the positions given. *The Admiralty List of Radio Signals* gives a code by which they signal their exact

Station	Latitude	Longitude	Remarks
A	62° 00′ N	16° 00′ N	Between Faroes and Iceland
B	56° 30′	51° 00′	Denmark Strait
C	52° 30′	35° 30′	Mid-Atlantic
D	44° 00′	41° 00′	Mid-Atlantic
E	34° 00′	48° 00′	Between Azores and Bermuda
H	46° 00′	70° 00′	Gulf Stream
I	59° 00′	19° 00′	Rockall Area
J	52° 30′	20° 00′	West of Ireland
K	45° 00′	15° 00′	West of Finisterre

Table XII*e*. Positions of ocean station ships

position, besides the radio frequencies on which they keep watch. A sailing yacht can often tell when she is in the vicinity of an ocean station ship, besides its approximate bearing, from the presence and course of aircraft flying high over the ship's position. The ships are fitted with radar, and as they spend a long period on station, they always seem to welcome a quiet period of friendly ocean gossip by flashing or semaphore with a passing yacht, which has more time for such pleasantries than their normal high speed clients, intent on reaching New York in time for breakfast.

Pilot charts.

Probably the best guides on which to work out the strategy of a cruise are the ocean pilot charts published by the U.S. Hydrographic office, Navy Department. These valuable charts are produced monthly for the different oceans and give a wealth of information about all that goes on in the ocean, including, for instance, little tit-bits to cover North Africa, such as what happened to the bottle thrown overboard by Second Officer Shoemaker of S.S. *Fort Mims,* and the bright lights seen by Second Officer Rabeau on a voyage from Portugal to Boston which were either the Aurora Borealis wandering far south or some strange afterglow.

Even the backs of these charts are covered with some topical subject vividly illustrated with pictures, verse and quotations, such as the poet Virgil's views on birds as weather prophets, or the pilot of a DC4 airliner's impressions of a tempest. There is only one serious fault in these pilot charts, which is that their modest cost of thirty cents is hard currency for yachtsmen outside the dollar area.

XIII

Wind and Sea

THE strategy of a cruise is planned largely on the general movement of the air masses and ocean currents. Hour to hour tactics, which in a military sense are defined as movements in the presence of the enemy, depend chiefly on the local wind and sea.

Wind.

Wind is the horizontal movement of air over the earth's surface. At the height of a yacht's sail its speed and direction are influenced by four factors:

(a) The movement of air from high pressure to low pressure areas, at a speed in proportion to the pressure gradient.

(b) The earth's rotation which continuously tends to deflect a moving body at right angles to its line of motion. This is due to the geostrophic force and although this can be calculated by anyone with a sound knowledge of the differential calculus besides a few more mathematical tricks, even the keenest yachtsman does not yet carry a 'geostrophometer' at the mast head (if there is such a thing). In the northern hemisphere the deflection is to the right, in the southern hemisphere to the left.

(c) The centrifugal force on the moving air when its track is circular, such as round a depression.

(d) The friction between the wind and the earth's surface. This is most when the surface is hilly land, and least when it is smooth sea.

The wind on a sail is therefore affected by such changing and complex forces that it is constantly varying both in strength and direction.

Turbulence.

The continuous gusting and shifting of the actual surface wind is known as turbulence. To a sailing vessel the amount of turbulence is almost as important as the mean strength of the wind. For instance a mean wind of 20 knots (Force 5), gusting between 6 knots and 34, puts more strain on a yacht's equipment than a steady wind of Force 7, gusting between 28 knots and 32.

The amount of air turbulence depends on three factors:

(a) The speed of the wind.

(b) The rate of fall of temperature with altitude, called lapse-rate.

(c) The surface of the sea.

In a typhoon off the China coast in 1937, which I was able to observe closely, a stationary anemometer showed winds gusting to 164 knots and lulling to 60 knots at the height of the storm; that represents a pressure on a square foot disc alternating between 80 and 14 pounds, owing to this exceptional turbulence. The anemometer trace showed that the wind speed later varied between 100 knots and zero every few seconds over a period of nearly two hours. It is this turbulence that makes a hurricane force wind so utterly different from the effect of standing up clear of the wind-screen in a car going seventy miles an hour.

Polar air has a large lapse-rate and accordingly makes for turbulent conditions. This is often apparent in the cold front of the depressions that form on the polar front and move eastward across the oceans, giving cold squally winds that in the northern hemisphere are often from the north-west. The log of *Samuel Pepys* on 16th July, 1952, in mid-Atlantic showed that at midnight a very shallow trough of low pressure passed over with a cold front; this gave no more than a trace of rain, but a wind shift brought in a breeze varying between calm and 20 knots, which the helmsman likened to sailing on the upper Thames in a dinghy that sometimes lay becalmed in the lee of a building, and at others forged ahead as the wind slipped through a gap.

Tropical maritime air has a small lapse-rate, and therefore brings winds steady both in strength and direction, such as the trades. In the north-east Monsoon which blows tropical maritime air undisturbed over a thousand miles of the sea, it was normal at one time to race dinghies in Trincomalee harbour with full mainsails until the anemometer reached 28 knots—the lower limit of Force 7. This was only possible because no gust would exceed 30 knots and no lull drop to 25.

The particular discomfort of the Doldrums to a sailing vessel is caused by the small pressure gradient giving very light winds, with the high lapse-rate of equatorial air giving great turbulence unlike the stable conditions of tropical maritime air. Thunder clouds at any time give an indication of a high lapse-rate and warn of the presence of turbulence and squalls.

Disturbance of the sea surface only affects the air for a short distance above it, but this is the stratum that interests the small sailing craft. In coastal waters it is often noticed how the turn of the tide seems to increase the wind strength, although in fact the mean wind is unchanged, but the turbulence is greater. In the open ocean a heavy sea will increase the turbulence of the air; this is particularly noticeable in the Gulf Stream whose current, sometimes running locally at 5 knots, often causes a confused sea; yet as soon as a yacht crosses out of the fast running waters of the Stream, not only does the sea at once become more placid but the wind feels more modest as well.

It is an utter fallacy to believe that open waters always enjoy steady winds.

Measurement of wind.

Wind strength is measured by the Beaufort scale, in which the various Forces represent mean wind velocity at a height of 33 feet above the sea. The correct Beaufort scale number does not show the force of the strongest gust, which will be an amount greater than the mean depending on the turbulence. In the typhoon mentioned in the last page the anemometer recording, during the height of the storm, showed that the mean wind speed was 110 knots, or Force 17 on the Beaufort scale, although two gusts exceeded 160 knots.

As a very general guide, in cyclonic winds above gale force the fiercest gusts will be about 40 per cent higher than the mean wind force. Conversely a yachtsman noting an actual wind velocity of 50 knots by the anemometer at his masthead should not record the wind as Force 10, which is a whole gale; it may well be only Force 7, which is not a gale at all. Very close to the surface of the sea the wind strength will be far less than the mean velocity of 33 feet, so the reading of a hand anemometer held by a man in the cockpit will give no true comparison with the Beaufort figure; on one occasion with a moderate wind in the open sea, sails were lowered and a hand anemometer held 16 feet up the mast recorded 35 per cent higher than another identical instrument held 3 foot 6 inches above the sea level, yet well above the gunwale of the boat.

Measuring wind strength from the synoptic chart.

A good check on the estimated wind can be read off the synoptic chart, that is, the chart showing at any moment the positions of isobars, for any position within the area of ample reporting stations. This actually gives the geostrophic wind, which is approximately the wind speed at 2,000 feet altitude and is comparatively steady in velocity. The relationship between the geostrophic wind and Beaufort scale wind at an altitude of 33 feet is variable as it depends on turbulence. However, a reasonably accurate approximation can be made, and at least it will be possible to see when the wind has been grossly over-estimated, which is a very common occurrence aboard a small yacht. As isobars are drawn at intervals of 4 millibars on the synoptic chart, Fig. XIII, 1, has been calculated to show the approximate Beaufort scale wind at different latitudes by measuring the distance apart of these isobars. It

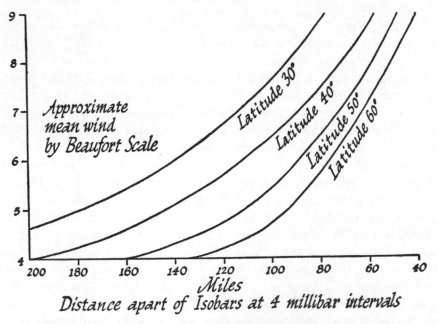

Fig. XIII, 1. Approximate wind in different latitudes read off the synoptic chart

will be seen that to produce a certain wind force in high latitudes the isobars must come closer together than in low latitudes; conversely a certain pressure gradient will cause a stronger wind to blow in the tropics than it would cause in the British Isles.

The pressure gradient cannot be found by a single observer. For instance, a yacht near the centre of an intense stationary depression would experience a nearly steady barometer, although there was a steep pressure gradient giving very strong winds.

It is of great interest after a voyage to compare the yacht's log with the daily synoptic charts, particularly at the times bad weather threatened or was experienced. This not only enables a check to be made on wind estimations, but also assists weather forecasting on future cruises. For the North Atlantic ocean these can be obtained for 2½d. from the Meteorological Office, London.

Sea.

An active disturbance on the surface of the water is normally known to the seaman as 'sea'. He does not use the word 'wave' for this overall description as in certain circumstances, particularly in a storm, the state of the surface is too utterly chaotic to be composed of recognisable waves, but is more a conflict of many waves of different characters.

Swell.

Swell is the dying disturbance after the wind has stopped blowing, or when waves emerge from the generating area. Instruments can record swell coming from disturbances many thousands of miles away and travelling at half the speed of the wind that generated it. In the zones of the westerlies swell very seldom runs ahead of a storm to give warning of its approach, but swell gives a good indication of the general weather conditions, particularly when a depression passes on the polar side of the vessel. In tropical regions swell is one of the most valuable warnings of the presence of a revolving storm.

Waves.

Simple waves, or undulations on the surface of the sea, behave according to known mathematical formulae. These perfect waves only occur in practice in the form of swell coming from an area of strong winds to pass through an area of near calms. However, modified wave form makes up the sea under most conditions.

The simple wave has four characteristics, as shown in Fig. XIII, 2. First there is its length, which is the distance from one crest to the next. In practice it is easy grossly to under-estimate wave-length, particularly from the height of eye in a small craft's cockpit. Then there is the period of the wave, which is the time it takes for two succeeding crests to pass a fixed point; it can be measured by recording with a stopwatch the

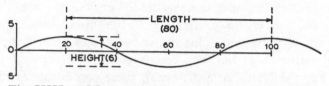

Fig. XIII, 2. Measurements (in feet) of a simple wave

time interval between one crest and the next passing a floating object or a foam-patch. Next comes the speed of the wave, which is very hard to guess in a slow-moving craft. However, these three factors, length, period and speed are all interconnected, so that if one is known the others are readily calculated. As the period is the easiest to measure from a yacht, the other two may be ascertained by formulae as follows:

Length in feet $= 5.1 \times$ (Period in seconds)^2

Speed in knots $= 3 \times$ Period in seconds

The last, and perhaps most important, characteristic of the wave is its height, measured vertically from trough to crest. It is not connected mathematically with the other factors, as a swell wave will run on for hundreds of miles maintaining its length, speed and period, but gradually losing height at the rate of half the wave height every time it travels a distance in miles equivalent to its length in feet; thus an 8-foot wave 500 feet long will be 4 feet high after 500 miles and 2 feet high after a thousand miles. Wave height can best be measured at sea by taking up a position in the vessel so that when she is upright in a trough the wave crest appears in line with the horizon; the height of eye then gives the wave height.

Movement of water in a wave.

Until the wave begins to break, the water does not travel along with the wave, but a particle of water on the surface will move forward with the crest, and come back an equal amount with the trough. The maximum velocity at the crest of the wave is given by the formula:

$$\text{Velocity in knots} = \frac{2 \times \text{Wave height in feet}}{\text{Period in seconds}}$$

Thus the maximum speed of water at the crest of a wave 300 feet long and 12 feet high would be 3.2 knots.

Creation of waves.

The factors influencing the creation of simple wind waves are the velocity of the wind, the time it had been blowing, and the fetch, or distance to windward in which it is blowing over the sea. The fetch may be limited by land to windward or by the comparatively local extent of the wind's influence. Within coastal waters the size of the waves is usually limited by fetch; in the open sea the size is chiefly limited by wind velocity.

In practice the turbulence of the wind creates a variety of waves of different lengths, which grow in height, rapidly at first and then at a lesser rate. The length of waves forming increases at a slower rate than the height, so they become steeper until the limiting steepness is reached when the mean height is about one twelfth of the length. After this any further energy supplied by the wind causes the wave to break.

Figures XIII, 3, 4 and 5 show the growth of waves under certain

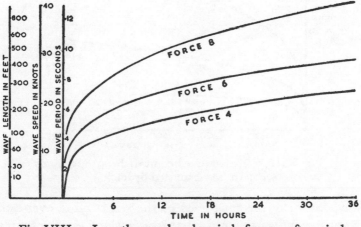

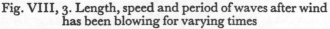

Fig. VIII, 3. Length, speed and period of waves after wind
has been blowing for varying times

theoretical conditions. An approximation to these conditions will usually be experienced in practice.

Table XIII*a* shows the actual characteristics of waves compared with the apparent wave experienced by a moving yacht. It is clear

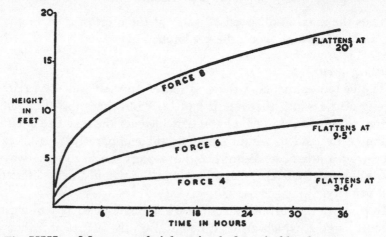

Fig. XIII, 4. Mean wave height gained after wind has been blowing for varying times with unlimited fetch

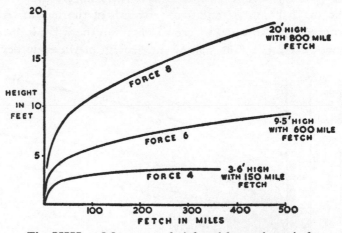

Fig. XIII, 5. Mean wave height with varying winds when the sea is limited by fetch

from the table why the roughness of the sea is often over-estimated when going to windward; for instance in a short sea (for the open ocean) of 82 feet wave-length a small yacht beating to windward would meet

Plate 17. A big wave breaking is awe-inspiring, but in the open sea it is relatively safe for a well handled small craft

Plate 18. A craft which runs for shelter may not see from outside that the harbour entrance is as dangerous as this

Plate 19. Big strains come on the spars and rigging as the main boom dips with *Rapparee* of 42·5 ft. overall running under spinnaker in a stiff wind off Beachey Head

Plate 20. Cutting out the damaged section of a metal spar in *Bolero* of 73 ft. overall before rebuilding it at sea of aluminium, wood and resin glass

perhaps seventeen waves a minute, while the same vessel running would be overtaken by only some seven waves a minute.

Apparent frequency of Waves from yacht		Actual Wave		
Running at 6 knots	Close hauled (48 degrees to wind) at 4.5 knots	Period	Length	Speed
Seconds	Seconds	Seconds	Feet	Knots
8	3.2	4	82	12
8.2	4.1	5	125	15
8.5	5.1	6	184	18
9.8	Too rough	7	250	21
10.4		8	326	24
11.3		9	413	27
12.0		10	510	30
13.0		11	617	33
14.0		12	734	36

Table XIIIa. Apparent and actual wave characteristics

Table XIIIb shows the mean waves that might be expected in the open ocean after various winds have been blowing for certain times, starting from a calm sea. Nature ridicules averages, and the seaman is concerned with the extreme sea that may endanger his vessel; in practice it is likely that the highest wave will be forty per cent greater than the mean, or higher still when such factors as currents affect the movement of the water. With the stronger winds the wave height will usually be limited by fetch in the open sea; thus a Force 8 gale will only raise 17 feet high mean waves in twenty-four hours if the wind is blowing over the sea for 500 miles to windward; a Force 6 strong breeze needs a fetch of 200 miles to reach 8.5 feet in the same time.

Rough sea.

In a strong wind waves of different lengths, and therefore velocities, build up to form a rough sea. The fastest waves will move at the speed of the wind forming them, and possibly even faster, but these waves are low and have only a small influence on the sea. The predominant waves, which are the highest, will probably work up to about two-thirds of the wind speed, but the varying velocities of different wave systems

M

will cause them to ride up on the tops of one another so that the maximum height of the sea will normally rise to 1.4 times the height of the predominant waves.

Size of waves.

In the North Atlantic waves up to 600 feet length, whose velocity would be about 33 knots, are quite usual; in the Southern Ocean, where the Roaring Forties storm unhindered by any land, waves are often as

Time wind has blown (From calm)	Mean wave height in open sea in feet				
	4	6	7	8	10 on Beaufort scale
1 hour	1.0	2.5	4	5.5	9.5
2 ,,	1.2	3.2	5	7.5	11.5
4 ,,	1.6	4.0	6	9	15
6 ,,	1.8	5.0	7.5	11.5	19
12 ,,	2.4	6.0	9	13.5	22
20 ,,	3.0	8.5	11.5	17	
3 days	4.5	11.0	17	20	

NOTE.—Actual highest wave would be 40% higher in normal conditions.

Table XIII*b*. Mean wave heights in the open sea with different winds blowing for varying times, assuming unlimited fetch

long as 1,000 feet moving at 44 knots. The difficulty of measuring wave height means that opinions differ about the sizes of the largest waves. Several estimates of North Atlantic winter waves have exceeded 75 feet, such as that from S.S. *Majestic* in 1923 when the wave crests showed above the horizon on her bridge, 89 feet from the water-line. There is little doubt that waves higher than 40 feet are very exceptional, and only occur when gales blow from the same quarter for several days, or in a hurricane. In summer cruising in the North Atlantic a 20-foot high wave is about the tallest normal limit, except for areas such as the Gulf Stream where the character of the sea is made so much more complex by current. Low waves are often under-estimated, while high waves are almost invariably exaggerated.

In a small yacht the difficulty of climbing up the mast will usually limit wave measurement to about 20 feet, but the occasions when this is insufficient will be very few; for instance during winter and summer combined, only 15 per cent of all wave heights in the North Atlantic or Southern Ocean exceed 20 feet. When the wave height exceeds 20 feet, the imagination tends to overwhelm careful observation in a small craft.

Shift of wind.

A system of waves that has any semblance of regularity is not dangerous to a small yacht if properly handled, until the waves reach the stage of breaking heavily.

However, when the wind shifts appreciably, the disturbance from the old wind becomes swell, and the new wind will build up a different wave system that conflicts with the swell. The resulting sea will be confused, and the quicker the wind shift the heavier will be the confusion of the sea. Some of the most dangerous seas to small craft are caused by the rapid change of wind near the centre of a cyclonic disturbance, the worst of all being in a tropical revolving storm, when hurricane force winds may shift ten to twelve points within a few minutes.

Effect of currents on sea.

It is well known how in coastal waters the tide setting against the wind steepens the seas by reducing the wave-length. When the tidal stream runs fast enough to cause overfalls, such as off Portland Bill or in the Pentland Firth, a contrary gale raises seas that are really dangerous. Precisely the same thing can happen when a fast running ocean current causes overfalls; the most outstanding example is the Gulf Stream where so many yachtsmen cruising round the world have reported their worst weather.

On a calm day, without enough breeze to flicker a match flame, the Gulf Stream simmers in irregular patches, some perhaps only fifty yards across. It is always restless, and the first gentle breeze kicks up a sea out of all proportion to the wind force. Thus *Samuel Pepys* could sail within 44 degrees of a Force 3 breeze in calm inshore waters, yet found on occasion in the Gulf Stream that she could only point within 70 degrees of a similar breeze, due to the troubled sea, and strong tide relative to the wind speed.

In a gale the Gulf Stream is one of the most magnificent and frightening spectacles in all the ocean. The waves seem too impatient to form into ranks with long crests, instead the sea becomes a mass of separate steep crests, each moving independently, and breaking haphazardly. Occasionally two converging ridges will meet with a violent smack and rear up in a sharp-featured pinnacle or clapotis. The crests, which are too short to justify the name of waves, mount so steeply that in sunshine shades of azure glow beneath the frothing white tops as the light shines through from above. When the sky is gloomy, such crests look vertical-faced as they mount over the stern of the yacht, while the vivid white plume, outshining the dark bosom of the sea, makes the whole wave look as though it is overlapping. Only when the waves are seen sideways-on is it possible to judge the gradient of the face, which is then seen to be much less than it appears when seen from beneath it in the trough (see Plate 14).

Often a swell is noticeable across the direction of the wind, but at times it will be quite smothered by the wildly boiling crests, so that one loses sense of direction and feels that the wind has suddenly shifted.

Breaking seas.

The greatest open water danger of all comes from heavy breaking seas. Then a large mass of water moves forward at the speed of the wave or even faster, in the same way as waves break on a beach. The violence of the wave-break varies with the height of the breaking top and the square of the wave velocity. Fortunately it is seldom the longest, and therefore fastest, waves that break in a storm, but usually the predominant waves that reach about two-thirds of the wind speed.

Some accounts record the whole face of a wave breaking, which is certainly the appearance of a wave breaking a little distance astern when the spray surges forward down the trough. However, no vessel could survive the onslaught of a wall of water perhaps 40 feet high and moving at 35 knots. Seen from the side it is clear that only a comparatively small portion of the total wave height curls over and breaks. Graham recorded in the Gulf Stream towards the end of a three-day November gale, up to Force 9, that the breaking tops appeared to him to be 5 feet high when the height of the sea was 30 to 40 feet; aboard *Samuel Pepys* in nearly the same position after three days of gale, reaching Force 12, it was estimated that the tallest breaking tops were 6 to 8 feet with seas up to 40 feet high.

From the cockpits of such small craft it is most unlikely the breaking wave tops were under-estimated. From a very large ship, hove-to in the Bay of Biscay in December when it had been blowing Force 12 by instruments for an hour after many days of wintry gales, I estimated breaking tops as 6 feet high; when the wind rapidly eased to less than gale force as it veered eight points, the breaking tops were estimated to be 7 feet high, with the wave height 38 feet.

Effect of very strong wind and heavy rain.

In very strong winds the violence of turbulent gusts is sufficient to scoop the tops off the waves, tending to flatten the crests and reduce their danger. When this happens the dense cloud of driving spray makes it impossible to differentiate between air and water. The effect is even more marked in heavy rain, and more so still in hail. In the Gulf Stream in June I have seen an unpleasant sea about 8 feet high battered into near calm within five minutes by an exceptionally violent hail squall blowing at gale force. As the squall eased and the hail gave way to light rain, the sea increased again.

In a severe storm the most dangerous seas are sometimes encountered after the wind has begun to ease.

Noise.

Apart from any other effect of wind and sea on a yacht, the noise of a storm has an appreciable effect on her handling. Not only does it prevent any spoken word on deck, but it may even make communication by voice impossible below. Worse than this, the shrieking of the wind over a long period, intermingled with the savage snarl of the breaking wave, is a heavy strain on the human nerves.

XIV

Bad Weather

THOSE who venture on long sea passages will almost inevitably meet a gale at some time and, although this will be a rare event, it is an important factor in the design of the craft, her gear and her organisation. A gale must be as much a routine matter to the deep water yachtsman, even if uncomfortable and perhaps slightly dangerous, as is a fire to the fireman.

Oddly enough it is not the invigorating fast sails under perfect conditions, or even inspiring coastal scenery, that leave the most lasting experience on the mind. Years afterwards the fierce grandeur of a gale at close quarters is remembered in every minute detail, just as it struck the mind at the time. Calms at sea also carry the same vivid memories for those who do not motor away and leave the experience untasted.

Rough sea and gale.

To the deep seaman who is particular about precise classifications a rough sea means that the waves are some 14 feet high, and a gale means a sustained wind speed at a height of 33 feet above the water of at least 34 knots. This does not make him respect any the less the furious seas which may be bred in the Solent, although they could only be classed as slight by the textbook; nor the wild gales that are bred in every yacht club bar, although they are known to the Meteorological Office as yachtsmen's gales.

Stark figures from the Meteorological Office show that at Portland Bill, fully exposed to all winds, there are on average only 1.2 gales throughout the whole four months of May, June, July and August; the Scilly Islands only manage 1.5 gales in all these 123 days. Cruising in such coastal waters within the normal summer season there is no need to meet rough seas at all if the yachtsman heeds to the radio forecasts that ensure no gale occurs without a warning, even if some six warnings occur without a gale.

The fact is that until ocean racing forced the need to go to sea on a definite date and perhaps remain there for two or three days on end, really rough weather was quite unknown to most yachtsmen, except the very few who ventured into the oceans. The averages show that you must remain at sea in the Channel for about a hundred whole summer days to get a full gale; my experience seems to follow this rule, as having spent five days a week at sea during several years in the Channel and Irish Sea, I then experienced only two summer gales in those waters; they were twelve years apart and each lasted under three hours. Nor did the coastal sailing trawler often experience real gales, as their meagre profit would have disappeared had they risked sailing gear and nets in these conditions.

The result of this common ignorance of gale conditions in a yacht is that bad weather is feared more than is justified. Encountering even a modest blow is considered as being 'Caught out' and often in the past those who told of their success in riding out a gale were those with sufficient imagination to create the gale, and at the same time created fearful counter-measures that were more frightening than the gale itself. It was rather as though, never having seen the savage Cyclops that they feared, the local inhabitants surrounded his cave with obstacles that would trip *them* up if he should look out.

None of this implies that it is not extremely tough-going to beat to windward in a fresh wind blowing up-Channel over the spring-tide ebb; but little real danger is essential, as it is simple enough to stop thrashing to windward. Portland Race can be hell in a modest breeze, so can pounding ashore on the Long Sand shoal in a moderate easter. The art of pilotage should avoid either of these situations.

Bad weather seamanship.

Bad weather seamanship, in the strict sense of handling a vessel at sea, only really starts when she is too far off-shore to run back to the shelter of the land. It is the most satisfying art of all, as success depends entirely on the men aboard, with the vessel they have selected and prepared; it is too late then to wish for something different, and there is no possibility of consulting anyone else. No sport is more magnificent than deep water sailing in bad weather and none requires more courage, nor sustained effort of body and mind; nor does any pay a bigger dividend to careful preparation.

Effects of bad weather on small craft.

The safety of his vessel and crew must always be her master's first consideration when sailing for pleasure, so it is important to discuss just what dangers are involved in bad weather.

Loss of men overboard is by far the most imminent danger in a gale. In the first Transatlantic of 1886 six men were lost in this way and ever since then the sport of sailing has seen a steady toll of life from this cause. Once a man is separated from the yacht his chance of survival is small, and the yacht's crew may be seriously weakened by his absence. This most vital of all rough weather seamanship is controlled by organisation, design and equipment far more than the actual handling of the craft at the time. It is dealt with in some detail in the various chapters on these subjects, besides that on personal safety.

Damage to equipment may occur due to the strength of the wind, the violence of the yacht's motion or the weight of the sea. This damage may be to masts, spars and rigging on deck, besides such equally important matters as cooking apparatus below. Up to a certain limit this can be controlled by suitable equipment, maintained in perfect condition, and securely rigged or stowed. However, beyond that limit, the stresses and strains are greater than the equipment can withstand. When cruising it should be possible to keep well within these limits by reducing the strains in good time; it is as unseamanlike to have equipment that is too heavy for the crew to control as it would be to fit a rudder that will only steer the ship under simple conditions.

In racing off-shore the situation is very different. E. G. Martin wrote, 'The chief difficulty in sailing a good race lies in judging rightly the moment when legitimate hard driving becomes recklessness.' This judgement requires seamanship of the highest degree; the decision requires an accurate assessment of the ability of the crew, just as much as the strength of the gear; the crew contains far more variable factors. Many ocean racing skippers must remember occasions when in retrospect they realise that the ship was eased more than necessary, and perhaps more than their opponents' vessels; probably the same ones will also remember occasions when they drove men or material beyond their limits.

The greatest danger is not so much the actual damage from the gale, which may be considerable, but the effect of this damage starting off a train of accidents. It is when grappling with a sheetless sail, shaken as though the wind were some giant terrier doing it to death like a rat, that men go over the side; it is the struggle for hours with an ill-secured dinghy or damaged spar that leaves the crew so exhausted that the storm seems more violent and even the will to fight for the safety of the ship flags.

Overwhelming of the ship by the violence of the waves breaking over her and damaging her hull is a danger which is controlled to the largest extent by the actual handling of the ship at the time. Large vessels have been seriously damaged, and even lost, in seas that would have been perfectly safe had they been handled differently. Running for shelter, or perhaps racing for harbour to land a good catch of fish, must have cost many lives and ships. Size is absolutely no criterion of safety, but shape has an important effect.

Speed.

Danger to men, equipment and hull is largely dependent on the speed of the vessel in bad weather. If she is stationary, or nearly stationary, little harm will be done even in very bad conditions, at least until the breaking tops of the waves exceed the height of the vessel's freeboard; this is likely to mean a whole gale (Force 10), except in areas where the current is running rapidly in a different direction from that of the wind. When sailing on the wind it is obvious when the vessel is driving too fast, as she will pound violently, perhaps bury her nose into the waves, and minor damage will begin to occur. When running it is less obvious, the speed is exhilarating, and sometimes the yacht will race ahead, wave-riding with the sea frothing up on either side of the deck; then no clear warning or damage occurs until she is seriously pooped, and may broach-to under the next wave. Surf boards can ride on the wave tops for long distances, but no full-bodied sailing vessel can hope to do this in the open sea for more than two or three seconds and then only when the waves are comparatively short; a 400-foot long wave moves at 25 knots, so it is an obvious fallacy to hope to avoid pooping by keeping up with the speed of the waves.

When a vessel is near her maximum a small increase of speed will make a big difference to her wake; conversely when running, a slight easing of the spread of canvas may make her progress very much safer.

Pooping.

Pooping occurs when the stern fails to rise to an overtaking wave. Although the wave cascades over the stern of the yacht, pooping is controlled by the whole shape of the vessel from bow to stern; it is not just a matter of buoyancy in the extreme after part of the vessel but of the fore and aft motion of the yacht as a whole. It is probably a matter of the momentum, which is proportional to the square of the speed, that the faster the yacht is travelling the more likely she is to get out of step with the wave, and her stern may then fail to lift in time. The decision when to ease speed while running must be largely a matter of experience, but it is certainly possible to gauge the feel of a yacht's movement, and realise when she is beginning to 'get above herself' instead of conforming to the movement of the waves.

A yacht may also be pooped when a steep wave breaks over her stern. Then there is no chance of her stern rising to the wave, whose vertical or even curling face is higher than her freeboard. Again speed is an important factor, as the wake from a fast moving vessel invites an uncertain wave crest to break just in that position where it does most harm; the greater the disturbance of the wake the more this effect is noticeable.

Heaving-to.   (See Fig. XIV, 1.)

This is not necessarily a rough weather evolution, but a simple method to checking the yacht's speed without lowering the sails. She is steadied by the pressure of the wind and makes very little headway, while moving slowly to leeward. It does not require a yacht with a long keel, nor any particular rig, to heave-to; most well designed yachts will do it readily, including light displacement vessels with short keels and high aspect ratio. In a sloop the headsail is backed by hauling aft the weather sheet, the mainsheet is checked, and the tiller secured a-lee; some cutters, particularly if they have a long bowsprit, will need to lower the jib before backing the staysail. It is not wise to heave-to for any length of time with an overlapping genoa, as this will be hauled against the weather shrouds and suffer chafe.

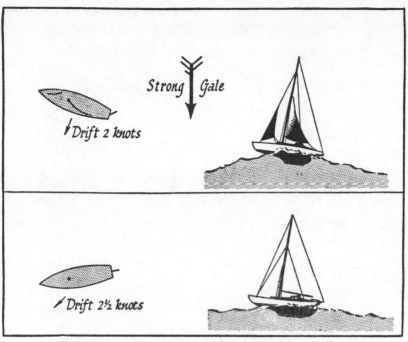

Fig. XIV. 1. Heaving-to with a backed headsail

2. Lying a-try across the sea

The real advantage of heaving-to in this way is that the vessel looks after herself, so if she is first put on the starboard tack to secure right of way, the crew can go below to rest or prepare a meal with the least amount of motion on the boat. She is perfectly safe until the wind force puts too heavy a strain on her gear, or the breaking tops of the waves become too high. E. G. Martin recorded that he hove-to safely in the 52-foot square-sterned *Chance* for forty-eight hours in the North Sea when the wind averaged from 65 to 78 miles an hour. The fetch would probably have limited the wave height on this occasion, but this was a hurricane of Force 12, described by Beaufort as 'that wind which no canvas will withstand', so perhaps the sail-maker has improved his art since the Admiral produced his scale in 1806.

Hove-to literally means to stop the vessel, but the same tactic can also be used to reduce her speed when on the wind. When cruising there may come a time when the discomfort of pounding into the waves is unacceptable or, when racing, it may be that there is fear of her seams

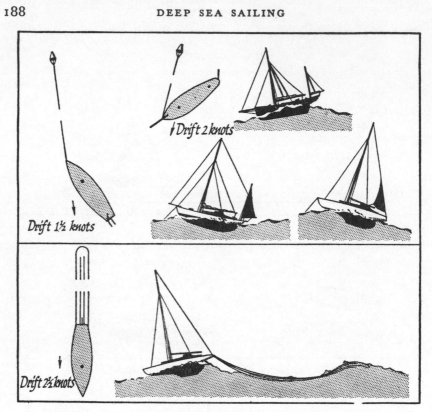

Fig. XIV, 3. Lying to a sea anchor with or without a steadying sail

4. Stern to sea with warps streamed

opening up; then it often happens that a small reduction in her speed by taking some weight on the weather jib sheet will stop the pounding. During the Wolf Rock race of 1949 I sailed *Minx of Malham*, 30 feet overall length, to windward in a Force 8 wind with a fairly steep moderate (12 foot high) sea; under trisail and storm jib she pounded so heavily sailing at 4 knots that it was impossible even to remain lying in the lee bunk, and the piledriver action as she leapt off the steep tops felt as though it would drive the mast through the keel. With the storm jib partly backed her speed came down to 3 knots and she sailed to windward in a way that might not have been considered comfortable to everyone, but at least could do no harm.

Lying a-try or a-hull.   (See Fig. XIV, 2.)

This is another simple tactic which consists of lowering all sail and letting the yacht drift where she will. She will normally lie broadside on to the sea, presenting her greatest buoyancy to the waves, while in strong winds the resistance of mast and cabin-top will help to steady her. She will roll more than when hove-to under backed head sail, and her drift to leeward will be greater. Aboard *Samuel Pepys,* 30 feet long with a 6-foot deep keel, lying a-try in wind Force 8, the leeway was estimated as $2\frac{1}{2}$ knots and her forward motion about $\frac{3}{4}$ knot.

Oil can be used to some advantage when lying a-try as it spreads out to windward to give some protection; however, the slight forward speed of the yacht will prevent the surface film from being fully effective. A deep keeled yacht normally lies more comfortably a-try than does a very shallow one, which, having less grip on the water, skids about the waves less happily.

Lying a-try is effective in full gale conditions, and perhaps even worse. However, a wind Force 12 would exert a thrust of some two tons on a typical 45-foot long sloop and heel her far over to leeward; also once the breaking tops of the waves are higher than a yacht's freeboard, it would be folly to offer the whole length of the ship to them, and the safest course in such survival conditions is to offer the least resistance to wind and waves by presenting the bow or stern.

Lying to a sea anchor.   (See Fig. XIV, 3.)

Unaided the sea anchor will not keep any normally designed yacht head to wind; even the three masted dug-out canoe *Tilikum* lay five points off the wind under a sea anchor without any sail hoisted, and the naval whaler lies much the same with a keel nearly as long as her gunwale.

The sea anchor is normally used in conjunction with a mizzen, so as to lie pointing closer to the wind. Voss records that by setting a leg-of-mutton spanker on his mizzen mast with the sheet hauled hard in, *Tilikum* could lie within two-and-a-half points of the wind. Even if a yacht has a mizzen mast it is hard to set an effective riding sail as opposed to a driving sail, while in a single-masted yacht it is more difficult still.

In trials under fresh wind conditions in a small sloop with pronounced cut away stem, it was found that she lay broadside on to the sea when a-try, while when the sea anchor was streamed right forward, she actually turned away and lay with the sea anchor and wind on her quarter. This agrees with Claud Worth's experience as illustrated by a diagram in *Yacht Cruising*.

The sea anchor method has various disadvantages even aboard craft which will lie nearly head-on to the sea. The yacht is drifting astern, comparatively fast on the crest of a wave and not at all in the trough, which puts a severe alternating strain on the rudder. When I was lying to a sea anchor in the South China Seas aboard a naval whaler with only the mizzen mast stepped in wind Force 7, the rudder broke clean off. In 1951 *Nova Espero* had the same trouble sailing east-bound across the Atlantic, when her rudder was broken while the yacht was lying to a sea anchor. This accident also showed up another difficulty in that a vessel drifting astern is not under control and, with her broken rudder held over by the stern way, she seems to have broached-to stern first. Yet another limitation of the sea anchor is that it relies completely on a sail, so in really strong gales, such as that which no sail can withstand, the system is ineffective. Voss encountered such a severe wind sailing aboard *Sea Queen* in the Oya Siwo current off Japan, when he was lying to a sea anchor with a mizzen sail hoisted. The mizzen sheet parted, the sea anchor carried away, the yacht turned turtle and lost both her masts; but still Voss persisted that lying nearly head to sea with a sea anchor was the answer to the yachts-man's storm. *Vertue XXXV* was also lying to a sea anchor when she was dangerously damaged during extremely bad weather in the North Atlantic.

From all this it is hard to escape the conclusion that the sea anchor provides a good enough way of lying-to in the open sea, so long as the weather is not too bad. In coastal waters it has other good uses, such as checking drift when the crew cannot manage a yacht off a lee shore.

Stern to sea.   (See Fig. XIV, 4.)

If the bow cannot be pointed into the seas, the stern always can. The stern usually has less freeboard than the bows, and the after part of the cabin top or dog-house is normally the weakest as it is pierced for a hatch; with the wind and spray coming from aft it is more likely to be necessary to batten down than if it were coming from forward, and this means added discomfort. Yet the advantages of keeping stern

on to the seas in really bad conditions are such that this seems the only
method that has not given rise to some stirring drama of overcoming
damage and danger in wild seas; that is when the speed of the yacht
has been reduced to the minimum.

There is nothing new about the method. St. Paul records how his
ship was 'exceeding tossed with a tempest, and was let drive'; she was
only lost fourteen days later when she went aground approaching
the land under mainsail. Slocum was forced to this tactic although
it drove *Spray* straight towards Cape Horn when 'no ship in the world
could have stood up against so violent a gale'. He paid out two long
ropes to steady her course and to break combing seas astern; she
never shipped a sea. He reports 'even while the storm raged at its
worst, my ship was wholesome and noble'.

The ship remains under full control of the rudder, as she is moving
in the direction she was intended to go, and in sympathy with the sea.
In irregular seas, such as a Gulf Stream or Aghulha Current gale,
waves will come from directions differing as much as 40 degrees from
the mean, so it is valuable to be able to steer the stern into any menacing
steep crest. Running under bare pole without any brake the speed may
be too high to give safety from pooping. *Samuel Pepys*, whose rigging
is simple and windage reduced to a minimum, recorded her speed under
bare pole as 3.9 knots with wind Force 8; on another occasion with
wind Force 9, which represents a 45 per cent greater wind pressure
than with Force 8, her speed was logged as 5.3 knots. These speeds
would be much too high for her to run in heavily breaking seas,
although on neither of these occasions were the breaking tops dangerous.

Storm Warps.

The most effective way of reducing a yacht's speed when running
is to stream a warp astern in a bight with the two ends secured on each
side of the counter, the bigger the warp used, both in length and cir-
cumference, the more effective it is as a brake. This bight can be backed
up by streaming astern single warps with any objects like fenders or
sail bags attached.

The bight of rope moving slowly over the surface leaves a narrow
lane of comparatively calm water and tends to discourage waves from
breaking in the dangerous position just over the stern. Even in wind
Force 11 to 12, when the wind pressure is three times as great as for

Force 8, *Samuel Pepys* ran safely ahead of warps, and her crew noted many close up profiles of breaking waves tops 6 to 8 feet high, when the total wave height must have been over 30 feet; yet the warps seemed to prevent submarine views of such waves breaking over the stern.

A great advantage of streaming warps from aft compared with streaming anything from forward, particularly at night, is that all the work can be done either from or very close to the cockpit, and the warps remain under the immediate control of the cockpit. A disadvantage is that some ships will need to be steered throughout the storm; yet this may be no disadvantage at all as it seems rather an insult to a good gale to go below and wait for better sailing weather—an insult the gale might resent; besides this a storm, endured at such very close quarters as the cockpit of a yacht, is an experience that would prevent any man feeling his life had been dull, even if nothing ever happened to him again.

The best method of lying to a gale.

Each of the four methods of riding out a gale in a small craft has its strong advocates among really experienced sailing men. Comparisons are difficult, as once the wind is above the strengths we are accustomed to judge, it is well nigh impossible to gauge it correctly, unless a synoptic chart can be achieved afterwards that will give the probable wind force.

Every craft will behave in her own way under the same circumstances, and it may be quite different from that of any other vessel. Some boats will not lie a-try restfully, others will not heave-to comfortably, and some will only ride out a stiff gale safely in harbour.

An interesting comparison of the different methods is recorded by Commander Graham aboard *Emanuel*. He mentions that in a Gulf Stream gale in November his craft received heavy blows from the waves when lying a-try and hove-to; however after his mizzen had carried away and the yacht had been put before the wind with hawsers streamed astern, he could recollect no very severe shocks, nor did there appear to be any strain on the rudder.

Oil.

The use of oil for small craft in heavy weather is so well known that its value is obvious. Nor is it only very small craft that can benefit from it. Captain G. M. Fletcher told how one of his first jobs at sea as an apprentice had been to spread oil from the stern of a large unwieldy freighter as she steamed very slowly before a heavy Western Ocean winter gale. The method was to half fill the pan in the crew's head right aft, then give a pump or two every few minutes; each time he dozed off into a seasick coma, the heavy smack of a wave breaking over the stern, followed by a cold douse of sea through the door, would remind him of the value of pouring oil on troubled water.

The practical difficulty in the use of oil is to spread it over that portion of the sea where it will protect the vessel effectively. This is very difficult when lying to a sea anchor, so someone contrived an ingenious device with an endless whip running through a block on the sea anchor bridle; however, the gear looks so complicated to lay out from the fore deck of a yacht in rough weather, and ropes become so unmanageable when oil sodden, that it would be best done with the help of a motor launch in harbour!

With the yacht running really slowly before warps, the oil can either be pumped through the head, or if this effort and the cleaning afterwards is too laborious, it can be streamed on either quarter from oil bags or the cans suggested in Chapter III.

Simplicity.

The key to all rough weather handling of small vessels is careful preparation beforehand, and severe simplicity when the time for action comes. The noise of a storm at sea is such that not only are orders quite impossible, but the human mind loses practically all its power to direct the muscles in any operation with which they are not thoroughly familiar. The violence of the sea makes any physical movement a painful and strenuous effort; even getting a few feet from the cockpit to the bows is not just a couple of minutes' difficult crawl while holding on tight, it becomes a lengthy struggle for existence at the end of which a man is streaming with sweat in spite of periodic dousing into the waves. The cockpit feels the only safe base for operations on deck, and seems the safer if it is deep enough for the feet, knees and hips to get a grip inside; whether the cockpit is full of water or not is quite immaterial to safety in a yacht built with this intention, and a cockpit drain must be large if all the water is to escape before the next wave comes inboard.

Even in modest conditions, such as half a gale in the open sea,

N

everything is many times more difficult than when sailing in a quiet breeze, so the necessary evolutions should be correspondingly simpler. Lowering a heavy gaff in a heavy sea, even if the spar is sprouting with vangs and steadying tackles, is a hazard that would send up the wind force at least a couple of figures on the Beaufort scale in the mind of any normal being. Often the least efficient gear on deck is that for reefing, and requires a yacht chandler's store of purchases, reef earings, gallows and topping lift tackles, besides studding half the sail with Spanish pendants that anywhere else would deserve the highest condemnation as loose rope ends. So complicated is this reefing gear that the methods of its use for years provided one of the most regular topics of discussion in the yachting press.

Certainly in small craft roller reefing can be entirely efficient. It is so simple that its operation, when designed and fitted, cannot even provide a whole paragraph for a yachting author. To reef one has only to open the gate of the slide track, lower the main halyard with one hand, and turn the reefing handle with the other; the reverse process may be a little more difficult as occasionally it will be necessary to stand up to push the slides into the gate.

In nearly all yachts the halyards are efficient and simple, as they are frequently used. For this reason it is seamanlike to rely on the halyards as much as possible when varying the amount of sail to be set in brisk conditions.

My hell, should that be my destination, will have a truly diabolical torture. It will consist of incessant gales in a lumpish great yacht, no freeboard, gaff rigged, with a bowsprit half a cable long; it will have a giant sea anchor with tripping lines, outhauls, floats to keep it up and otter-boards to keep it down. The only variety from reefing the vast main-sail (with a thousand reef points and earings too large for their blocks) will be reefing the bowsprit, housing the topmast and building sea anchors out of polished cabin doors; all in raging gales that will persist until the job is done. Yet should I go to Heaven, surely there will still be an occasional brisk gale, rode out in a simple little yacht manned by such a perfect crew as accompanied me on various races across several seas and oceans.

Comfort and Health

THE success of any cruise will depend to a large degree upon the health and comfort of the crew. Comfort means satisfactory mental and physical conditions, which may well be quite different from amenities such as soft arm-chairs and bed-side lamps. Health is not so much a matter for the doctor, who deals with any failure in health, as straightforward seamanship in keeping the crew in good condition. Accidents may occur, and at sea a doctor cannot normally be called however serious the injury, so some preparation should be made for such a possibility; this is not a matter of first-aid but of 'only-hope', so there is little use in the type of first-aid book that in so many cases gives the action to be taken as 'apply a tourniquet and summon a doctor without delay'.

Clothing.

Probably clothing is the factor that affects physical comfort more than anything but food. In bad weather this is particularly so, and indirectly clothing has a big effect on the safety of the yacht.

The object of clothing is to keep the body warm and dry under a great variety of conditions and yet not restrict movement more than can be avoided. It is a difficult object to achieve as in some watches a man may sit for hours almost motionless in the cockpit, and in another he may, without warning, spend an hour or more working really hard on deck. It is important that a man should start his watch clothed ready for all that may occur, or at least with all necessary clothing immediately to hand. Otherwise he will be reluctant to do something he knows should be done, because it involves the extra effort of dressing up, or he will get wet and spend the rest of his watch in discomfort.

No single outfit of clothing has yet been devised that is adaptable enough for all conditions, and the heavy suits that combine outer and inner covering have the disadvantage that, when once thoroughly wet, they are very hard to dry in a small yacht.

The best compromise is an efficient waterproof outer coating, with a separate inner or warming layer provided by a variable number of jerseys, trousers and stockings to suit the occasion. Should any water leak through the outer skin, probably only one layer of inner clothing will need to be dried, and as it is comparatively thin it can readily be dried on the next suitable day. Duffel coats look impressive ashore with seaboots and a pipe, and they are a well-known convention for those who like to act a part on or off the stage, but they are very little use on a long voyage in a small craft, as they get wet very quickly and dry very slowly.

Waterproof clothing.

Waterproof clothing may consist either of the oilskin variety that prevents any passage of water in or out, or the finely woven cotton whose fibres swell when damp to become waterproof, yet when dry they will allow damp air to escape. In really heavy spray only the oilskin or plastic type will keep out the water for any length of time. Plastic on a linen base can be made light and flexible, yet really tough and durable, besides avoiding the hot-climate tackiness of the old-fashioned oilskin.

Almost as important as the material of the waterproof clothing is its fit. Ill-fitting weather clothing is a common cause of a miserable watch or reluctance to go forward to shift a headsail; while clumsy clothing is so difficult to get into when the yacht is moving actively that a man may arrive on deck exhausted. When the watch below are needed in a hurry, clumsy clothing means that either a man must go without it and get wet, or take so long that he is only in time to clear away the shreds into which the sail has disintegrated.

The long oilskin coat, even if it comes well below the knees, still leaves too attractive a gap for the sea to splash up from below. The hem must either be cut so tight that it will restrict movement or it will be so loose that the foot of the coat flies up in a wind and may catch in a block besides exposing a large amount of the inner clothing to the spray. For comfort on the exposed deck of a small yacht, waterproof trousers are essential, with a large overlap between them and the top garment to ensure a water-tight joint.

The top garment is best designed as a blouse to increase water-tightness, and the inner flaps of the sleeves need rubber sponge joints, as elastic cord is less comfortable and will not last so long. The most difficult joint to keep water-tight is the neck; no amount of scarves and towels will really overcome the persistent force of gravity that eventually urges any drop of sea within the oilskin collar down to the small of the back. The best solution is a hood fitting with a rubber sponge joint close round the face; the disadvantage is that little can be heard when the hood is over the head, but it can be lowered back off the face when spray is less than neck high. In strong winds with spray, the unprotected eye cannot look to windward, so a small peak to the hood is most effective, as appears to be the experience also of the various sea officers of different countries that have adopted a peaked cap as part of their uniform.

Footwear.

A normal pair of sea-boots weighs about seven pounds when empty, and a good deal more when full of water, but they are still excellent wear for muddy streets, or the wet deck of a big ship, aboard which the motion is moderate and the spacious decks are surrounded by really man-proof guard rails or life-lines. In a small sailing craft, where sure-footedness on deck is essential, something far lighter is needed. If the sea temperature makes it possible, the extra agility from light canvas shoes with non-skid soles makes them the best footwear. For colder seas a really light rubber boot with non-skid soles is the best alternative.

Bare feet are most convenient in hot climates, but the toes need to be well hardened before they can tolerate collisions with the many things on deck that invariably get in their way on a dark night. It is worth remembering that the tops of one's feet seem particularly susceptible to sunburn until tanned.

Gloves.

Fleece-lined leather gloves that are so excellent for motoring, or even driving a power craft from a sheltered position, cannot be kept water-tight and quickly fill up, after which they are difficult to dry out. Gloves may have to be taken off quickly for any job requiring detailed manipulation, so a gauntlet with a strap will not do. The best solution is wool, which will still provide some warmth to the hands even when soaking wet.

Sleep.

Sleep is essential eventually, even if a man can go on for a long time without it. One of the most valuable assets to a seaman is being able to snatch sleep in small quantities at any time of day or night.

When racing it is the principal functions of the skipper to make the best use of the energy supply of his crew, which can only be re-charged by sleep; it is bad racing tactics, and perhaps even bad seamanship, to overdrive the crew until the reserves of energy are exhausted. However, sometimes, perhaps at the critical point in an exciting race, the supply may run very low; equally when cruising there may be times of particular trial, such as struggling out from a lee coast-line in bad weather, that exhaust the crew unduly.

The unfortunate thing is that over-exhaustion often prevents sleep, and so delays the re-generation of energy. Under these conditions it might be advisable to use a sedative such as Seconal that will produce drowsiness but not interfere with simple action if really needed. Naturally it should not be given to the whole crew at once, but if a proportion are helped to sleep well in this way, after a few hours they will be fit to resume their full duties again.

Often the ability to sleep is reduced by cold in a wet bunk, so that the cure of this state is not just a matter that affects the individual using the bunk, but indirectly the safe handling of the ship. Persistent deck leaks can often be deflected from a bunk by drip screens, or strips of canvas secured temporarily by drawing pins, that will lead the water down where it is less of a menace.

There is little difficulty about keeping awake for long periods in an emergency but if the excitement is not enough Benzedrine tablets could be used. These require a medical prescription, and should be handled with the usual care for such drugs. They delay sleep, and can therefore only safely be used for an emergency of limited strength, with the certain knowledge that the emergency will be followed by a quiet time for sleep.

Wind sails.

In a hot climate the atmosphere below decks can become so oppressive that sleep or work is impractical. This is especially so in such conditions as running before the Trade Winds, when the wind velocity is small relative to the hull, and the sun is nearly overhead at noon. A white hull is much better than a dark-coloured one, as white reflects the heat while black absorbs it; it is also helpful to keep the decks wet with a mop.

However, the greatest relief comes from the use of a wind sail, a canvas screen or trunking that directs the wind down the hatch. If this is rigged over the fore-hatch it is quite astonishing what a difference is made to the atmosphere below decks, even when scarcely any wind can be felt passing over the deck.

Washing.

Salt water soap, such as Tepol, is quite effective in removing dirt and grease. Few things are more conducive to discomfort in a small vessel than greasy crockery and cabin soles. Most soapless detergents, such as Tide, are effective for clothes and personal washing in salt water, but it is pleasant if both clothes and the men can sometimes be rinsed in fresh water, such as a shower of rain.

Cockroaches.

These pests will inevitably come aboard in hot climates, usually in the form of eggs amongst fresh vegetables, and hatch out into tiny cockroaches soon after they get aboard. If not attacked assiduously they will find some utterly inaccessible corner of the ship in which to breed, and soon turn to thousands which will carry the dirt of the bilge on to the food that is still to be eaten. Possibly many tropical stomach disorders are due to this.

Alcohol.

The extent to which alcohol is carried on board depends on the taste of the owner and his crew, besides the amount of stowage that can be found. Some need it as a stimulant or tonic, others are themselves stimulants and need no tonics. There is little doubt that even a modest amount of alcohol affects the judgement, besides the co-ordination between mind and muscles; should it come to a difficult rough weather job on the foredeck, even one tot of whisky may well make the difference between success or otherwise, and perhaps between safety and danger.

No harm can be done if it is possible to have a drink, knowing that nothing much will be required for three or four hours. If a man comes below wet and cold after a long night watch, numbed toes and fingers often prevent his getting to sleep; alcohol actually raises the temperature of the extremities for perhaps an hour at the most, so a drink will be valuable in helping him to sleep. Rum is the most effective.

A drink relaxes the nerves, so even in the most intense race there may be occasions, such as a calm, when it is valuable to 'switch óff' the nervous output of eager enthusiasm for a short period. However, anything more than a very modest consumption under these conditions may lead to some feeling of depression just at the time when the wind comes again.

Seasickness.

Seasickness seems an endless joke to those not suffering, either because they are ashore or because they have overcome it. It is also a major menace to safety in a small yacht. As often as not, when a personal error is made at sea, it is due to one or other of the many forms seasickness takes. In a cruise the difference between pleasure and misery may depend on overcoming seasickness; in an ocean race it is as important as several feet of rating, or many square feet of canvas.

It is often a consolation to sufferers to know that remarkably few people are totally immune from seasickness; probably the number is under 3 per cent, although some put up with far worse conditions than others before they succumb. I have yet to be a shipmate in a small vessel with anyone totally immune, although it took such jobs as hanging head downwards into the bilges, when the yacht was bashing to windward in a really unpleasant sea, to prove that this was true.

Many of the different remedies tend to help, but as a seaman with no medical qualifications, I am quite confident that the efficiency of my crews has increased vastly since modern drugs such as Avomine became available; in fact this drug appears to have solved the problem of seasickness in a great majority of cases. It seems to be similar in principle to Dramamine, that is so much used in America with excellent results, but Avomine does not appear to bring on the drowsiness that sometimes occurs when Dramamine is taken. Dr. Pye mentions in his book *Red Mains'l* his amazement at the effect of Dramamine in curing his wife, even using the word miracle; he also records that it had an unexpected side-effect with her, in that after taking it she had to do her share of cooking, while previously this had not been possible at sea. Dramamine in some countries goes under the brand names of Gravel or Andramine.

Most laymen tend to be wary of drugs, fearing that they may cure one thing to cause some other harm, but I could never detect any side-effects or discomfort after taking Avomine. As part of the tests before using it at sea, a set of four star sights were worked out against time; then after taking a double dose of the drug and waiting a reasonable time to ensure it was absorbed, I worked through another similar set of sights and found the time taken was unaltered.

Constipation.

Most yachtsmen sailing off-shore are warned against constipation, with its encouragement of seasickness and general reduction of efficiency. A host of marvellous remedies is usually included with the warning. However, it is a state that probably shows that the balance of the diet is wrong, and the real cure is more care over the feeding.

Burns.

Burns are the most likely injury aboard a small vessel, as the violent motion may easily throw a boiling kettle or hot pan off the stove. Immediate treatment and care that nothing contaminated comes in contact with the wound are vital to prevent infection. In the difficult conditions of a small craft in a rough sea it is safest and most convenient to have ointment in collapsible tubes, similar to tooth-paste tubes, then the sterile ointment can be squeezed straight from the tube to the wound, and laid on in roughly parallel lines, before being covered with sterile gauze. As the wound will have been sterilized by the heat that caused the burn, quick action may prevent any contamination.

An antihistaminic cream, which apparently has not been used enough to qualify for any more homely name than Dibromopropamidine/phenergan, has been found most effective in curing burns and reducing the pain. When *Samuel Pepys* raced across the Atlantic a tube of this ointment and a packet of gauze was kept in immediate readiness in a commanding position near the galley. This treatment was so effective that no burn was experienced throughout the voyage and the ointment could only be tested ashore, before and after the cruise.

If nothing else is available ordinary bicarbonate of soda, or baking soda, dissolved in water can be put on a burn as a compress. Speed is more important than measurement for the treatment of burns, but the best proportion is two teaspoons to a cup of clean water. Bicarbonate of soda has many uses, not only is it valuable for the treatment of burns and the cooking of cakes, but it also is effective against sore throats and indigestion, and also acts as a tooth cleaning powder, and an antiseptic.

Sunburn.

Sunburn is another common complaint. A frequent treatment is to say, 'I told you so, and you'll know better next time.' While both of these pieces of advice are invariably true, neither will cure this often very painful state. As pain is the main symptom, the usual means of alleviating pain, such as aspirin or codeine, may be necessary as well as the direct treatment of the burnt skin with calamine lotion. Certainly a man with a badly sunburnt back will be quite useless for working the ship for some days.

Drowning.

Speed is the first essential when dealing with someone unconscious from drowning. Whatever method of artificial respiration is used it must start at once, as the delay of perhaps even a few seconds may be fatal. All those in close contact with the water, such as anyone aboard a yacht, should be sufficiently familiar with artificial respiration to be able to start on the job at once; it is not enough to leave this ability to one member of the crew and trust that he is aboard and does not happen to be the patient, when the emergency occurs.

The mouth-to-mouth method of resuscitation is now generally accepted as the best, and can be carried out anywhere. Briefly it consists of putting the apparently drowned person on his back, pulling back the head as far as possible, then pinching the nose to close it, while the rescuer takes a normal full breath, then puts his lips around the casualty's mouth and exhales forcibly. This is continued until breathing has restarted, and the attempt should continue for at least a full hour.

This seems quite simple, but few things really turn out to be so simple without skilled demonstration followed by practice. A valuable assistance to resuscitation can be a simple method of cardiac massage to restart the heart. This can best be learnt at a first aid class.

Appendicitis.

Probably anxiety about appendicitis even equals anxiety about. tropical revolving storms in the minds of most yachtsmen setting forth on a long cruise, if anyone aboard still has his appendix intact. If any skipper reads W. A. Robinson's *Voyage to the Galapagos* before setting out, he will insist on each potential crew member having his appendix removed before the voyage. Certainly Mrs. Pye underwent this operation immediately before leaving England to cross the Atlantic in *Moonraker*, although there was to be a doctor, her husband, aboard.

It may be that only one thing is worse than being a skipper at sea in a small vessel with an appendicitis case on board, and that is to be the case oneself. One January day I was at sea aboard an ex-trawler yacht *Dayspring* in rough weather about 15 miles south of Portland Bill when visibility was poor, and the situation only tolerable so long as we remained hove-to. It was then that one of my two shipmates showed signs of appendicitis. Without an engine, rather under-manned with a third of the crew out of action, and uncertain of my position, there were few things that I wanted to do less than attempt a landfall on Portland Bill. However, one of those few things was remaining at sea with an appendicitis case. Portland Race showed little sympathy with George Moyes' pains, but fortunately all went as well as it could under the circumstances, and a successful operation was achieved as soon as we reached harbour. Oddly enough the following November, when at sea in the Bay of Biscay aboard a vast ship in bad weather, another temporary shipmate developed appendicitis that was dealt with by an emergency operation on board; the patient turned out to be the brother of George Moyes.

If there is anyone aboard with his appendix intact, it would be well to have some antibiotic in the medicine chest, with detailed instructions from a doctor on its use. In any case, anyone with abdominal pains that might be appendicitis should never be given a purgative.

Medical equipment.

The medical equipment needed aboard will depend on the cruise to be undertaken, but a doctor's advice is best sought on this, and his signature will certainly be needed for the items that can only be supplied on prescription. It is always of interest to a layman that when one doctor advised on the most suitable medical outfit, should another offer his assistance, he will condemn half the items and order others in their place. This seems to show that the matter is as much an art as deciding the best rig for off-shore sailing, or even how to lie in a gale.

Whatever is carried should be stowed in a wooden box or rust-proof metal case. This should be kept in a dry place that is accessible both for use in emergency and frequent checking. Some items, such as adhesive tape, will not last long in the tropics once the tin is opened. Every item must be plainly marked with its name and purpose. (See Table XV*a*.)

Bandages
  24 1 inch wide
   6 2 inch wide
   2 3 inch wide
   2 4 inch wide
  (all 4 yards long)
1 pound white absorbent lint
1 pound cotton wool
4 packets gauze
	Adhesive tape
	  1 tin 1 inch wide
	  1 tin 2 inch wide
	  1 tin 3 inch wide
	  2 tins elastoplast dressings
	
	1 sling
	1 pair scissors

Calamine lotion   (sunburn)
Avomine   (seasickness)
Morphia   (intense pain)
 	
Benzedrine   (delays exhaustion)
Seconal   (assists sleep)
 	
Dibromopropamidine/phenergan cream
                                   (burns)
Succinylsulphathiazole   (diarrhoea)
	Codeine (pains and headaches)
	Dettol (antiseptic)
	Cascara (constipation)
	Liquid paraffin (,,)
	Penicillin lozenges (sore throats)
	Iodine in bottle with glass stopper
	                                 (sprains)
	Chloroquine (malaria)

Table XV*a*. Sample contents of the medical box of a small yacht

Medical knowledge.

It is important that several members of the crew understand the use of all the equipment carried, otherwise it is perhaps useless and possibly dangerous. Many laymen, particularly men, are nonplussed when faced with someone else's injury or treatment for the first time, so detailed instruction by a doctor will be valuable. Once when aboard an American yacht in an isolated Long Island harbour, one of the crew damaged his back, but fortunately a well-known surgeon was found aboard another yacht anchored nearby. An ambulance was ordered by radio, and the doctor came over by dinghy to order a morphia injection. The yacht's medical chest was well equipped so her owner handed the doctor a box containing everything necessary for the injection. But the doctor was a yachtsman as well as a surgeon and handed back the box saying, 'Here's your chance, Commodore, while it's not blowing a gale, and there's a doctor handy to stop you from making a mistake. Next time it may be harder, so the practice will be useful.'

When racing from Bermuda to Sweden in *Belmore*, the ocean was in grim mood on a day when we were a trifle closer to Iceland than America or Scotland. But it seemed a devil of a long way from anywhere when one of my crew became ill. I was certainly grateful then that Hans Rozendaal, a yachting friend and New York doctor, had, before we set off on the voyage, seen that we had ample medical stores, besides some instruction in their use.

XVI

Meeting Other Ships

IN the open sea one of the warmest pleasures comes from sighting another ship, although much anxiety and perhaps the greatest danger come from the chance of finding it too close.

When fog streams past the cockpit carried by a clammy wind, the ocean feels bigger than ever; the waves are less friendly as they jerk into view perhaps less than a cable to windward. Then the first moan of a ship's siren, quite close but direction uncertain, makes one grip hard on the cockpit coaming as the hair stands up on the back of the neck. The next few minutes are mental torture, made acuter by the thought that one came to this situation of one's own free will. At last the bulk of a great ship looms through the fog boundary, and passes safely down the yacht's side; there is a wave from the bridge, repeated from a group dressed for the stoke-hold further aft. In a few seconds she is lost to sight, and her siren's now friendly note dissolves into the murk astern. Such passing greetings make as warm a welcome as any planned reunion with one's oldest friends. The ocean feels less hostile, and even the fog loses some of its eerie discomfort.

Navigation lights.

Some consider that large light boards, secured in the rigging port and starboard, are the mark of a sea-going yacht. The object of these boards, when fitted in a steam ship, is to limit correctly the arc through which the lights are visible. In a sailing vessel so fitted, the arc of the light will depend on the amount of her heel, so the boards are ineffective as well as clumsy. The rigging of a small yacht is a poor place for lights, as the lee side is partly screened by the headsails, the spray level is at about its highest, and the give in the lee shrouds tends to shake out the light.

The rule of the road requires that a sailing vessel of less than 20 tons gross need carry only a combined lantern, and if it is impracticable to fix this, it should be kept lighted and exhibited over the correct arcs in time to prevent a collision. Under this rule it is sufficient to keep the lantern in the cockpit and show it when another vessel comes near, so long as a good look-out is kept.

The modern trend of sailing cruiser, with no bowsprit and a pulpit forward, is fortunate in having a fairly good site for a combined red and green lantern, secured immediately below the top rail of the pulpit. It is unlikely to get knocked off, it is exceptionally free from spray, and has an uninterrupted view ahead round to abaft both beams. The only limitation to this position is that it is comparatively low and will not be continuously visible from any distance even in a slight sea.

There is really only one position aboard a yacht from which a light can be seen by another vessel with certainty, and that is at the mast-head. An all-round white light at the mast-head is the best way of making known the presence of the yacht when either no watch is being kept on deck or the weather makes it hard to see much while nestling close among the waves in the cockpit. This light only con-forms to the rule of the road if such a small vessel is assumed to be in the same category as a pulling boat under sails, yet it is the only light that has been used by many single-handed yachtsmen in the open sea, who are more concerned with common-sense safety in their own unusual cases, than with rules that also must take account of blame should there be an accident.

The fact is that the system of navigation lights developed when craft moved relatively slowly, and visual lookout was by far the most important factor towards avoiding collisions. This is no longer so, and in most large ships the officer-of-the-watch is tucked away in a sheltered compartment surrounded by numerous devices to assist him. One of the most valuable can be radar, and particularly in low visibility, he is likely to concentrate on his radar screen far more than on visual look-out, and indeed this is almost certain to give him the first warning of the presence of another large vessel. Probably it will not tell him of the presence of a small yacht, so there is surely an excellent argument for such craft to carry particularly effective lights; no steady light is ever so noticeable as a flashing one, so I believe that the correct answer would be for sailing craft to carry flashing navigation lights to stress that they have limited ability to get out of the way of power driven vessels. Another point is that they usually have rather limited battery power, so on long voyages show lights that might just be visible the correct distance on a clear dark night, but in slightly hazy weather they cannot be seen very far off. The same applies to the oil lamps that a small sailing craft might carry. A flashing light can easily be made very much brighter for the use of the same amount of electric power during any one night.

It really seems rather absurd that at the moment the craft showing the most visible lights is the hovercraft, which is the one which must most often have to get out of the way of other craft.

Electric navigation lights.

Electric navigation lights can be thoroughly reliable and are so much more convenient than any oil lights, that their practical efficiency is far greater. For a mast-head light, electricity is clearly essential.

Slips of red and green transparent material, that will go inside the lens of the ordinary hand torch, if needed, can be carried as secondary lights. In practice it is surprisingly difficult to improvise a green shade. Once when I was sailing *Marabu*, 58 feet, in the English Channel, the glass of her starboard light was smashed to small pieces by a swinging block, so I ordered a search aboard the ship for something to adapt a white light to the correct colour. After a long delay one of the crew was satisfied, having lashed a lettuce leaf round the clear glass; little light came through, and that was not green, but he argued confidently that the light was lit and the leaf was green. Shortly before this he had given up a career at sea in favour of politics.

Fog.

Most small yachts carry a fog signal, either worked by a hand-operated plunger, or by mouth. Usually neither has a very powerful note and as the noise is made close to the water the sound will be dispersed rapidly except in the calmest weather. The plunger type can make the greatest noise at its best but as it has moving parts that can be damaged and a leather washer that can dry up, it is less reliable as a piece of equipment that may not be used for months on end, than the simple blowing tube type. If the sea is even slight or moderate the range of the signal is greatly increased when it is operated from a height of say 12 feet. Working the plunger device from up the mast would be about as simple as using a stirrup pump when climbing up a rope, however it is quite practical to jump aloft with the vocal fog tube and trumpet from the cross-trees when the signal from another vessel is heard.

The best defence of a small yacht in a fog, when on the steamer routes, comes from aural alertness on deck and below. There are cases when the approach of a steamer has first been heard from below owing either to the propeller noise travelling through the water, or even to a fog signal being in some odd way audible in the cabin when it had not been heard from on deck.

Radar reflector.

More and more merchant ships are fitted with radar sets that enable them to proceed at their normal speed in low visibility, confident of picking up an echo from another ship in good time to avoid a collision. Usually these sets are tuned so that the large wave of a rough sea will not show on the screen, and this means that a 10 ton wooden cruising yacht will not show either, as it is far smaller than such a wave.

The use of radar therefore increases the danger to small yachts unless they are fitted with some device that will give a strong echo to the transmitting ship. A temporary reflector can be made from strips of wood, or even canvas on a rigid frame, coated with aluminium paint;

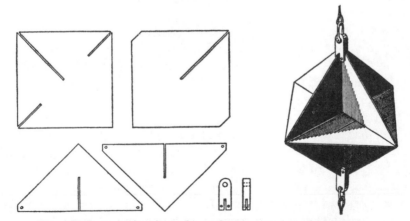

Fig. XVI, 1. A simple radar reflector cut out of aluminium sheet which will stow flat when not in use

o

however, to return radar rays coming from any direction the angle between the reflecting surfaces must be correct. The model shown in Fig. XVI, 1, is effective whatever the angle of heel, and however it is hung, even if swinging or twirling. The design was required to be completely efficient, take up practically no room when not in use, weigh very little, cost less and be easy to set up. When this was satisfactorily achieved for *Samuel Pepys* by L. E. D. Wise, the gadget became known as the Wisdom. It is cut out of thin aluminium sheets that stow flat when not in use.

Signalling.

The value of being able to communicate with another ship is obvious but it becomes drastically urgent when, failing other methods, she comes close enough to read the yacht's name on the stern, oblivious of the 5-foot high sea that makes the yacht's crew detest such close attention.

The name.

The yacht's name should be painted in letters at least a foot high on a strip of canvas that can be displayed when needed. The canvas cockpit dodger will normally do well for this purpose as well. Boldly formed letters painted in black will enable any ship to identify the yacht at a perfectly safe distance.

Flags.

Theoretically the perfect way to exchange messages is by the use of the international flags and code. This provides a simple hoist for most messages likely to be needed; the sender need only be able to read his own language and to be free from colour blindness, while the receiver also needs colour vision and the ability to look up the message in his particular language.

The practical limitation to the system, when used by a small yacht, is that the flags never seem to be visible to the reader. This limitation is very real, as from a sailing yacht I have never known the system to work at sea. If the sails are lowered to show the flags more clearly, the steamer assumes that the yacht is in some trouble and steams up close to ask verbally what it is, without waiting to read the flags.

If variety of messages is required, beyond some standard hoist that can be kept ready under a pillow, a great deal of space must be given up in the yacht so that any of the forty flags in the code can be found readily. Even the flags themselves, without inglefield clips and bundled into a sack, will be as heavy and bulky as a spare main sail for a ten tonner, but far less useful. The fact is that in a small sailing yacht there is not space aloft for sails and flags to be efficient at the same time. The best use for the signal flags is in harbour—for dressing ship, if one can afford this colourful luxury; even then someone should be ready to go to the mast-head at sunset to clear the top flag when it gets caught up.

Semaphore.

This is a fast and simple daylight method of signalling that can be sent by most Boy Scouts, but can normally only be received at sea by a naval signalman. No equipment is needed for sending messages as a man's arms can be seen through binoculars at a distance of half a mile, so semaphore is particularly useful for daylight signalling with a warship, coastguards or ocean weather ship. The fact of sending a message in this way will make its reader assume that he can reply in the same way, and also at the same speed; so if a yachtsman rips out his message at twelve words a minutes, a test chiefly of physical agility, he must be able to read semaphore at the same speed, which is a severe test of every sort of ability when the yacht is moving around at sea.

Flashing.

Flashing in Morse code is by far the most effective method of visual signalling for a sailing yacht by day or night. It requires only simple equipment, is readily understood by practically all sea-going ships and has excellent range. But it does require far more knowledge of the Morse code than can be obtained by reading the dots and dashes out of a pocket diary as one sees them signalled.

Special signalling lamps, such as the Aldis, are not entirely suited to a small yacht at sea, although excellent in harbour. A good torch that can be focused to a broad beam of light is simple to maintain, and will be visible at a surprising distance. The long hand torch with five single cells, such as is commonly sold in country areas where rabbits abound at night, has been successfully read in sunlight by a signal station five miles away, while on a clear night at sea, signals have been exchanged with ships up to seven miles' distance. Such a torch costs a guinea, weighs a pound and a half, and with proper seaman's care lasts a couple of Atlantic crossings without refilling or injury.

If a mast-head light is fitted, this is excellent for flashing at short ranges, except that it will be necessary to bring a lead on deck with a controlling switch, so that the light can be flashed with the other ship in view. Wandering leads or switches on deck have a tiresome habit of failing in the middle of a message, unless the equipment is so heavy that it incidentally becomes bullet-proof as well as waterproof. It will probably be found that in a small yacht such complications are soon abandoned in favour of the torch.

Before starting to signal, a position must be selected with the body firmly supported so that the torch can be kept trained; it must be high enough so that the wave tops do not eclipse some of the symbols, and it must have a good sector of visibility so that a shift of position is not required half-way through the message. The expert signalman can read whole sentences at a time, the normal yachtsman will do best to have another man write down the letters he calls out, and not make back the signal 'T' for a word received until the writer confirms that he has a word that makes sense.

Aboard most merchant vessels the officer-of-the-watch will have to read messages without help, so it is important to allow him ample time between words to write down each one separately. It is also valuable to write down the message before sending it off so that the sender will not have to divide his attention between signalling and English composition.

The ability to read Morse code needs some practice, but it is well worth this effort by one member of the crew on board a yacht in the open sea. The sun shines for hours and days on end, so that the navigator can perfect his sights before the landfall; meals follow in quick succession, so the cook that fails for lunch can do better for supper; but only one ship may be sighted on a long voyage, and nothing is more annoying, after waiting days or weeks for such a chance, than to see her disappearing over the horizon with the miserable note in the log 'Failed to establish communication with unknown ship'.

Radio.

Communication with another ship by radio requires far more knowledge and ability than is needed to signal with a torch. It is neces-

sary to know the radio watches she keeps, which depend on the number
of operators on board, and the frequencies to which she is tuned; it
will also still be necessary to read Morse code, except in the case of two
ships using a pre-arranged voice frequency.

Near the shore the value of two-way radio communication is far
more important than in the open sea. When aboard the lifeboat in
Pentland Firth during the stormy winter of 1953, the coxswain told me
that he would almost prefer to go back to his sailing lifeboat than to be
deprived of his two-way radio.

In a small yacht, unless there is a practised operator on board, radio
transmission in the open sea is really only useful for distress purposes.
If a transmitter is carried for this purpose, each member of the crew
should be thoroughly familiar with the procedure for transmitting a
distress signal, otherwise the whole purpose of the apparatus may be
lost. It is not enough to know that the set should be tuned to a certain
frequency; each man must actually move the necessary dials so that
he has tuned to this frequency.

Radio distress procedure.

Having switched on the set correctly, which may well involve some
local, little private trick like pulling the light leads off the battery
terminals and wedging the radio leads in position with a toothbrush,
the procedure for a yacht fitted with voice transmission is:
  (i)   Tune to 2,182 kcs.
  (ii) Say 'MAYDAY MAYDAY MAYDAY, this is (yacht's name)'
        three times
  (iii) Give Position
             Nature of distress
             Type of assistance required.

This signal should not be addressed to any particular station or
ship, but stations may answer on the same frequency.

The best times are at 15 and 45 minutes past each hour, and for
three minutes afterwards, but a distress signal may be made at any
time. If battery power is limited and the time can be afforded, every
effort should be made to transmit only at the best periods.

Transferring at sea.

In the case of emergency it may be necessary to transfer an injured man to a passing ship, or even to take aboard essential replenishments of food and water. In the open sea this should normally be done by boat unless grave urgency makes the risk of serious damage to the yacht acceptable.

A merchant ship lying stopped, drifts faster to leeward than a sailing vessel sheltered from the wind by the hull of the larger vessel. The drift may be as much as 2 knots in a strong wind, so once alongside to leeward, the yacht cannot get clear undamaged even with an engine. It is unlikely that she could go alongside to windward in any but exceptionally calm weather.

For boat work in bad weather use must be made of the comparatively calm water in the lee of the ship. A freighter or passenger

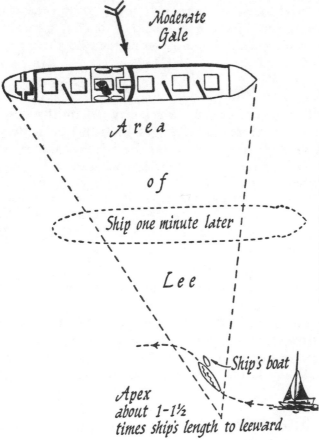

Fig. XVI, 2. Transferring a wounded man or stores from a ship at sea in a gale. Although a stopped ship will give a lee of smoother water, she drifts to leeward fast in strong winds and once alongside her lee side a yacht cannot get clear

ship when stopped lies approximately beam on to the wind and her lee forms a triangle whose apex is one to one-and-a-half times her length to leeward. The boat should remain within this sheltered area of sea, yet the yacht must not allow the ship to drift close enough to take her wind. Fig. XVI, 2 shows that in a stiff wind a ship of 400 feet length reaches the position of the apex of her lee two minutes after it began to provide shelter.

If the yacht uses her own dinghy or float, the ship will drift down on it so long as it is slipped within the area of the ship's lee. However, unless it is a powerful boat, it will not be able to get clear again to leeward in anything more than a moderate wind. If the ship uses her own lifeboat it can be lowered when the ship still has slight headway and steered out from the ship's side on a boat rope. The transfer of men or stores from ship's boat to the yacht is helped because there is nothing to foul the yacht's gear aloft; however, in rough seas it may have to be done very quickly within the area of the ship's lee.

In every case the yacht must have everything prepared in advance; if an injured man is to be transferred he must be ready on deck, perhaps in a temporary stretcher made of spare spars, oars and a mattress, and certainly wearing a lifebelt. All boat work in the open sea is liable to be dangerous both for the yacht and the crew of the ship's boat; crushed limbs and broken strakes are likely, so the risk should not be taken lightly. The dorymen that are lowered over the side of their parent vessels daily to fish on the Grand Banks are experts with specialised craft.

Transferring stores from a trawler.

On sighting a trawler after many days at sea there is often a strong temptation to ask for, or accept the offer of, fresh fish. If the sea seems calm the job of transfer looks simple enough; yet it is a safe guess that the sea never will be completely calm in the open ocean, although the low swell may not be noticeable until two craft are nearly alongside each other; then, if both have masts, the swell becomes obvious.

A direct transfer can be made safely only if both vessels are under way and under full command. A trawler, or very small ship, will probably have a low enough hull to allow a good deal of wind into the yacht's sail; then it becomes safe for the yacht to sail to windward of her on a broad reach, edging in close enough to pass the stores over on a line, or even to throw them over if sufficient fielding space can be found on deck clear of the sails.

For a really small trawler a safe approach can be made with the yacht to leeward in a steady wind; then fish or small quantities of stores can be thrown into the yacht's mainsail, and caught under the boom.

The safest way of transferring stores, if this is practicable, is by floating them astern on a line that is picked up by the yacht.

Abandoning the yacht.

A yacht will only be abandoned at sea after particularly trying circumstances that have left the crew incapable of navigating her. They will probably be equally incapable of making a plan to leave the ship safely, unless it has been considered beforehand. There will also be a psychological tendency to feel that the danger is over as soon as a rescue ship is seen approaching. Many lives have been lost at sea unnecessarily, due to confusion when abandoning a vessel.

Once the decision to abandon the yacht has been made, each member of the crew must know exactly what is required of him. Never must any be left in doubt as to whether the intention is to abandon ship, or merely to seek assistance from another vessel.

When preparing to abandon the yacht in bad weather every man must don his lifebelt, and wear proper safety harness or secure round his waist a strop with an eye strong enough to take his weight in wet clothes. Any gear that it is hoped to salve should be ready on deck packed in sail bags, each with a line attached. When the rescuing ship comes alongside, the first object must be to secure the yacht with lines fore and aft, so that nobody is left behind tending the yacht until it is too late for him to jump for the ladder. It is also unsafe for a man to start aloft when the yacht may drift aft and spear him with the crosstrees or wipe him off with the rigging.

Rigid discipline is never more essential than at the moment of abandoning a ship. Each man should be ordered personally when to go, and then take his turn climbing aboard the rescue ship; in a heavy sea with the ship rolling, it is important not to mount the ladder until the yacht has reached her highest point relative to the ship's side, otherwise she will crush the man on the ladder before he can climb clear. I have seen this happen to a doctor sent over in a boat at sea to give medical aid in another ship, so that he became a patient with a broken foot. If conditions make it possible, some of the crew can be told to take with them the ends of the lines secured to the sail bags with gear; these bags should not be hauled aloft until all the crew are on the ship's deck, as there must be no diversion from the main object of saving all the crew uninjured.

The concussion between a ship and a yacht lying alongside in heavy weather is very violent. The noise of crunching wood gives the impression that she must sink any moment long before this happens. Standing on a yacht's deck it is easy to be thrown over the side, which will almost certainly be fatal if it is between the ship and the yacht.

Towing in the open sea.

Towing a small yacht in the open sea is a thoroughly dangerous job, and unless shelter is close, the risk of towing a yacht that cannot be navigated by her crew is such that few masters would consider it a reasonable proposition.

Reporting through Lloyd's.

The most effective way of being reported at sea on speaking to a merchant ship is to make arrangements with Lloyd's intelligence department, whose address is Lloyd's, London, E.C.3.

A deep sea yachtsman may write to the Head of the department, giving particulars of his proposed trip and his yacht, and the names and addresses of the people he wishes to be informed should the yacht be reported.

At sea any ship may be asked to report the yacht to Lloyd's of London. If it is felt that flag signalling might work, the single hoist from the International Code of MIL (Please report me by telegraph to my owners *via* Lloyd's, London) might be kept ready in large size flags, but I have never once found them to be read.

The ship should send a radio-telegram to Lloyd's, giving the name and position of the yacht, besides any other message that the yacht might pass. In practice this does not always happen with some foreign ships which wait until they reach harbour before sending on the message by cable. Any speaking reports received at Lloyd's are published in the shipping column of *Lloyd's List and Shipping Gazette*, and would be passed on to the general press if there was public interest in the particular yacht or voyage.

The cost falls on the owner of the yacht, and will vary considerably in different cases. In addition to the Lloyd's reporting fee of 7s. 6d. and the costs of sending telegrams to the people arranged beforehand, the major part of the cost will normally be the radio-telegram from the ship to London. Radio charges vary according to the land station through which the ship routes the message, and the nationality of the ship. The minimum radio charge is 1s. a word, but aboard a foreign ship the charges are subject in addition to gold franc rate of 2s. 4d. per franc. A simple reporting signal giving only the name and position may easily cost £3 and more, so it is obviously an advantage to report through a ship of the same nationality as the yacht. Thus a speaking report in mid-Atlantic passed through S.S. *Queen Mary* cost £1 6s. 6d., another a week later with the same number of words cost £3 8s. 2d. when passed by a foreign ship.

XVII

Yacht Business

THE paper work required of a pleasure yacht when cruising is simple; complications only arise if it is neglected. There are occasions when the plan of a cruise will have to take into account administrative regulations but, so long as these regulations are known in ample time, little inconvenience will result. For example, entry to some of the Pacific island groups can only be made at a certain port, and if this is not allowed for, the yacht might sail on to leeward of the compulsory port, and then be faced either with a beat back to windward, or omitting her visits to the whole group of islands.

Document stowage.

Probably one of the most important parts of the organisation of the yacht's business is arranging some locker or drawer aboard where the papers are always stowed and returned immediately after use. The perfect arrangement is a small cupboard with a list of the contents on the inside of the door. Gross inconvenience has sometimes been caused when an essential document has been left ashore and the situation is little better if, after three weeks of anxious cabling and 'strained relationships' with the authorities, the document is found slightly pulped below the fresh water tank in the bilge.

In very small vessels lockers, if fitted at all, probably cannot be spared for correspondence. A canvas wallet can be made and secured in some safe, dry place such as tacked to a partition forming part of the skipper's bunk space. The list of contents can be written straight on to the canvas and a really neat-minded seaman might sew in a separate pocket for each document, with a flap over the top that will prevent water drips from filling up the pockets.

Certificate of registration.

This is the yacht's official identification document and is required for the transaction of all official business. It is not essential to register a yacht if her registered tonnage would be less than fifteen but an unregistered vessel has no status outside her own country, and will not only cause extra work to her master but she will be an infernal nuisance to the various officials whose duty it is to administer the shipping, health, customs and immigration laws of their country.

A yacht can be registered however small she may be, so long as evidence of her life history can be produced, on application to the local Registrar of Shipping. Any gap in the chain of ownership since she was built makes registration very difficult. This official registration under the Merchant Shipping Act of 1894 is quite different from entry in Lloyd's Register of Yachts, which is an unofficial list produced by an important and influential society.

Charter-party.

If a yacht has been chartered by her owner, the charter-party explains why she is in the hands of someone other than the owner whose name is shown on the certificate of registration.

If no charter-party can be produced, a yacht under the control of someone other than the registered owner or master could be detained.

Bill of health.

A bill of health must be obtained from the customs authorities, or from the British consul, for any yacht going from one country to another. It describes the condition of the port from which the yacht sails, and can be 'foul', 'suspected', or if no infectious disease is known to exist in the port or its neighbourhood, it is 'clean'. It is usually printed in delightful terms that start by sending greetings 'to all to whom these Presents shall come', and after certifying that 'no Plague, Epidemic Cholera nor dangerous disorder exists in the Port or Neighbourhood', perhaps goes on to mention one case of chicken-pox. Many weeks later, and thousands of miles away, when the document next comes out of its wallet, one might pause a second to hope that the anonymous chicken-pox sufferer has returned to his lessons at school while the news of his health is being carried around the world.

Quarantine.

The governments of most countries protect their inhabitants from dangerous infectious diseases by imposing on newcomers a quarantine, a word originally implying forty days, until they are proved to be free of infection. Accordingly a yacht entering the waters of a new country must fly the quarantine flag (Q in the international code) and none of her company may land until pratique is given.

Pratique.

In some places customs officers, waterguards or pilots are authorised to give pratique to yachts entering with a clean bill of health. If the bill is 'foul', or 'suspected', the certificate of pratique will be issued by the port medical authorities, perhaps after a period of isolation.

Customs clearance.

The certificate of pratique, or sometimes just verbal permission, allows a vessel to enter the port, secure alongside if necessary, and her company to land. This certificate should be taken to the customs authorities, although in many cases a customs officer may board the yacht either with the medical officer, or sometimes representing him in addition to his other functions. The responsibility for contacting the customs rests with the master of the yacht, so it is no good claiming that the customs ignored the vessel. In Great Britain a penalty of £100 can be exacted for failing to report to the customs within twenty-four hours of arrival.

In some ports the different authorities are widely spread, and each claims ignorance even of the existence of the others. At the opposite extreme Anita Leslie tells in *Love in a Nutshell* how in Bequaia, amongst the Grenadines of the West Indies, a notice over one small office read, 'Treasury, Police, Customs, Post Office, Law Court.'

In countries where there is an import duty on yachts, the owner will probably have to sign an agreement that he will not sell the yacht, and unless he pays duty on her, she may have to leave the waters of that country within a limited period.

Cruising licence for United States waters.

Yachts of certain countries, including Great Britain, Canada, Jamaica and the Bahamas, may receive a licence to cruise in United

States waters for up to six months without entering or clearing, obtaining permission to proceed, or paying fees. This licence may be given by the U.S. customs under section 308 (5), of the Tariff Act, and is subject to the conditions that the yacht does not enter in any trade, or violate the law of the country in any respect.

If intending to visit United States waters, it might be well to contact in advance the treasury attaché in the embassy of the country to which the yacht belongs. Many yachtsmen have found that the U.S. customs officials administer the laws of their country very strictly and conscientiously, so that if they are not accustomed to entering foreign yachts at any port, there may be considerable delay. On the other hand Newport, Rhode Island and Miami, Florida, for example, have ample practice, and carry out their functions very rapidly. It is reported that when T. O. M. Sopwith arrived in Newport with *Endeavour I* to challenge for the America's Cup, Walter Dring, the U.S. customs collector, lent him a dollar to pay for the cruising licence, asking that it be repaid only when he had won the cup. Many non-American yacht owners have since been grateful to the same officer for his efficient clearance, in and out.

Passports.

It is an advantage for each member of the crew to take a passport when visiting a foreign port, in case he should decide to leave the yacht and continue his journey in some other way. For certain countries a visa is required from one of its consulates or embassies before leaving, and these may take several days to be completed. Passports are not essential for members of a registered vessel's crew, professional or amateur, so long as their names appear on the crew list.

Crew list.

It is advisable to carry a crew list, although not essential if no professional crew is carried. This shows the name, age, place of birth, date and place of joining, besides height and weight, of all the crew. This seems simple enough, but when the time comes to make out the list for a yacht's crew, it is inclined to lead to much shouting from the customs house across the harbour, such as, 'Where was George born, and what does he weigh?' the second part of which usually brings back a very delayed hail of, 'About seven pounds, I suppose, same as a normal baby,' unless the owner has set out with every fact gleaned in advance.

Should the cruise have to be abandoned, the crew list might prove a great advantage at some isolated place, as all the crew entered on it can be treated as distressed seamen. Any British ship is obliged to take aboard distressed British seamen at the rate of one for every fifty tons burden. The yacht's owner would still have to pay a reasonable sum for his crew's passage and maintenance, but they might otherwise have to wait much longer and pay far more for a passage towards home.

Duty-free stores.

Duty-free stores for the consumption of the crew of a yacht going on a foreign cruise can always be obtained if the yacht's registered tonnage exceeds forty. For such vessels the master makes a declaration with the customs officer, and obtains clearance for his vessel. It is an interesting conjecture to wonder why the lower limit of forty registered tons was imposed, unless it was considered that this was the smallest vessel that would set out on a foreign cruise at the time the regulation was drafted. Customs officers are today lenient for smaller craft.

Customs licences.

In Britain a craft of under 40 tons must be licensed by the Customs if it goes more than 36 miles seawards from any port of the coast unless she is being used at the time exclusively for pleasure by her owner. It remains his pleasure under this regulation, if someone else is in charge under his direction without remuneration, or a member of his family has his permission to take her.

Weights and measurement.

The metric or the English system, sometimes with modifications, is used in nearly all countries bordering the sea. The English equivalents of the commonest metric units are:

    1 Kilo   = 2.2 pounds
    1 Tonneau = 2,205 pounds
    1 Litre   = 1.76 pints
    1 Metre   = 39.4 inches or just over half a fathom

In some countries, including the United States and Canada, the ton is 2,000 pounds, and the hundredweight, or cental, is 100 pounds.

A shipping ton anywhere is a measure of space, not weight, being 40 cubic feet of merchandise.

In the United States the gallon is 0.83 of the British new or imperial gallon.

Where the kilometre is used it always has the same length, but the mile is far more adaptable. Compared with the nautical mile of 6,080 feet there are many different miles shown that might be used in local directions, as shown in Table XVII*a*.

British statute mile (5,280 feet)	0.86	nautical miles
Danish mile	4.06	,, ,,
German geographical mile	4.00	,, ,,
Italian mile	1.00	,, ,,
Norwegian mile	6.097	,, ,,
Swedish mile	5.77	,, ,,

Table XVII*a*. Lengths of a mile in various countries ashore

Many yachtsmen exploring new places ashore on foot will feel sympathy with Anita Leslie's experience in Carib Land, when a mile and a half was to be an elastic unit that continued to be the distance of her destination however far she walked towards it.

Salvage.

Salvage is the money paid for saving a yacht from loss or damage. Salvage differs from saving life, for which no fee is demanded from those saved. When danger to life does not exist, or no longer exists, lifeboatmen or anyone else may attempt salvage of a yacht, and will be entitled to reward if they are successful.

Where possible an owner should make an agreement before salvage commences on the lines of Lloyd's open agreement. This is based on a 'no cure—no pay' basis, and leaves the remuneration to be settled by arbitration. If the yacht would have been lost but for the salvor's voluntary efforts, and should these efforts require skill to perform and expose him to danger, then he may be entitled to an award that is a substantial portion of the value of the yacht.

When the owner feels that his yacht is not in danger, but for his own convenience he wants a tow from another vessel while he and his

Plate 21. *Bolero* had dry decks as she ran under spinnaker and reefed mainsail before a grand westerly gale in mid-Atlantic

Plate 22. A magnificent great Atlantic roller taken at the same time would certainly fill the cockpit of a small yacht running before it should it break over her stern

Plate 23. Concentration all through the hours of darkness was an important factor on board *Belmore I* of 36·5 ft. overall, seen finishing second overall in a Bermuda race

crew remain in full charge of his yacht, then he should come to an agreement with the towing vessel before the tow is passed, and no salvage will be involved. Once the crew have left their ship in the open sea, it would be very hard for them to prove that they had been bound elsewhere on a social visit.

The Press.

Sometimes the Press, either locally or on a wider basis, may take an interest in the cruise of a yacht. Then it is likely that journalists will want to come on board soon after the yacht reaches harbour, at a time that is most inconvenient to the owner, just as he is feeling rather harassed by officials carrying out their duty and residents offering hospitality, while he has not yet adapted himself to the uncontrolled life ashore, compared with the well-ordered regime he has led at sea.

The result may be that the reporter gets scant welcome and no information, so with the need to write something to justify the time and effort of his visit, his story may wander into conjecture. The owner will read this with scorn, and can only pray that his yachting acquaintances will not read it also. He has only himself to blame.

The journalist usually wants a long list of detailed facts on which to base an accurate story; to the crew many of them appear dull and totally irrelevant, but he cannot faithfully report without far more information than will appear in his story, particularly if he has no technical knowledge of the subject. The solution is for the owner to appoint in advance a well-informed member of his crew to assist any reporter that should seek information; the person doing this should have readily available all the details of the yacht and her crew, her programme and her equipment. After a little practice he will learn what is wanted and get through all the basic background in quick time, anticipating such regular requests as the names, home town and age of all aboard; if any feel at first that any of these questions only concern themselves they soon find that it is better to give the figure of their own choice, rather than leave their age as a guess of the reporter.

If anything of interest has happened, the reporter will certainly want some short account from the owner, and it is churlish to withhold affairs of the sea that are no man's private property. If the reporter has already been well-informed by answers to his detailed questions, this brief statement need not take much time at a difficult moment.

P

XVIII

Storm at Sea

IT seems appropriate to end a book on deep sea sailing with the description of an actual storm encountered by small yachts in the open ocean. Storm is the time against which many of the preparations are made, and although it is experienced seldom, it is something that all deep sea yachtsmen must be prepared to face, perhaps without warning. The story is told of the storm as it was seen at the time from one yacht, but the presence of three others nearby made it possible to analyse the situation more closely when they exchanged information afterwards. It brings out many of the points that have been discussed in more detail in their various chapters of the book.

The storm took place within the area bounded by Bermuda to the east, Cape Hatteras to the west, and Nantucket to the north. It is an area notorious for fierce gales. It was there that Slocum in June met his worst weather at the end of sailing round the world in *Spray*; there too Robinson in *Svaap* met his worst weather, but for him it was at the start of a voyage round the world. Gales there may come suddenly, yet last long, as the warm waters of the Gulf Stream spewing out from Florida Strait stir up the stable air of the Horse Latitude and cry havoc when waves form on the polar front that often lies in this vicinity.

By chance four yachts were bunched together some 500 miles from the American coast at the time the storm raged most violently. All were British, newly built, and bound for America. *Vertue XXXV* had left Falmouth, England, forty days before with just two men on board, bound for New York. A sloop 25 feet long, she displaced under five tons; very toughly built, of heavy displacement, she had already on that voyage come undamaged through six North Atlantic spring gales.

The other three had left Bermuda in company, bound for New England to compete in the ocean race from Newport to Bermuda.

Cohoe and *Samuel Pepys* both weighed under five tons and were light displacement sloops with excellent racing records. *Samuel Pepys* had aboard a full racing crew of four men, all experienced in off-shore sailing; *Cohoe* had two of her racing crew and one extra man with far less experience. Finally there was the cutter *Mokoia*, a medium displacement cutter of some seven tons weight; she had on board two of her racing crew and a girl. Each of these last three yachts, with full racing crews, later that year competed in the Transatlantic race to win the first three places, with only a few hours between them after sailing 3,000 miles in twenty-one days.

On 24th May, 1950, the synoptic chart showed a large anti-cyclone centred a thousand miles east of Cape Hatteras. Conditions seemed settled with light easterly winds in the area north of Bermuda. There was no hint of a depression forming. Yet within twenty-four hours the storm was establishing itself right among the yachts. At first only the two yachts that had lagged behind due to smaller crews felt the strength of the wind; then the storm caught the leader a hundred miles to the north and later *Vertue XXXV* sailed into it from the east. By this time the first two to meet the gale were among calms in the centre, but later they emerged to encounter strong gales once more. The storm lasted four days, and only moved sixty miles throughout its life.

At 1800, May 25th, *Cohoe* and *Mokoia* ran into gales. First *Mokoia* hove-to under storm trisail, and soon afterwards *Cohoe* hove-to under bare poles. Both logged strong gales from the eastward, and continuous heavy rainfall. Next morning the wind moderated for them, although the barometer continued to fall. By noon *Cohoe* had Force 3 wind from the south, while *Mokoia* some ten miles to her north had light westerly winds. Of that time the skipper of *Cohoe* wrote in *North Atlantic*:

'The scene presented the appearance of a city after an air-raid. The bombing was over and the chaos remaining. There was a huge swell coming from two directions, and the sea was heaped in complete confusion . . .'

Later she emerged into strong gales again for many hours before the depression filled, but these two yachts were apparently in the central area of the calm air and confused sea during the thirty-six hours that the storm was at its height.

On the evening of 25th May, *Samuel Pepys* sailed on to the north-ward, little suspecting any change of weather. Hoping to let the others catch up, she had lowered her mainsail, but was reaching fast under a

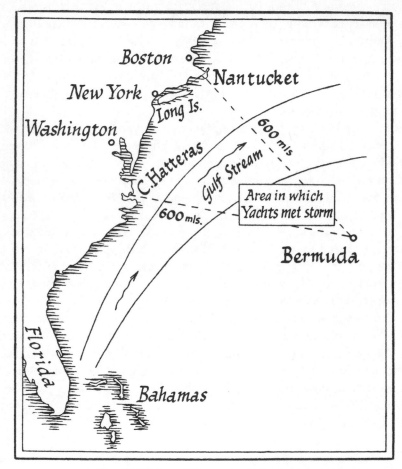

Fig. XVIII, 1. The area of the storm

genoa in a moderate sea with continuous rain. I had under my com-mand a really good crew, although this was our first experience of sailing off-shore together in *Samuel Pepys*. As mate was Stephen Sampson who had skippered various yachts successfully in ocean races; he was tall and slim and everlastingly sought for better ways of doing any job. The bosun was Pat Ovens, a Royal Marine Commando officer who

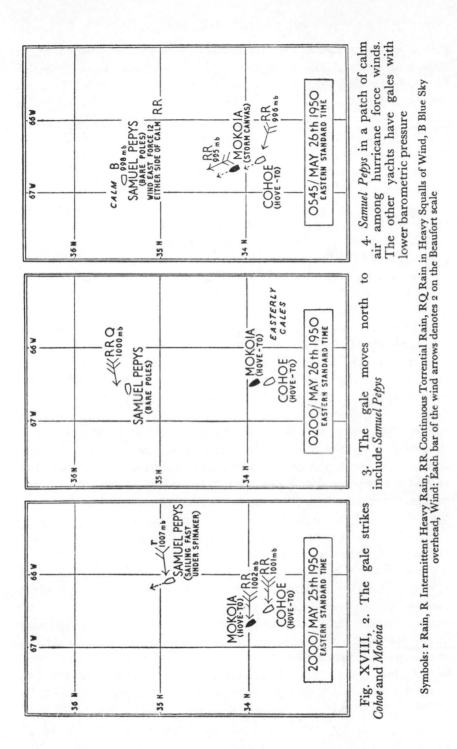

Fig. XVIII, 2. The gale strikes *Cohoe* and *Mokoia*

3. The gale moves north to include *Samuel Pepys*

4. *Samuel Pepys* in a patch of calm air among hurricane force winds. The other yachts have gales with lower barometric pressure

Symbols: r Rain, R Intermittent Heavy Rain, RR Continuous Torrential Rain, RQ Rain in Heavy Squalls of Wind, B Blue Sky overhead, Wind: Each bar of the wind arrows denotes 2 on the Beaufort scale

was as quick witted as he was strong; short and wiry in build he combined vigorous *élan* with the ability to play tricks with the differential calculus. As carpenter was Chief Petty Officer Flux, an exceptional seaman, who had learnt his sailing first under Uffa Fox and then John Illingworth, surely moving from the sublime to the superb. Fluxie added exceptional physical and mental robustness to his great experience.

At midnight the storm caught us. As the barometer plummeted, violent gusts struck the yacht. All sail was lowered, and the boat put into the trough of the sea while we watched for any change. After one hour the barometer had checked its fall and the wind's mean easterly direction was unaltered. The torrential rainfall and screeching gusts all suggested that she might be in the path of a tropical revolving storm, or hurricane. Yet the instructions for avoiding such storms could no longer be carried out, as the wind was too violent for any canvas to withstand it.

The situation, as it appeared at 1 a.m. in the middle watch, was the very one that had been studied most carefully, not because it seemed likely but because it was the worst position we could imagine for a yacht in the open sea. It was assessed that the loss of the tall Bermuda mast was probable, there was only the precedent of Voss for this. With no engine or wireless in a lonely part of the ocean, survival needed the preservation of all food and water, so nothing could be discarded to lighten the ship. Next it was assumed that crew fatigue would be a danger, should a breaking wave smash in the deck or cabin. In fact this happened to *Vertue XXXV* on the second day of the storm, and her survival may well be due to the fact that her crew had recently finished a meal that sustained them for the prodigious task that saved their ship. Finally came the danger of crew being washed overboard; this seemed the greatest hazard of all.

It was clearly best to direct the boat end on to the sea to reduce the chance of a wave breaking over her. In wind too strong to allow any canvas aloft, she could not lie head to sea with a sea anchor over the bows. However, she could readily be steered stern to sea, as a helmsman could always be kept on deck with such a strong crew. (Fig. XVIII, 3.)

Samuel Pepys was turned to the westward, with the wind still increasing its rage from the east. Even without sails the windage of the bare mast was driving her through the water at near maximum speed. To slow down the yacht, the anchor warp of nylon was streamed astern in a large bight from each quarter; added to this, several lengths of hemp were streamed out as extra brakes. It was surprising to feel the soothing effect of these warps on the waves, which no longer broke in the narrow lane immediately astern of the yacht.

The night was black. The outstanding impression was noise, the shriek of the wind in the rigging and the din of the waves all blending into one devilish clamour, as the tepid rain hammered against one's head.

Moving around was not easy in these conditions; small wonder that a new helmsman taking over was caught off course for a few seconds while shifting into position. At once a sea came pounding over the quarter, filled the cockpit and slammed against the cabin. The ship was battened down, so little water went below. Until one had been on deck for some time it was hard to believe that each succeeding wave would not wash over her, yet if the helmsman could meet each wave squarely with the stern, she would rise quietly with the sea, and nothing but spray would come aboard.

The problem became chiefly a psychological one. With very experienced helmsmen no exceptional difficulty was found in steering the stern into the seas even in the dark; nor was unusual physical strength required. But it was decidedly frightening to hear the furious snarl of a wave breaking astern above the continuous roar of wind, rain, spray and waves hurling themselves at the boat.

I prayed earnestly for the dawn, and went below to look at the barometer; it was falling steadily, but there was a slight easing of the wind, still blowing a full gale. Man is a creature of the daylight, and I felt that if I could but survive the night unharmed, all would be well. When dawn should have broken, angry darkness held its own.

Slowly light seeped through the rain and spray. The dawn was more frightening than the night. The sight of the huge combers building up astern was devastating. The whole surface sometimes became a dull, frothy white, save for the black path etched out by the warps astern. In the driving spume one could scarcely see beyond the next crest even when on the top of a wave.

With the self-excuse that I had been up all night, but really from sheer horror of looking at the seas, I went below to write up the log, and ate a bar of nut chocolate. If on deck the ocean had felt overwhelmingly hostile, below the cabin seemed like a prison cell. The worst impression was that of utter helplessness; one felt the skipper needed to be constantly on the alert, but there was so little he could do about anything.

A spurt of water shot through the tiny peep-hole left for the helmsman to communicate with those below; the water jet sagged, then turned to driven drops. I looked out and saw Fluxie signal to me to come up. Conversation was impossible on deck, but it was obvious that he just wanted support; he too was frightened by the sight and noise of the seas. Curiously I found his anxiety reassuring. It did not seem to matter being afraid if a man of his calibre was feeling the same. In any case it felt better to be lending support to another.

Strengthened in this way, one could look round more objectively. In all the furious assaults of nature, the outstanding feature was the concentrated fury packed into the noise of each sea as it curled over to break. One compared it with the seas of winter gales breaking on the shore, but there was no likeness between them. Was this due to the position down below the crests, or were there some special devils in these seas? It was the noise of the curlers that chiefly caused the fear. Otherwise the general tumult, the violent motion, the mingled rain and spray, the angry, dim colourless light and the salt air, all mingled together in a diabolical cocktail of sound, sight, taste and feel.

At 5.45 a.m. on 26th May, the wind fell dead. (Fig. XVIII, 4.)

The sudden change was staggering. We had run into a patch of blue sky; colour sparkled; the rain dried up and spray had ceased to drive. On deck our voices were freed; words no longer atomised in the storm.

'Look at that Everest, sir,' Fluxie shouted, forgetting that his voice had not to compete with the elements, 'it's breaking all ways at the top.'

The sea was hopelessly confused. Pinnacles of water would surge up without any form or rhythm. It might have been the dream of a modern sculptor with toothache. One longed for some wind to steady her, but as urgently dreaded the return of its overwhelming power. The boat's motion was chaotic in the heavy pregnant air; one felt sympathy for the rat in a terrier's jaw. Yet the two below had somehow wedged and lashed themselves into their bunks. It takes a seaman to rest in such conditions; but every moment they could lie down when off watch strengthened our defence.

'I suppose we're all right, sir,' said Fluxie doubtfully, 'it scared me to look at them curlers astern.'

'Yes, we're all right,' I replied without much enthusiasm, 'but the real thing is what happens next.'

'You've got to look at 'em to keep your stern pointing right; but—what does happen next, sir?'

'The strongest wind comes after the calm, Fluxie. We seem to be in the eye of a storm.'

'I'll bet no one else has looked into the eye of a storm; not from a boat this size. What are we going to do now, sir; can she stand any more of this stuff?'

'She's stood it so far, Fluxie, and we've done all we can. We're all ready, so there's nothing left but to pray.'

The urge to pray was deeply insistent; we were both silent for a minute.

'We'll pull her through, sir.'

Warm-hearted, loyal Fluxie. No finer man could exist to share one's anxiety. There was colour and blue sky, but the mental relief that had come when the wind no longer blew, fizzled out like a spent rocket. All round she was hemmed in by a curtain of angry swirling blackness. Seven minutes of unnatural pause seemed an age.

Savagely the wind pounced again.

It was still from the east. I struggled to check the course from a second compass, surprised that it did not blow from a new direction. She was still heading to the west with the wind astern.

The clock's hand clung to every minute of time, but at last an hour of anxiety was passed. The barometer was pumping up and down vigorously as she dived and soared with the waves, but the hoped for rise had not come. After the barometer had checked its fall in the calm air, it had begun to fall again slowly. This was a bitter disappointment; perhaps the depression was still deepening.

At last came a slight easing in the wind's screech, confirmed with the stopwatch by longer intervals between the gusts. This heralded a shift in direction.

Any change was for the good, so I went below to chew some dried fruit and nuts, pushing past Pat who was working at the bilge pump. The food tasted of salt, so did the fresh water drawn from the tap; the very air seemed salt.

Q

Soon I noticed the vehemence with which Pat was working the handle of the pump. Although he was being thrown around the cabin with the boat's motion, he attacked the machine as though he was battering the life out of some vile enemy; each stroke was accompanied by fierce abuse. In the bedlam of noise his words could not be heard, but the tune was staccatissimo. Dressed in oilskin trousers and a wet singlet there was rage in his every movement that seemed to reflect the feelings of the elements. I was relieved to see such reserves of energy, but as violence was the order of the day, only vaguely curious about the cause. (See Fig. XVIII, 5.)

Gradually the story came out. Pat had felt water pour into his bunk, and reaching up to a locker high under the deck, found his precious camera soaked by salt water. When the wind stopped, the yacht had rolled so far that momentarily she lay almost on her beam ends, before whipping back to roll the other way. The water in the bilge had run along the yacht's side to pour even into the highest locker.

Frequent work on the pump was needed to keep the bilge empty. Although water was driving through every possible crack from the deck the quantities showed that there must be a leak below. On any other occasion such a conclusion, when in a small boat many hundreds of miles from land, might have caused grave concern. I was gale-struck and my feelings were numbed by the all-powerful magnificence of the storm, so I merely felt that it was just another troublesome nuisance to search for the leak.

The search was difficult with stores or fresh water tanks carefully stowed and rigidly secured in every corner of the bilge. I removed my oilskins and crawled first through the small opening that led into the irregular space under the cockpit. It was there that, long after the storm, the leak was found to come from the hull outlet of a cockpit drain. But water gyrated madly as she tossed, so I achieved nothing but an urgent desire to escape from such a hole, little bigger than my prone body.

Right forward the sail bags were shifted, and laboriously replaced without result. Wrongly I assumed that the two ton cast iron keel had jerked with such momentum that it had opened up the seams in the hull planking. Content with this explanation, we continued to pump frequently.

By afternoon the wind had backed four points to north-east, and was down to a fresh gale; yet the seas were increasing in height, although they still showed no semblance of regularity. The barometer's slow fall continued. I wrote in the log the facts as I saw them—each letter an effort in that heaving, lurching hell. Then on the opposite page I drew little diagrams to try to solve the nature of the storm. These suggested that its centre was almost stationary, and still deepening, with the yacht in the dangerous sector. Finally was scribbled the note, 'Get to the north-west.'

In a fresh gale she could run fast under the tiny spitfire jib, which was amply strong for such winds. To go fast in such seas was hazardous, yet it seemed an even greater danger to remain in those waters.

It was no easy job to go forward even in daylight to hoist the small jib. With some two feet of freeboard, her nose plunged deep into the waves, and spray hurled in erratic showers over the deck. But Pat and Fluxie knew just when to hold on and when to move, as Sammy tended their life-lines from the cockpit. Next they hauled aboard the warps streamed astern as brakes, all save the bight of nylon; this would help to control her when she was borne forward on a wave top, and in danger of broaching to. When any particularly threatening sea reared up astern, she was steered round to gain some protection from the towed warp. But much solid water came aboard.

The height of the biggest waves was estimated at 35 feet, but judgement was difficult under those conditions. When a sea broke, the top 6 to 8 feet would curl over, and come crashing down its face in a seething avalanche. One could only shudder at the thought of one breaking over the yacht. It never happened. The barometer fell more rapidly, but for some time the gale grew no stronger.

Suddenly came a hungry, tearing gust from a new direction. The wind increased so fast that the waves themselves were momentarily shocked by the storm's passion, and the tops were wrenched off as concentrated spray. The wind had veered back to east and increased.

Once more the sail was lowered, and with every warp streamed astern, she tossed under bare pole, with the stern steered into each oncoming sea. Soon after, the sun set somewhere to the west behind the devilish black biting spray. (See Fig. XVIII, 6.)

Another night of storm was upon us. But even the night brought some hope of improvement. The barometer had stopped its fall, and for an hour or so had pumped up and down around the same mean. Had we but known it, this was the final crisis of the storm. It was then that *Vertue XXXV* was picked up by a wave and flung down with such violence that the cabin top was smashed in on the lee side.

The barometer began to rise. On the rise the wind often blows harder, but hope outweighs exhaustion when it is known that the shriek of each gust should be louder than the next to come.

At midnight the wind still blew with its full malignant spite. It had backed steadily four points to north-east once more, but in spite of this wind shift the seas seemed more regular. The stopwatch showed that on average a major crest passed at intervals of 11.8 seconds, giving a length of 700 feet, but the water between these crests had many hillocks and cross furrows.

By 1 a.m., with daylight just a few hours ahead, the wind was logged as Force 10, a whole gale, but it was better than the weather that had gone before. The barometer still rose slowly.

Half an hour later the wind tormentingly veered four points to east in a quick succession of gusts, bringing confusion to the sea surface once more. The barometer checked its rise. Anxiety jabbed fiercely at the tired body and sleepless mind, with the fear of the afternoon's events repeating themselves, and the mental picture of a wandering storm that might pass right over us once more. Stories came forcibly to mind of storms meandering aimlessly in the Horse Latitudes to strike time and again at some hapless ship.

I went below, and by the light of the waterproof torch drew more diagrams and figures in the log. The scribbled conclusion seemed urgent, 'Must gain distance to the N.W.' At least I did not feel we were running from the storm, but might gain distance from it.

After forty-eight hours of storm I doubted if I had the strength myself to go forward in the dark and hoist the spitfire jib. Fluxie yelled back between the gusts, 'I can get the spitfire on her. Just give me time, sir. I'll be all right.'

It seemed best to keep just two men on deck, any more could not help in the dark, and if she was washed down by a breaking wave as she forged ahead, there would still be two men down below. Those on deck would not stand too good a chance.

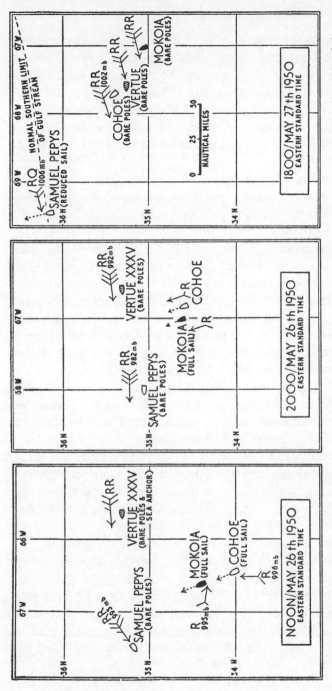

Fig. XVIII, 5. *Mokoia* and *Cohoe* have light winds from contrary directions, while the other two yachts are in gales

6. The barometer touches its lowest point in *Samuel Pepys*, and the storm is at its height. *Vertue* was damaged by the heavy seas about this time. *Mokoia* and *Cohoe* have rising barometers and light winds with very confused seas

7. *Cohoe* and *Mokoia* sail back into the gale area near *Vertue*, *Samuel Pepys* has worked clear of the storm but still has strong squalls and torrential rain

Fluxie set out from the cockpit, a life-line round his waist, crouching against the 18-inch high cabin top. I could see him no more, but felt his progress on the line. With 20 feet out he must have got forward, and I pictured him sitting down on the foredeck, with one leg each side of the stay, as he cleared away and clipped on the spitfire jib. The line went slack, perhaps as he reached aft for some obstinate lashing. Ages went by. Could he still be there? I gave a little tug on the life-line to explore.

No answer, save the whining howl of a raving squall.

My heart stood still. Then as the yacht recovered from the blow of that squall, back came the firm pull that seemed to say, 'I'm quite all right; just give me time.'

Steering with one hand, with the other I kept a feel on the life-line. There was movement as Fluxie shifted aft to the mast. He was feeling for the halyard in the dark. Soon it was cleared away and the moment of apprehension came as he started to hoist. The spitfire sheet, secured to a cleat beside the cockpit, came to life as the wind felt the sail's head raised from the deck. A few seconds later it was tamed from a writhing beast to a bar-taut straining rope as the wind filled the 50 square feet of canvas to drive the yacht ahead eagerly.

Fluxie scrambled back into the cockpit safely, and the sweat of relief poured down within my oilskins. I went below to read the barometer. He had been forty minutes out on deck, but time had been meaningless in what had seemed the longest trick of my life.

The barometer resumed its slow rise. My stopwatch came out again, as judgement was hopeless without it. The gust frequency was less, and they were shorter in duration. Then I timed ten wave crests passing, the mean was 11.5 seconds so even the sea was shorter. For the first time the bruises that covered my body and limbs began to ache. I ate some cream biscuits, wedged myself on the cabin floor, and took out the whisky bottle from its locker. Never has a tot tasted better. It was 3.30 a.m.

Back on deck the wind still tore at one's face, warmed by the neat spirit. But surely it had eased. I yelled at Fluxie, and the words got through first time: 'What do you make of the wind?'

'About flatters, I'd call it, sir, after all that stuff. But any other day it would be half a gale.'

He was right. The wind was down to a moderate gale, Force 7;

squalls no longer bit and the seas had lost their vicious snarl. They were as high as ever but almost regular. This might have been just another pause, and to my mind the Black Hole of Calcutta was a health resort compared with our area of sea. Nothing could be quick enough for me to get clear from it.

'Call all hands,' I shouted impatiently. 'We'll get the storm trisail on to her. Quick.'

Dawn broke more happily than its eve. There were still fierce squalls throughout the next few hours; they would bring down with a rush the reefed main sail that soon replaced the trisail. The sullen rollers were magnificent in their size. Rain drove in drizzly patches, but the grey light allowed a hint of colour to the scene. Sky, sea and spume were divided once more.

The storm was over. (See Fig. XVIII, 7.)

The other yachts, further to the south, still had another day and night of gale before them, although the depression was steadily filling up. Plotting back afterwards it was calculated that during the thirty hours that *Samuel Pepys* was almost entirely under bare pole, she had been carried 123 miles to the westward. This set was parallel to the Gulf Stream, but in the reverse direction to its normal course. The synoptic analysis showed that winds of Force 12 might have been expected near the centre of an intense depression that passed very slowly across the track of the yacht.

This story of the impressions experienced at the time surely shows that competing with a storm is largely a psychological matter. However bad the weather may be, the mind is less concerned with the weather at the time than with what may happen next; the exception is when someone goes outside the shelter of the cockpit, or is in imminent danger due to his own actions. It had seemed many times that the ship could not stand up to such punishment for much longer; yet she did so and suffered no more damage than the loss of all paint from the after side of her mast due to the sand blast effect of the spray, besides the disappearance of her masthead burgee. In retrospect it is clear that the risk accepted by twice hoisting the spitfire jib, in an effort to get clear of the storm, was not justified. Without this the yacht might have spent a few more hours within the gale area, but she would probably have been none the worse for it. Yet who could have foretold this at the time?

A tempest of such unruly force drove home the lesson that once it has struck, neither inspired ship-handling nor the most powerful efforts of the crew would make up for any failure in the yacht, in the training of her crew, or the stowage of her gear before the coming of the storm; it came without warning.

Since this account and its conclusions of 16 years were written, that storm has been analysed time and again. Was it a double-eyed depression such as since have sometimes been disclosed by radar in specially equipped hurricane tracing aircraft? Or was it a storm whose centre traced out a circular track in our area? Much work on these theories has been done, but probably we shall never know for certain, as there chanced to be no other ships nearby, and the development of today's storm tracking organisation in the North Atlantic was then in its early stages.